Jazzocracy

Jazzocracy

Jazz, Democracy, and the Creation
of a New American Mythology

BY
KABIR SEHGAL

WWW.BETTERWORLD.COM

BETTER WORLD BOOKS
5570 Current Road
Mishawaka, Indiana 46545
www.betterworldbooks.com

Library of Congress Control Number: 2007942112

ISBN: 978-0615-17693-2

This book was set in Adobe Caslon Pro by CurlyRed Inc.
Book design by Jennifer Marin
Cover design by Katie Clark

Printed in the United States on
50% post-consumer recycled paper

10 9 8 7 6 5 4 3 2 1

For My Father
Raghbir Kumar Sehgal

Table of Contents

"From a small spark, kindled in America, a flame has aris-
en, not to be extinguished. Without consuming, like the
Ultima Ratio Regum[1] , it winds its progress from nation
to nation, and conquers by a silent operation. Man finds
himself changed, he scarcely perceives how. He acquires a
knowledge of his rights by attending justly to his interest,
and discovers in the event that the strength and powers
of despotism consist wholly in the fear of resisting it, and
that, in order *'to be free, it is sufficient that he wills it.'*"

–Thomas Paine, *Rights of Man* (1790)

[1] The Final Argument of Kings (i.e.,war)

Foreword

During the 2004 U.S. presidential election, I became friends with Kabir Sehgal. Kabir's designated role was to escort Senator Max Cleland from state to state for the John Kerry campaign. Because Max had lost three limbs at the Battle of Khe Sanh during the Vietnam War, Kabir's job was to push the Senator's wheelchair through the caucus and primary seasons. Everywhere Max went, Kabir went too. A first-generation Indo-American raised in Atlanta, Kabir had the high-octane energy level of at least three men his age. Even though Kabir was still a student at Dartmouth College, he wasn't one-dimensional in any way. Besides helping Max get around, from time to time Kabir also offered advice to the Kerry Campaign on reaching the "Youth Vote." And as if he weren't already busy enough, in between Dartmouth classes and Kerry rallies, Kabir would jet off to play bass with trumpet legend Wynton Marsalis. Clearly, Kabir was a remarkable twenty-one-year-old, with an equally remarkable gift for multi-tasking!

Because I had written a book about John Kerry, titled Tour of Duty, I ran into Kabir quite often on the campaign trail where we had many far-ranging, and illuminating, conversations. In Iowa, for example, we discussed Duke Ellington and Romare Bearden. In New Hampshire, it was Albert Murray and Charlie Parker. In part because of his relationship with Wynton Marsalis, Kabir had developed heart-felt theories about the complex intersection of democracy and music. Some of his ideas seemed to be borrowed from such intellectuals as Stanley Crouch and Ralph Ellison. Others were fresh and original. At some point during our travels, Kabir told me he was interested in writing a book about *Jazzocracy*, as he phrased it. Quite naturally, I encouraged him. In fact, I invited him to New Orleans to spend a semester researching the subject at Tulane University as a visiting fellow.

For months I watched as Kabir launched himself heart and soul into this book. Occasionally we would get together in the French Quarter to brainstorm about his work. Let the record show that I spent quality time with Kabir not because he was my student, but because almost every minute with him became a revelation. Essentially we reversed roles; he was *my* teacher about jazz. One afternoon he explained to me why jazz was a "negotiation." The next morning our conversation focused on why Louis Armstrong was a "collagist." Channeling his inner Catskill comedian, Kabir could make me laugh with funny anecdotes about Duke Ellington in Syria and Dave Brubeck in Turkey. Sometimes he made huge intellectual leaps--such as his belief that Walt Whitman was an improvisational precursor to the jazz movement. Over and over again he equated the concept of "freedom" with jazz. He was, in a sense, a cultist.

As a text *Jazzocracy* is global in its outlook. Whether it's the French Avant-Garde of Weimar Germany or West African calls, Kabir's thinking knows no boundaries. He operates along the lines of

Duke Ellington's famous maxim: "No Boxes." Quite appropriately, he ends his narrative grappling with the cultural legacy of post-Katrina New Orleans.

According to Kabir, the U.S.—compared to European nations—too often neglects the role of culture in its society. I think he is right. By writing *Jazzocracy*, Kabir hopes to showcase the rich heritage of America's unique art form. Not only does he succeed—and succeed brilliantly, but *Jazzocracy* will also be remembered as the opening salvo of a truly great new American mind.

Douglas Brinkley
February 14, 2008

Preamble

A society's collective memory and self-expression manifests itself through art, or so thought American poet-saint Walt Whitman. As the *Atlantic Monthly* puts it, Whitman "sang of America and shaped the country's conception of itself."[1] He longed for an indigenous art that would declare America's cultural independence, a declaration that would achieve parallel footing with America's political independence. Whitman knew something about creating a unique American voice; he scribed a new world voice for poetry.[2] French author André Malraux wrote that the Egyptian statues of Ka are "more Egyptian than Egypt itself ever was."[3] [Art can arguably be *most* representative of the culture it represents because it codifies the ideals, values, aspirations, and experiences of a particular society.] We visit museums like the Prado in Madrid to better understand the life and times of Goya and the Spanish court. Artworks are the fossils of a society and instruct later observers of the qualities and intelligence of a certain people. Art objectifies culture and philosophy, translating the ethereal into the real—or as Malraux understood it, art was the "means by which the raw material humans experience becomes style."[4] Design becomes artifact, expressions turn into the permanent, the temporal transcends the topical.

Writing in 1922, American writer James Weldon Johnson recognized that the last test of a culture is the art that it produces:

> A people may be great through many means, but there is only one measure by which its greatness is recognized and acknowledged. The final measure of the greatness of all peoples is the amount and standard of the literature and art that they produced … No people that has produced great literature and art has ever been looked upon by the world as distinctly inferior. [5]

What would be the new world voice for American music? More importantly, how would that art sound? What audio art would sound the national *vox populi*? Step forward, America's art of jazz. As the first discernable form of American musical self-expression, jazz translated the raw American experience into a definite sonic style. In the sound that was created in the early twentieth century, one hears the tribal music from Africa, church songs from the Deep South, secularized blues tunes of the Mississippi Delta, and European instrumental arrangements. The music is a mélange of millions of Americans and a stylization of the raw American experience.

[I don't think it's an accident that jazz emerged as America's first indigenous art form. It may seem a stretch, but I believe that jazz music shares the sustained conversational nature of democracy that began in the inkwells of Thomas Jefferson, John Adams, and James Madison. The steady and democratic deliberations that one finds in Vermont town hall meetings and lengthy US Senate debates are found in jazz music. You could say that the designers of jazz unknowingly bestowed the music with democratic properties and ideas of equality, structure, improvisation, and liberty, but it's probably more intellectually accurate to say that the malleable nature of jazz allows later thinkers to frame it as musical democracy. Jazz music is an art form that involves steady and sustained musical conversation. Instead of reciting the notes on the page, the jazz musician makes music with fellow musicians. The spontaneity of the jazz solo carts the band in an unpredictable direction. Similarly, democracy is wrought by constant conversation and the making of decisions. There may be disagreement over the resulting bill or law, but there is agreement in how a decision will be reached: through constant conversation and the *making of democracy.*

I am reminded of Zachary Roth's anecdotal piece on Democratic Congressman Steny Hoyer in *Washington Monthly.* Hoyer was at a reception for teachers, and at the time pundits were correctly predicting that Hoyer and the Democrats would win control of the US House of Representatives:

> As Hoyer strode to the podium, he passed House Majority Leader John Boehner (R-Ohio), a politician with a reputation for schmoozing perhaps equal to Hoyer's own, and the two literally slapped each other on the back simultaneously. "Do you have the votes?" Hoyer asked Boehner, a propos, it seemed, of nothing except a shared love of the legislative process.[6]

Hoyer and Boehner are an imperfect example of bipartisanship or democracy, but the story illustrates a mutual respect for the opposition, following the words of Voltaire: "I disapprove of what you say, but I will defend to the death your right to say it." The discordant voice is not to be demonized or vehemently castigated. Instead, the opponents are merely instruments in the greater score of democracy.

Jazz and democracy are indeed built on the principles of equality and liberty. But in order to participate in these mediums, there must be a requisite spirit or willingness to engage. Democracy requires an active and participative citizenry that considers government a lever of change. Each citizen must recognize his or her place as a luminous note within the greater performance of democracy. One jazz musician acknowledges the importance of active participation and interpretation in *making* jazz music. He describes the innateness of jazz as the "democratic spirit of the music."[7] If structure and improvisation are the tangy ingredients to the democratic brew, then the participatory spirit is the secret formula.

Maybe I readily saw similarities between jazz and democracy because I split my time between touring with the Wynton Marsalis Quintet and serving as a special assistant on the John Kerry presidential campaign. *Build a crowd and perform.* The performances of Marsalis and Kerry were strikingly similar; both endeavored to unify discordant voices. Both engaged in steady and sustained conversations with concertgoers, band members, constituents, and voters. Though there was a goal in mind (a successful musical performance or winning an election), the future was always in doubt. Democracy is more than votes and elections. Democracy is built on the idea that power can be vested in the citizens; through constant dialogue, the prevailing sentiment will be enacted. The result is perpetually in flux.

"Each field of art has its own particular questions," writes *Philosophy Now* Editor Rick Lewis.[8] Jazz music in particular has provoked questions from its inception. Why was jazz initially associated with vice? Why did it gain a great audience in the Soviet Union and Nazi Germany? Did the music represent more than trumpets and trombones? Pablo Picasso's *Guernica* abstracts the Nazi bombing during the Spanish Civil War in 1937. The black and white mural shows the suffering and horror of the moment. The dead horse burns in the heat of a light bulb that hangs from atop. Just as Picasso's mural represents a refraction of the Spanish experience, so, too, does the American blues ballad reflect sensibilities of an American experience. The blues ballad is soft and emotive and helps the protagonist reconcile himself with the world in which he lives. The pragmatic optimism of the typical blues ballad reflects the American spirit of tragic optimism and overcoming difficulty. Through the blues, we conquer the blues.

Irish poet William Butler Yeats pondered whether the dancer could be separated from the dance. In jazz music, the performer cannot be separated from the universal vibrations emanating from the sticky valves and Zildjian cymbals; the notes are those of the performers, not a 1980s songwriter or conservatory composer. Jazz is not only about going through the motions or repeating a doctrine—*think, phrase, spit*. Jazz is inseparable from the musician because it originates from the African and African American tradition of *making* music. In many African cultures, music is integrated into daily life. Attending a music performance is almost a foreign concept. Jazz is an extension of the musician's sensibilities, individuality, style, coordination, and personality—an escape from the predictably pleasing tunes of a bar jukebox. Since the music is not written down, the musician must merge technical proficiency with personal experience and sentiment. American conductor Leonard Bernstein describes how composers are often considered more dignified than performers. He goes on to say that jazz musicians are both composers and performers, making them the most dignified of all.[9]

Duke Ellington played his orchestra as if it were a single instrument. Jazz writer Nat Hentoff writes, "Duke was an orchestra."[10] A music clinician tapped the rhythm to Ellington's "Peanut Vendor" on a stool for my high school jazz band. "Listen for your parts. Everything is there," he said. Sure enough, I heard the bass groove in his taps, the trumpet melody in his thumps, and drum pattern in his strokes. We heard music, not just wooden sticks hitting the wooden stool. Ellington's first job was to sell peanuts at Washington Senators baseball games; he ordered the noise of life into music. *Come buy those peanuts roasted today!* There was little separation between life and music for Ellington. Jazz music represents more than notes. It's a sonic conversation, a dialogue among the musician, his life and band members. The instruments are merely the creative tools for the jazz musician to enact musical democracy on the bandstand.

The jazz-as-democracy metaphor requires some explaining. Start with the basic idea of democracy, no bells or bassoons. Democracy is a government in which power is concentrated in the people. The Thelonious Monk Institute of Jazz cites Abraham Lincoln's often-quoted explanation: " … of the people, by the people, and for the people."[11] Democracy reconciles the interests of the individual with the group. For instance, Americans are granted the freedom of expression, but must also live with the freedom of expression of others. If I think all Americans should listen to jazz (I do), I must not impede on the wishes and actions of others to believe or act otherwise.[12] Perfect democratic societies occur when individuals are able to freely choose and bolster the group simultaneously. But perfect democratic societies are nonexistent. Democracy perpetually reconciles the dual (and dueling) interests of the individual and the group. And if Lincoln's brief explanation of democracy fails, we can remember Winston Churchill's remark: "Democracy is the worst form of government except for all those other forms that have been tried."

Jazz and democracy are built upon the mutually antagonistic ideas of equality and liberty, or structure and improvisation. One can virtually hear the *making* of democracy in the jazz performance: the flurry of the shout section of Duke Ellington's "Tutti for Cootie,"—*hush!*—piano chords purposefully placed. Blazing trumpet growling with intemperate worry. *Should I keep on shootin' this horn?* Political campaigns spark intense and heated debate. Each candidate takes his or her turn in the spotlight, much like a jazz soloist in a jam session. Democrats assail the incumbent on incompetent leadership. The

Republican incumbent prepares his assault on the distressed donkey. *What should I say back?* Election Day soon approaching—shout out the vote, shout out the message (*is this the shout chorus of a jazz tune?*), shout out your opponents, *be heard!* The ferocity undoubtedly reaches a cacophonous pitch in the terminal phases of the big band swing performance and in the last days of the political campaign. If democracy is the messy process of finding harmony within a legislature and among the citizens of our vast country, then jazz is surely the soundtrack of this epic movie. Jazz is democracy in sound.

By rejigging our ears, one finds harmony, not discord. The sustained conversation and interplay of ideas is musical democracy at work, the wrestling of many voices into a mandate for one, whether for a swingin' piece or an inspirational president. It's the pluribus to our unum. It may pass the giggle test, but one can create direct parallels between a jazz band and America's democracy in order to gain a better understanding of the jazz-as-democracy trope at work. One can compare the rhythm section of Count Basie's Orchestra with Congress. The rhythm section keeps the band together, providing the pulsating beat. If it gets too far ahead of the beat, the judiciary reeds or executive trumpets will squeal. If Congress passes an unconstitutional bill, the Supreme Court will strike it down from its perch atop the marble Acropolis. Checks and balances. There is a respect for sections and soloists in jazz and democracy. There is a dialogical process involved in *making* music. The jazz band can serve as a laboratory for understanding democracy. Every player has the freedom to express himself—to fill the music with personal sonic vignettes or clichés and corny nursery rhyme jingles. The band must support the unique identity of each musician and sonic fingerprint of every instrument while reconciling the sounds of other musicians.

I readily admit that the jazz-as-democracy metaphor can be found in other works. Authors Ralph Ellison, Albert Murray, and Stanley Crouch have advanced theories that conflate jazz with the *making* of democracy. Trumpeter Wynton Marsalis propagates the jazz-as-democracy claim in his *To a Young Jazz Musician*. Trumpeter Irvin Mayfield often alludes to this metaphor during his performances. I greatly respect philosopher-musicians because they can depart the circle of critics. Many jazz musicians see the jazz-as-democracy metaphor awaken as they travel across America, since they are in constant dialogue with concertgoers and fellow musicians. Strains of the jazz-as-democracy metaphor can be found in several academic works. Scott Saul discusses a similar argument regarding hard bop and freedom in rich detail in *Freedom Is, Freedom Ain't: Jazz and the Making of the Sixties*. Ken Burns's popular documentary *Jazz* also intimates the comparison. In an interview, Burns says:

> Jazz is open and free. And yet, jazz itself adheres to some pretty important rules. In some ways, people are playing within that, which is much like democracy. We're given freedom, but we know that freedom has to occur within certain bounds and constraints, not just of the law, but of other people's freedoms, and their desires to express it. So jazz becomes a mirror that way.[13]

Skeptical jazz scholars could dismiss this text as a hopeless rehash of the Ellison-Murray-Crouch-Marsalis-Burns line. What's more, the jazz-as-democracy metaphor has been dismissed in some quarters. English Professor William Maxwell notes that the jazz-as-democracy trope appears to bellow from Lincoln Center, the New York City-based institution that serves as a home for jazz music. Maxwell boldly questions this metaphor: "What American jazz fan could fail to respect such a bold claim to political as well as cultural authority, the music's descent into coffee shop sonic wallpaper redeemed in a healing shower of red, white, blue, and black?"[14] The jazz-as-democracy metaphor has ostensibly *saved* jazz. Maxwell understands the jazz-as-democracy metaphor to be a defense crafted by jazz intellectuals. The fading popularity of the music is to be quelled by elevating it in comparison to the vaunted democratic process. Others may question the usefulness of such an academic exercise, likening me to a twenty-first century Hans Castorp, galloping up Thomas Mann's *Magic Mountain*, only to become infatuated with an edgy intelligentsia.

I hope this text will serve another purpose. I do not wish to debate the jazz-as-democracy trope or serve as a mandarin for Jazz at Lincoln Center. I believe the jazz-as-democracy metaphor because it helps to explain America and what Americans value: a constant democratic conversation as a means to *making* decisions. This work not only explains the jazz-as-democracy metaphor but suggests how jazz can help direct and guide Americans. Like a classic American novel, jazz music yields lessons, symbols, metaphors, and tropes that can help to understand and decipher American culture.

Jacques Attali, one-time Special Counselor to the President of France, believes that communities are created by ordering noise. After all, a community must decide how to order and organize itself, separating the music of compromise from the noise of anarchy. Creating a representative democracy is a way of organizing noise. How else can three hundred million Americans sign off on legislation? Attali did not go further by addressing particular types of music. He did, however, consider some arts to be prophetic. Wagner sounded the Tristan Chord in his opera *Tristan and Isolde*, a departure from the tonal harmony of his era only a few years after the Communist Manifesto appeared in 1848. The half tone became permissible during the Renaissance with the rise of the merchant class.[15] French writer Gustave Flaubert reminded, "The war of 1870 need never have been fought had people read my *Sentimental Education*."[16] The jazz band was integrated long before Major League Baseball or other parts of civil society. Thought is antecedent to action, and the mutations of politics and policy could be heard in prescient arts of a past era.

[It is debatable whether art can be a forerunner of a culture. But art indeed represents the culture that creates it. When jazz was the music of popular entertainment, it reflected the jam session character of America, as millions immigrated to America in search of opportunity. What does popular music say of America today? Popular rap music often rewards the most brutal and demoralizing voice. To enact a vulgar stereotype speaks not to the beauty of America. Much of popular rap music shows what we don't want to become, instead of presenting a model to which we aspire. With heavy metal, ratchet up the dial and bedazzle the audio engineer. *Is it Dolby?* To the musical stratosphere, the amplified guitar shrieks its annoyance. After a point, amplification becomes noise and not music. It isn't musical consensus. It's the competition of volume. The loudest (or most crafty) individual gets his or her way. In fact, much of popular music is a return to conservative music making: two or three chord changes with rehearsed refrains and scripted lines. Isn't the height of predictability (and cliché) to know what the guitarist or rapper will burp next? The democratic habits of the American mind are not reflected in today's popular American music.]

Perhaps popular music echoes the visceral liberal-conservative culture wars. In the past several decades, and perhaps more revealing, the past few years, the fuming tension between liberals and conservatives has become more apparent. It would be one thing if this close division doubled as the euphoric euphemism that President Bill Clinton used after the 2000 presidential election debacle, "the vitality of our debate." However, one can point to the coarse, uncivilized, and crude dialogue as an Uncivil War of Rhetoric. This is nothing new in politics. Critics of Thomas Jefferson called him a "coward" and "anarchist." Another called him "the son of a half-breed Indian squaw ... sired by a Virginia mulatto."[17] Freedom of speech allows for vitriolic and hateful speech. Dissent is the highest form of patriotism, it has been said. But when such language bleeds into the apolitical world, like a thirteen-year-old who calls his classmate a "bitch" and "ho," it strikes me as a falling from grace. To break an arm in a mosh pit is an act of aggression and absurdity. If culture informs the mind, and if thought is antecedent to action, then how will America's culture instruct Americans in the years to come?

[Unfortunately, the American culture of today belies American values. American culture is failing America.] In a riveting commencement address, Dana Gioia, the Bush-appointed Chairman of the National Endowments of the Arts, offers a simple test. He likes to ask Americans how many *American Idol* finalists and NBA players they can name. He then asks them to name living poets, playwrights, musicians, and artists.[18] In the 1950s and 1960s, Gioia suggests that many Americans could name baseball players Mickey Mantle and Sandy Koufax as well as venerable artists such as Robert Frost, Georgia O'Keefe, Leonard Bernstein, and others: "I don't think that Americans were smarter then, but American culture was."[19] I agree. Our music has gone the way of commercial entertainment. I am happy that we live in a free market (a necessity for a democracy), but as Gioia observes, some things shouldn't have prices on them. Culture teaches what is "beyond price."[20]

[There is a loss of splendor and meaning in America's culture. Every culture has its own mythology—a collection of stories and beliefs that help shape a group and cohere its identity.] Many Americans recognize myths as another culture's religion, e.g., Greeks celebrated Zeus, Athena, Hercules, and Poseidon. Egyptologists have studied The First Dynasty tomb of King Wadj in which Horus is embodied by an airborne falcon, an image that shows the "distant realm" of God.[21] Samuel Floyd explains the myth of the trickster in African mythology in *The Power of Black Music*. The trickster is the scheming and puerile animal in African folk tales. The trickster is mischievous and up to no good. Stories involving the trickster are instructive, inculcating fear and wisdom in those societies that subscribe to the myth. The trickster appears again in early African American music and art.[22] But myths don't always deal with gods and goddesses. They can be central parts of secular life, mapping society every which way—the compass needle always pointing true. Myths may serve as lenses through which we perceive our world. They become storehouses of values. Erik von Kue-hnelt-Leddihn writes in his introduction of Alexis de Tocqueville's *Democracy in America*, "All nations have their 'sustaining myths' ... They are potent factors in forming a people because they have a 'pro-grammatic' character."[23] America's myths help to unify and bring or-der to society. Our mythology is our proverbial story—good, bad, and beautiful.

While this text explains the jazz-as-democracy metaphor, its main consideration is the rupture of America's mythology. Musicians are the mythmakers of modern society. They propagate the oral tradition and invent modern narratives to match the core beliefs of a culture. Instead of speaking to the trusted and true core beliefs of America—like self-reliance and the melting mood of diversity—many of today's popular mythmakers speak of vapidity, violence, and vulgarity. Many modern mythmakers rap of the angry black man and the rebel without a cause. These musicians have divorced myth from music. Their music perfor-mances are no longer rituals or enactments of meaning and myth.

There is no single American mythology. Hundreds or perhaps thousands of American myths exist; moreover, much of our mythology deals with violence and exaggeration: Billy the Kid, John Wayne, Davy Crockett, Paul Bunyan. In *Inventing Billy the Kid*, Stephen Tatum the-matically illustrates America's constant reinvention of Billy the Kid from criminal bad boy to the darling, romantic, and justified bad boy. The Kid embodied the frontier values of rugged freedom and individ-ualism, fighting against oppressive civilization. In the 1950s, the Kid changed from villain-hero to a rebel without a cause à la James Dean.[24] We've mythologized and glamorized the "rebel without a cause" in our movies, leaders, and culture. *I don't know what to do anymore. Except maybe die.* The real rebels, however, are those who slay dragons, conquer evil, and fight for a just cause. Self-reliance is the central trait for our American hero.[25] The jazz soloist and bluesman employ the highest of skills—improvisation—to express themselves and advance from the bunker of rhymes. Our dragons, unfortunately, have started to slay us, because our culture is increasingly divorced from beauty and myth.

In *Federalist* No. 51, James Madison asks, "What is government itself, but the greatest of all reflections on human nature?"[26] Government is a mirror that reflects man's true nature. Malraux reasoned that art is the supreme revolt against man's nature. If only for a moment, it teaches us to escape man's ultimate fate.[27] Art teaches of our potentiality and goes beyond price. Speaking to scholars at McGill University, author Rudyard Kipling said that in following the path of riches and reputation, folks should understand their destiny: "Some day you will meet a man who cares for none of these things. Then you will know how poor you are." Dust returns to dust. While popular music may entertain and amuse, it does not provide an escape from the banalities and profit motives of life.

What if American culture incorporated a smarter (and more accurate) set of myths? It once did. Jazz was ahead of its time when it came to race relations. It reflected the jam session character of the American experiment. The jazz-as-democracy metaphor accurately illustrates the way in which America separates music from noise and orders society. Walt Whitman believed that if America strayed from its values and unity, it could regenerate by exploring its native arts, since indigenous art acts as a tireless wellspring of principles and ideals. If democracy is the mirror of an American, then a jazz-inflected society is the beacon to which the American may aspire. Working towards a jazz-inflected society is to strive for the unattainable—Ouspensky's "Fourth Way," or Yeats's "Unity of Culture." The jazz-inflected society or "Jazzocracy" pushes the citizen to embrace meaningful music that incorporates myths that speak to core American beliefs. Let us return to musical and reasoned political democracy, one in which we choose to *make* and live with music, and to paraphrase Ralph Ellison, not to die with noise.

In this text, I have set out to accomplish two things: (1) to explain the jazz-as-democracy metaphor (viewing democracy through the kaleidoscope of jazz); and (2) to create a series of myths that can help re-center American music back to a more worthwhile purpose. In other words, how can the cultural liberalism found in the jazz idiom instruct American political and cultural democracy? In the end, my intent is to illustrate how jazz can help marry modern music with myth, and inform civil society and democracy. Yes, I want us to be rebels *with a cause, to re-center our culture back to challenging us with visions of the future. Check and balance our myths.* To borrow the name of a Louis Armstrong tune—Rhythm Saved the World. It can save American oral tradition and myth again.

French writer Victor Hugo once observed that there is nothing more powerful than an idea whose time has come. Jazz as a democratic process is certainly an idea that deserves attention, but I feel this work is meant to build on the jazz-as-democracy trope. The originality of my claim is that by understanding the jazz-as-democracy trope, one can determine an appropriate set of myths to better understand America. One can use jazz to forecast where America is going and where it needs to be. We can re-center our culture by tying our American music with myth, and recover our lost beauty. The jazz-as-democracy metaphor is a means to understand the end of this text—to overtly mythologize America through the trope of jazz (see Chapter 3).

For the sake of clarity, I use "jazz" in a liberal way, referring to the entire genre that encompasses early New Orleans style, big band (swing), and bebop. It is not my intention to wade into the confusing jazz wars: what is or what isn't jazz music. In order to focus my argument and musical trope, the jazz big band and smaller jazz combo are the laboratories for the jazz-as-democracy metaphor. My analysis is not intra-jazz but jazz compared to other art forms. I could broaden my definition of jazz to early African American music, but I use jazz to simplify the metaphor, since it was the first mainstream and widespread recognition of African American music in popular culture.

I am not trying to sanitize the history of jazz or write a historical analysis of the music. Jazz can be a tough parlor game with Louis Armstrong's marijuana use, John Coltrane's heroine addiction, and Charlie Parker's narcotic abuse. *Bird wanted more air.* A skim of Miles Davis's autobiography will introduce the reader to the coarse lives of many of these jazz legends. Miles admitted as much: "I think I have a lot of the devil in me."[28] Drug abusers may produce first-rate art, but that doesn't turn the creators into saints. The reverse may happen, too. Eloquent artists produce vulgar art that venerates wretchedness. Refined men and women don't spell sunny music. Rather, out of the swamp of dirt blooms the lotus of jazz. Democracy is also a full contact sport. Letting your opponents unwittingly hang while you profit. Slamming the downtrodden in favor of the rich. I'm not trying to mythologize the many personalities involved in musical and political democracy, nor am I trying to debate specific policy or advance a panoramic warning for American democracy.

This book is not meant for jazz insiders. That book has already been written. Gary Giddins's *Visions of Jazz* spans a century of jazz, delving into intricate detail with lyrical prose. This book is not meant for philosophers of aesthetic theory (see Immanuel Kant's *Critique of Judgement*). Nor is this text a guide for political scientists. This work is a medley of ideas inspired from literature, political science, music, and mythology. I draw upon eclectic sources to express a point: [America's cultural mythology has ruptured, and jazz can help press America onto the flowerbed of beauty. In jazz we hear an echo of ourselves]

I receive no pleasure in criticizing other types of art. In fact, I struggled with how to treat rap music and popular entertainment. It is the height of elitism to justify a preference by insulting someone else's preference. Jazz music stands on its own. The best way to convince someone of its merit is to play a Duke Ellington recording. In order to illustrate the rupture of America's oral tradition and mythology, it was necessary to contrast rap music and popular entertainment with America's classical music of jazz.

Before I prattle on, I should address the nettlesome issue of my qualifications to write on this topic. Why is an Indo American from Atlanta exploring an African American origination? Or, as my friend calls me, a "Coca-Cola Curry Cowboy." I'm a jazz bassist who picked up a pen. Hardly a professional writer, I grew interested in this topic. I also ardently believe that we are not African Americans or Indo Americans. We are Omni-Americans—influenced by a shared experience.

I've been listening to jazz music and performing it since fifth grade. My sister brought home a tape of her middle school jazz band that out-grooved Aerosmith. My lips blistered when I played the trumpet, so I switched to the bass. The low bass grooves always attracted me. "Don't play the bass lines on your horn," my band teacher Mr. Wimmer scolded me. Ever since elementary school, I've been in bands. I've played with my middle school jazz ensemble, high school jazz ensemble, college ensemble, professional musicians, and even started some new groups. But it wasn't just the notes that interested me. It was the quintessentially American nature of jazz that started the proverbial itch. *Why is jazz American? Why does it speak to me? Why does it uplift others?* My investigation began in earnest. This amateur musician was to become an amateur jazz scholar.

I ventured to explore the jazz-as-democracy metaphor as a senior fellowship topic at Dartmouth College, my alma mater, but the committee to which I presented my topic looked bewildered and befuddled. An engineering professor in the back of the room pelted me with a question: "Why not compare jazz with food?" A million answers came to my head but produced a traffic jam. My mouth sealed with silence. It was a lost cause because I was still painting with a broad stroke, and in the academic world, theorem-like reasoning tops personal rationale. If there isn't a syllogism, how can one trust personal observations?

With a willing and novice pen, I have researched and written on the jazz-as-democracy metaphor. I lived in New Orleans for many months, researching at the Roosevelt Center for American Civilization at Tulane University. Using both personal observation and historical analysis, I learned how art can codify and represent a culture. From close inspection of the works of noteworthy scholars, I learned that art can help to instruct a society, or at least serve as a model to which we can aspire. One can look at a government or society through a prism of art. When democracy is viewed through the kaleidoscope of jazz, one realizes that conflict is just as much part of the democratic process as resolution. Harmony and agreement are oftentimes defined by their opposites: disharmony and disagreement. To have one, you must have the other.

The two works for which I am most grateful in understanding the nexus of jazz and democracy are Robert O'Meally's *The Jazz Cadence of American Culture*, and Alfred Appel's *Jazz Modernism*. Section two of O'Meally's volume entitled *"Jazznocracy"* was particularly helpful, as a host of authors discuss the process of making jazz and democracy—such as Crouch and John A. Kouwenhoven (who wrote *The Beer Can and the Highway*). The authors in O'Meally's work advance differing claims: jazz as process or jazz as individual freedom. My work sides with the jazz as (democratic) process, which arguably subsumes the jazz as individual freedom argument: Doesn't democracy call for individual liberty? O'Meally's section "One Nation Under a Groove" also helped to shape my argument. Samuel Floyd's *The Power of Black Music* helped me understand the adaptation of African music to African American music, which I explore in Chapter 1. Appel's style and verve stimulated and encouraged me to dispense with formal prose, instead jazzing the text with asides and preambles, making this work *my* solo.

I bring attention to three works that guided my research for Chapter 2: S. Frederick Starr's *Red and Hot*, Michael Kater's *Different Drummers*, and Jeffrey Jackson's *Making Jazz French*. Chapter 3 benefited from James Oliver Robertson's *American Myth, American Reality*, Joseph Campbell's *The Power of Myth*, Richard Hughes's *Myths America Lives By*, Lewis Hyde's *Trickster Makes the World*, Albert Murray's *The Omni-Americans*, and perhaps the most insightful analysis of America's musical culture: Martha Bayles's *Hole in Our Soul*. Bayles traces the trajectory of American popular music, and where it is now—fallen from beauty. Many of the anecdotes I use to humanize the sometimes dense academic and theoretical jazz jargon comes from Bill Crow's *Jazz Anecdotes* and Miles Davis's autobiography.

More specifically, the first chapter, "Yankee Doodlin'," chronicles the similarities between jazz and American democracy, building on the works of the aforementioned scholars. The flick of a drum, the flutter of political freedom. "The (International) Sonic Bomb" explores how jazz served as an extension of freedom and democracy, particularly in foreign lands, particularly those who lived under oppressive governments. The Soviet Union, Germany, and France are contrasted. Before overtly mythologizing a Jazzocracy, it is helpful to look outside-in, gaining a second opinion on the nature of America's native self-expression. The last chapter, "Rhythm Saves the World," suggests why and how Americans ought to aspire to the beacon of a jazz-inflected society. Finally, in the Epilogue I try to show that I am not all mouth as I look at some concrete ways to reincorporate the myths of the jazz-inflected society into the broader American mythology.

This book is about change, it is about the politics of improvisation. It was written while on two tours, one a presidential candidacy and the other, a jazz tour de force. The timbre and tone are instructed by this parallel narrative, it is participatory, plodding, pedantic and playful. This book is political, it is social, it is historical, it is lyrical and it is musical. This book is an examination, a tour, a call-and-response. It finds an America at a crossroads, a contingent socio-historical confluence of awakening identity or crass collapse. This is who we were. Now, who will we choose to be? It challenges readers to re-imagine the potential for civic performance, to reject the coarsening of our youth by the petty and gilded aggression of the angry urban town-callers. This book is about the past and it is about the future, it is about the democracy we were and the one we hope to become. Both jazz and democracy are participatory arts; they are accomplished in their making, the triumph of the verb over the noun. We are the citizen performers: doing is achieving, playing is amending. This book is jazzy, the verse free-flowing, the tone improvisational, and this collection of words is my (at times, confused) solo. Enjoy.

Chapter 1
Yankee Doodlin'

"The greatest blessing of our democracy is freedom. But in the last analysis, our only freedom is the freedom to discipline ourselves."
—Bernard Baruch

A young Miles Davis rejoined Charlie Parker (nicknamed Bird) who was recovering from a pernicious drug addiction. Bird constantly challenged Miles to play at his peak potential. Miles noted how a night on the bandstand with Bird could lead to a full exchange of conversations among band members. The band struggled with how to congeal with Bird the maestro and keep up with his musical entrepreneurialism:

> [Bird's] creativity and musical ideas were endless. He used to turn the rhythm section around every night ... Bird would play in such a way that it made the rhythm section sound like it was on 1 and 3 instead of 2 and 4. Nobody could keep up with Bird ... Every time he would do this, Max would scream at Duke not to try to follow Bird ... [29]

Books have been written about Bird's musical genius. He and trumpeter Dizzy Gillespie are the most celebrated progenitors of the bebop movement, which placed an emphasis on musical virtuosity and technical proficiency. To perform with Bird was like being paired with Tiger Woods at the Masters:

> See, when Bird went off like that on one of his incredible
> solos, all the rhythm section had to do was stay where
> they were and play some straight shit. Eventually Bird
> would come back to where the rhythm was, right on
> time … You had to ride the music out.[30]

Sometimes it's better to just get out of the way of a master musician. But that doesn't mean you stop playing. Despite Bird's proficiency, he still needed the band for support. Without the group, Bird remained a soloist. The musical conversation on the bandstand respected every player's individuality. Bird could throw off the band, so the drummer Max Roach warned his bandmates not to wander after Bird. Miles adapted to Bird by playing "up" and being ready for the unexpected, the constant surprise.

When Miles added pianist Bill Evans to his group, he had to rearrange some of his compositions to fit Evans's style of playing. Evans played "underneath" the band and suggested a firm classical style, influenced by the works of classical composers Ravel and Rachmaninoff.[31] And when the Bill Evans Trio lost its bassist after the tragic death of Scott LaFaro, Evans understood that the musical dialogue would change. His new bassist Eddie Gomez approached the instrument with his own unique style and individuality. The *making* of the music would change to reflect each member of the trio.

The jazz musician learns to "tell a story" with his solo. These stories are what some scholars consider an "encoded exchange of personal narrative."[32] The continuous call and response in a jazz performance functions as the *making* of conversation. In jazz, "the presence of this kind of dialogical process is constant throughout a performance as *sustained antiphony*."[33] There is constant conversation and sustained *making* in the jazz performance. Jazz pianist and scholar Vijay Iyer recognizes the musical speech latent within most jazz performances. Analogous to speech, jazz is antiphonal, process-oriented, and contains "*semiotic* dimensions, which enable sonic symbols" to point to other compositions or parts of the same song.[34] *Speak. Sing. Play.*

Once I was playing a gig at an Atlanta restaurant. Jacques, a guitarist, was sitting in with my trio, "The Jazz Pioneers," for the night. We played the standard tune, "Equinox." The melody features notes of long duration, creating a soaring and continuous line. Jacques' solo took the tune in another direction as he filled each beat with bursts of notes. He played louder and higher. The restaurant-goers strained to make conversation over his amplification. Colin the drummer leaned over to me and said, "He's playing too much bullshit." C-r-r-r-ack—he whammed a stick on the snare drum, shocking Jacques back to attention. Jacques stopped playing. The pianist filled the gaping void with three measures of lush chords. Having understood Colin, Jacques reentered his solo with a more subdued approach. Jacques and Colin didn't exchange verbal words, but they were still conversing. This sustained musical dialogue is the *making* of jazz. In *Swing That Music*, Louis Armstrong writes, "There are more than four hundred words used among swing musicians that no one else would understand. They have a language of their own."[35]

Jazz composer and inventive bassist Charles Mingus conveyed his tunes aurally. He wanted his band to hear how the music sounded to him. Mingus and his drummer Dannie Richmond would provide the necessary support or "grid" for other musicians to converse. His drummer explains, "Mingus and I feel each other out as we go but always, when the time comes back into the original beat, we're both always there ... we find a beat that's in the air and just take it out of the air when we want it."[36] The *making* of Mingus's music is not something that lives on the staves and in the bars of the sheet music. Rather, it awakens in the interplay of musicians and personalities.

The *making* of music has always been central to the African and African American musical tradition: "African Americans have their favorite tunes, but it is what is done with and inside those tunes that the listeners look forward to, not the mere playing of them."[37] The joy of jazz isn't found on a recording or in a memorable melody. A "jazz recording" is an oxymoron: A recording limits the performance to only one possibility. The live jazz performance, instead, presents the novelty of surprise. The joy is in the surprise of what may come next. This is a distinct departure from the music of the European conservatory, where technical proficiency is rewarded, and flubbing a single note invites red ink from critics. Anyone can participate and contribute to the pastiche of tuneful colors. *All are welcome, all aboard.*

It might sound obvious today, but democracies value the living over the dead. Thomas Paine argued against monarchy by claiming that nobody should be able to govern after death or "beyond the grave."[38] The British Parliament once said to William and Mary: "We do most humbly and faithfully *submit* ourselves, our heirs and posterities, for ever."[39] Paine believed power should be vested in the living citizenry. The living can alter and amend government in order to fit the times. The living can *make* music that is more reflective of a particular culture. To recite the music of a late composer is to cede personal imagination to the tomb. The *making* of jazz is alive, participatory and invitational at its very root.

The jazz-as-democracy metaphor requires some explaining. It is terribly difficult to define democracy. It's a word that carries not only exacting meaning but can regenerate and emblazon a lost spirit to a disaffected people: Paine wrote to George Washington with the hope that New World democracy would regenerate the government and society of the Old World. The same spirit of openness and humble invitation found in African music is part of our deep democratic tradition. Our political democracy is most awake when it is served by a deliberate call and response discussion. Walt Whitman contends in *Democratic Vistas* that the history of democracy is unwritten because of the self-regeneration implicit within the democratic process. Democracy awakes when we rise from our proverbial slumber. To participate, though, means to possess a spirit of activism. An activist spirit provokes our citizenry to debate and foment change, to make and to process. Whitman wrote how democracy can occur as the highest form of interaction between citizens manifested by literature and arts. Since no mainstream indigenous form of American music existed during Whitman's life, he felt that the creation of such an art would be a composite and democratic experience.

At its core, however, democracy means that power is decentralized; it is a system of government of the people, by the people, and for the people, so said Abraham Lincoln. The people must make the decisions—not the king's court or magistrates. But this often makes for a complicated, heated, and an arduous process. The negotiation and compromises among the sundry citizens of the United States is the process of democracy. It is through the exchanges and conversation that democracy is borne out; the democratic tradition awakes when we *make* it so. Through this democratic discussion comes a decision, harmony, and *claritas*. Music is the ostensible organization of noise, just as government is the organization of society. Trying to find order, a simple score for society, is the work of government. The ordering process, the way of *making* music, differentiates between jazz and noise, democracy and anarchy.

After the colonialists declared their independence, there was a strong desire to create an honest mirror, a direct democracy. The separations of powers and the checks and balances of our current federal system did not exist. Instead, power was concentrated in the people's body, the legislature. Representatives were to be elected every year, and in Rhode Island and Connecticut, twice a year. Stringent term limits were enacted. America was to be governed by several large and boisterous town hall meetings. Bills could not become law under the Pennsylvania Constitution until they were publicized in town circulars, accepted by town convention, and finally enacted in the ensuing legislative session.[40] The establishment of a democracy was a new phenomenon. Some in Europe looked aghast at America's fledgling democracy. A Frenchman wrote to Benjamin Franklin with an offer to serve as America's new king. Because of his Norman roots, the Frenchman felt qualified to rule the new country.[41] But early Americans knew they didn't want another king. America's first attempt at democracy was very much about the *making*. Citizens wanted to make their government a carbon copy of the prevailing whims and confusions of the masses. The mob ruled in the name of liberty.

It wasn't until the Constitutional Convention that the filter of republicanism eschewed the "politics of liberty" in favor of the representational democratic tradition we recognize today. The founding fathers recognized the importance of a centralized and powerful government. Wouldn't it be a mockery if each state conducted its own foreign policy? It would be like Scotland and England waging international wars under different flags, argued federalist John Jay. The federalists also presciently warned about the possibility of states warring with each other. Who or what would regulate such a dispute?

No matter how virtuosic your lead alto saxophonist may be, he or she needs the support of the center. Operating at the fringes leads to disorder and anarchy. The politics of liberty, the "one man, one vote" principle, can be found in most jazz combos, but the power of the center must prevail. However, jazz critic Martin Williams recognizes the importance of individuality and its non-threatening position towards the group: "It is as if jazz were saying to us that not only is far greater individuality possible to man than he has so far allowed himself, but that such individuality, far from being a threat to a cooperative social structure, can actually enhance society."[42] It is the conversation between liberty and security, checks and balances, improvisation and group play that connects jazz with democracy.]

I admit that to explain the jazz-as-democracy metaphor is an exercise in relativity. It is difficult to prove the absolute veracity of any metaphor. But the humanities and social sciences are arguably the provinces of such relativism. And an exercise in relativity is not one of futility. We think in frames and images. In their defense of metaphor, Professors George Lakoff and Mark Turner claim that metaphors are ubiquitous: "Metaphor allows us to understand ourselves and our world in ways that no other modes of thought can."[43] The metaphor of "life is a journey" shapes how we perceive our lives, e.g., "making their way in life," "giving their lives some direction," and poet Robert Frosts' "Two roads diverged in a wood, and I—I took the one less traveled by…"[44] Metaphors aren't just part of the poet's artillery of rhetorical devices. They can help shape us. After all, notes Murray, man's perception is "forever jumping out of focus."[45]

Professor of Foreign Policy Michael Mandelbaum uses a horticulture-as-democracy metaphor to explain how representative government must be grown from an underlying society. Flowers and trees need suitable soil, water, and sunlight in order to grow. Similarly, democracies require appropriate climate and conditions in order to take root and bloom: "The equivalent, for a country, of the climate and the soil for horticulture, the social basis of its political system, is its political culture … skills and habits that have accumulated over time."[46] A democracy can only be wrought if the underlying culture supports it, or by a tendency to negotiate and *make* conversations as a means to making decisions. A democracy without the institutions of civil society or lawyers to litigate is like planting a sunflower in the Sahara. The horticulture-as-democracy metaphor instructs that democracy takes time, often generations, to learn and institutionalize. A democracy can arguably be installed by force, but in order to flourish, it requires the fecundity of democratic habit and engaged minds, and sometimes even art, as the codification off creative expression.

The jazz-as-democracy metaphor can furnish an additional image to conceptualize both things. By recognizing the call and response tendencies of jazz and democracy, we can eventually recognize the importance of an art that reflects our true democratic tradition of *making*. The tradition of making is the broad similarity of jazz and democracy. Security and freedom are necessary to moderate this *making* of change. The activist spirit that pervades democratic discussion is found in the jazz jam session. *Making* doesn't mean a free-for-all or mob rule. The three-branch system incorporated appropriate checks and balances to bring grid-like order to government. That is, the making of democracy requires the grid of security and the liberty of improvisation. To participate in the democratic process requires an activist spirit. Don't dally over the chord changes of apathy. The musical incarnation of democracy, evidenced with jazz, deposited democracy into aesthetic action.

With a working definition of democracy, let's move onwards to jazz. We can start with Merriam-Webster: Jazz is an "American music developed especially from ragtime and blues and characterized by propulsive syncopated rhythms, polyphonic ensemble playing, varying degrees of improvisation, and often deliberate distortions of pitch and timbre ..." Early in its history, jazz was associated with sexual promiscuity. Some towns like Zion, Illinois banned the music because it was an apparent vice like tobacco and alcohol.[47] American dancer Ada "Bricktop" Smith remembered that once she ran into pianist Jelly Roll Morton who couldn't decide whether to be a pimp or piano player. She told him to do both.[48] In fact, "jazz" was a synonym for fornication in some circles.

As for the history of its denotation, several theories have emerged, all of which have skeptics. Perhaps "jazz" was named from a person's name like "Jasbo" Brown who played piccolo and cornet.[49] Others believe it was derived from vaudeville performances. Yet another competing theory is that it came from Africa, a word that meant "to speed things up."[50] The French word "jaser," which means "to chat," led to another theory. Some "jazz" artists did not particularly like the word; Duke Ellington suggested "Negro music" and "America's classical music." Alternative words were suggested to describe the music: "Amerimusic," "jarb," and "crewcut."[51]

Any and all definitions are problematic and are sure to furrow the critical brow. But I will try to condense the definition of jazz simply to this: A modern music that emphasizes the *making* of music, reconciling the interests of the individual with that of the group. With this shorter definition, I hope to get to the crux of what makes the jazz-as-democracy trope helpful: The process of governing and making music calls for everyone's voice, filtering each voice through the prism of republicanism with the centrality of the rhythm.

To explore the jazz-as-democracy theme is to delve into what is American about America. America is an idea writ in sound, color and imagination; it is iconoclastic, democratic and fiercely innovative. Most recognize that jazz is an American art. But what is it that makes it American? An appropriate place to start our journey is with what erstwhile editor of *Harper's Magazine* John Kouwenhoven asked in his 1954 essay: "What's American about America?" He suggests that dichotomies of materialism and idealism, revolution and conservatism, and individualism and collectivism are fundamentally American.[52] Battling opposites create tension, out of which emerges a resplendent and harmonious nation. He offers Santayana's architectural image as an example: "The American mind was split in half, one half symbolized by the skyscraper, the other by the neat reproductions of Colonial mansions..."[53] Balancing opposites, negotiating and compromising with different viewpoints, asserting one's individuality and respecting the group, these are the makings of America.

If we were to sketch a list of some of those things that are quintessentially America, many of them would share a commonality: the process of making a conversation in which the individual is reconciled with the group. A sober red, white, and blue slate of Americana can reveal shared properties to our American values. Many quintessentially American things are all about the discussion and not the decree. And from the *making* process of democracy emerges a certain democratic spirit—to listen to another perspective. To make means to participate. It is an activist and democratic *spirit* that saved America from itself in the 1860s, 1890s, 1930s, and 1960s.[54] It is an activist spirit that is to be resilient and self-amends, plays another chord, or redrafts stalled legislation.

The democratic tradition cannot easily be replicated, packaged, and Dumbo dropped into another country or organization. De Tocqueville wrote of how Mexico used parts of the US Constitution on which to build its own democracy, but the results were different.[55] It's not that democracy requires thought, but as Mann believed, "Democracy *is* thought."[56] In order to build the necessary democratic institutions of government, the citizenry must possess a cultivated and sophisticated activist spirit. The spirit of democracy is evidenced in the civil society of volunteer organizations that builds houses for the poor, discusses legislation punishing driving under the influence, and sings in the town square during Christmas season. Months after September 11, 2001, volunteerism increased dramatically, emblematic of America's civil society and its "grace under pressure."

A democratic spirit has been perennially tilled from soil beneath the city grids and skyscrapers. De Tocqueville wrote, " ... the township was organized before the county, the county before the State, the State before the Union."[57] The New England colonies, stretching as far back as 1650, placed a premium on liberty (power in the hands of the local people). Historian Charles M. Andrews argues that the colonies respected the Crown and were not democracies.[58] But they were largely autonomous, thanks to their geographic distance from their imperial overlords. Some in England suspected the colonists were creating an "unmixed democracy" similar to that of Athens, where the people comprise the governing body.[59] But colonists denied such intentions, claiming that unmixed democracies were impractical, and that democracy would devolve into "olocracy," or "government by the rabble."[60] In the colonial townships were planted the seeds of democracy. The blossoming flowers grew in the colonial gardens, nectar to be collected come 1776. The very fact that colonists were organizing townships around democratic principles indicates the early activist spirit necessary for a vibrant democracy.

De Tocqueville wrote about the large associations that form in order to discuss common issues. The Vermont town hall meetings are representative not only of political democracy but civil democracy, for every citizen has a vote and must live with the social ramifications of his or her actions. Today's incarnation of participatory democracy can be found on Web sites like Meetup.com that serve as virtual forums for democratic gatherings. Jazz played its role as an integrated force in civil society: White musician Bill Evans performed with black musicians and integrated bands toured Europe. It was difficult for white audiences to respect jazz and not respect the black musicians. The differences of opinion provide for different democratic hues not only in political democracy, but American civil society. The invitation of jazz and democracy is open to all.

Professor Kouwenhoven provides twelve examples that illustrate America the beautiful, including the Constitution (*duh*), the Manhattan skyline, chewing gum, and jazz.[61] These examples are "quintessentially American" because they reflect discernable American values. Writer Gerald Earley noted that two thousand years from now, America will be known for the Constitution, baseball, and jazz.[62] These slices of Americana share the propensity for conversation and negotiation, for a process of making. They openly invite the democratic spirit of activism and self-amendment. All these examples share the same birthplace of America and take on a magnificent manifestation of Americana.

Quintessentially American: The United States Constitution

The importance of a constitution to a democratic nation cannot be overstated. Paine wrote "a constitution is *antecedent* to a government."[63] It contains values and principles of the collective people. The US Constitution is America's Bible. It serves as the gospel in legal circles and political debates. The Constitution safeguards America's democracy from being usurped. The thirteen colonies drafted the Constitution because of the inadequacy of their prior agreement, the Articles of Confederation, ratified in 1781. The Articles gave the colonies a unified front when dealing with Europeans, but it augured ill for executing the matters of government. Congress could make decisions but could not enforce them. It couldn't levy taxes (and war debt-heavy states refused to ante up) or print money. Each state was its own fiefdom, operating independently of its neighbor states. The individual burden placed on the state had not worked, for America was on the brink of failure, thanks to amassing debts.[64]

After ridding themselves of the yoke to the British Empire, the colonialists arguably overreacted with their proclivity for a direct democracy. The "politics of liberty" encouraged a vigilante spirit. Perhaps the best example was Army captain Daniel Shays and his cohorts (named the "regulators") who were angered because of excessive taxes. Shays and his armed companions tried by force to prevent the courts in Western Massachusetts from taking the bench. Shays's rebellion was thwarted by the local Massachusetts militia, which was financed by local merchants. The lack of central authority created a vacuum for citizens to right their perceived wrongs.

The nation's leaders watched Shays' rebellion with distress. It could have led to George Washington's epiphany of the need for a stronger central government. In fact, most of the leading federalists who advocated for the adoption of the Constitution bore military experience. They recognized the importance of security for their new state. Alexander Hamilton, the aide-de-camp in Washingon's army, experienced first-hand the inability of the state to raise funds for war. He was one of the first to call for a potent central power around which to organize America's political democracy. In *Federalist No. 9*, Hamilton reminds the reader to learn from the dismantling of Greece and Rome. America was in need of a government that could thwart external attack and avoid internal corruption.[65] Spare a spoonful of sympathy for the Articles. It was because of this compact that America recognized that the improvisatory vigilantism of post-colonial life was insufficient for the security of the new nation.

The Constitution demonstrated that the central government would hold rank over the states. With the introduction of checks and balances, the power of the legislature was diminished.[66] The framers adroitly embedded cross-purposes in the Constitution: To unite against the enemy and to divide individual state strength so that power wouldn't be concentrated in one entity.[67] Instead of concentrating power in each state, the Constitution was designed to find an equilibrium between the "two rival governments," those of the nation and of the state.[68] The framers feared the ascendant powers of states (the individual) and thereby went to lengths to restrict power. Madison wrote Jefferson on the need for federal judicial control over state laws in October 1787.[69] The Constitution did not endeavor to squelch each state's independence but to moderate it.[70]

The brilliance of Madison was that he chose not to change or flummox human nature. He recognized the power of ambition and suggested that if men were angels, no government was necessary. Man demonstrated Machiavellian inclinations when betrothed to power. Madison pitted ambitious and competing interests *against* each other but *within* the same federal system. With the federal system, the second coming of Daniel Shays could choose a path to power within the system instead of rebelling against it. He can *make* democracy by participating within it. In America's democracy, man may not respect anyone else, but he respects the law because he is implicitly part author, a stake-holder in the contract of democracy. This respect gives the *making* of democracy a legal and moral force. Violence is indeed antithetical to democratic values and principles. Instead of viewing opponents as warring enemies, democracy teaches that opponents must be treated as a contrary interest. Compromise and negotiation are encouraged.[71] Peaceful elections replace violent revolutions and coup d'états as a means of changing government. The federal system registered in the Constitution is built on the cornerstone of reconciliation, as it mediates the atavistic "mutually antagonistic" ideas of equality and liberty that debuted in Athens.[72] Though as Paine predicted, "What Athens was in miniature, America will be in magnitude."[73]

The federalist system was a result of several compromises that balanced competing interests. The great debate about whether the nation would be either a league-federal government model or population-federal government model was settled with the Connecticut Compromise that created a bicameral legislature composed of the House of Representatives, based on population, and the Senate, where each state is given two representatives. Fiery was the debate over representation: The Delaware delegation was directed to leave the convention if the Constitution did not include equal suffrage.[74] Additional compromises included the "3/5 Compromise," where five slaves counted as three free men (this compromise was born out of the Connecticut Compromise, where population determined representation), and the process of electing a president, which was perhaps the most difficult compromise.[75]

"The sovereignty of the United States is shared between the Union and the States," observed de Tocqueville.[76] This sharing of sovereignty and power is what makes the Constitution an instrument of federalism. The *making*, the negotiation, and the conversation of different interests helps to vest power in the people—not usurped by one excessively ambitious government branch. Tocqueville compared the balance of power to France, where the King held authoritative power, whereas in America the President has limited authority. An intricate series of checks and balances were installed to decentralize power in the Constitution. The President appoints Supreme Court justices who are to be confirmed by the Senate. The legislature can impeach a justice. The judiciary determines the constitutionality of the legislation. In the Constitution's primary role as reconciler between individual state and collectivist union, it ironically made the individual stronger, but not at the expense of the union. That is, states elbowed for power during the Constitutional Convention, but instead of the state becoming stronger in response to the Union, the individual did ("We the people … "). The Bill of Rights protects the rights of individual citizens. We as individuals contribute taxes to Uncle Sam and rush troops to battle in order to defend him.

The triumph of republicanism resulted when the Constitution was adopted. The Federalists advocated for a republican government that was analogous to a "filter." They were worried about too much democracy. Mob rule populism. A filtration process would eliminate philistines from legislative bodies. Men of merit would rise to the top, just like those who participated in the Philadelphia Convention. Men with virtuosic minds and capabilities would make for reasoned and cool, deliberate and logical debate. For instance, the complex method of electing the president (and electoral process for US Senators before the Seventeenth Amendment) guarded against the "tyranny of the majority."[77] Instead of a vengeful smattering of uneducated lawmakers, an enlightened coterie would serve as the *makers* of America's republic.

In order to *make* democracy, one must understand the rules of the game: the grid-like security of the rules and the ability to self-amend and improvise. The Constitution is inordinately extensible. Kouwenhoven compares the Constitution to the city grid. The checks and balances and articles create "the underlying beat which gives momentum and direction to a political process … 'a harmonious system of mutual frustration.'"[78] City grids are difficult if not impossible to redraw. One must adhere to the physics and geometry of the city's plan. One can't eliminate a third of a city and start over. We must respect the limits of a property within the grid and improvise with the lot we have. The Constitution is no different. The Bill of Rights outlines the freedom of speech, the freedom of religion, and a host of other rights. These rights are the grid on which we can rely. The text of the Constitution is the grid that unites and brings order to the dueling interests of individual and union.

But the Constitution can also be improvised upon. The grid allows for new laws, interpretations, ideas, and amendments. Contrast this with the French Constitution(s): The 1789 Constitution established a liberal constitutional monarchy; the Constitution of the Year VIII (adopted in 1799) created the Consulate; the 1814 Charter reestablished monarchy; so it was with the Constitutions of the Second French Republic, Second French Empire, French Third Republic; and the many compacts not included in this brief list.[79] We often take for granted the grid of American democracy, our Constitution. Other countries like France encountered difficulty in drafting a document that acted as a reconciler, compromiser, burden sharer, and self-extender. The purple Iraqi fingers point to problems with creating an Islamic grid for democracy. The improvisation, or vertical steel of the US Constitution, is manifested in the thousands of resolutions, bills, and laws passed every year with the possibility of self-amendment.[80] That a four-page document has been able to unify a country for over two hundred years is nothing short of extraordinary. If the Constitution were not extensible, man's penchant for improvisation may have eviscerated the document instead of engaging in the open-ended democratic process.

The self-amendment process recognizes the imperfection of man: We make mistakes. But the grid allows for us to right our wrongs.[81] Amendments are not only self-corrective but adaptive. The Constitution may appropriately fit the current times but it can be amended to adapt to the future. The Constitution indeed adapts and lives. The improvisatory amendment process is an American innovation; the British were skeptical of self-amendment, yet as of the early 1990s, less than 4 percent of constitutions worldwide did not include a self-amendment process.[82] The amendment process has made the Constitution (and state constitutions) into a renewing organic entity. The average state constitution has grown from 19,300 words when they were first written to 24,300 in 1991.[83] State constitutions tend to be longer then our national compact and illustrate the extensible nature of local governing documents. Indeed, changing our country's grid should not be taken lightly, but we creatures realize our shortcomings. Because of its basis in popular sovereignty, our Constitution's amendment process is the second most arduous in the world.[84] Nevertheless, the grid must be extended, for example, to include greater civil rights and women's rights, to rid ourselves from the blues of society.[85]

Quintessentially American: The Manhattan Skyline

To envision the grid of the Constitution takes an imaginative mind. But the city grid and skyscraper are as real as concrete and steel. In the Manhattan skyline, Kouwenhoven sees what Whitman described: "A dry and flat Sahara appears, these cities, crowded with petty grotesques, malformations, phantoms, playing meaningless antics."[86] Placed under the "moral microscope," New York the mirage appears, baiting the innocent bystander's itch for opportunity and desire. But placed under the lens of jazz, the architectural racket symbolizes a "man-made Sierra" that represents the grid and anti-grid of America's making.[87] Acclaimed architect Le Corbusier considered the Manhattan skyline "hot jazz in stone and steel."[88] Each building asserts its individuality, an improvisation off the Constitutional grid. But when viewed from afar, the skyscrapers are frozen in conversations of steel girders and concrete beams. Erected in 1928, the Chrysler Building was crafted with an external art deco style that was part of the architectural vernacular of the time. Rockefeller Center, built in 1932, and the Empire State Building, built in 1931, are not uniform in ornamentation. In fact, they're just the opposite.

What of the Freedom Tower, the building to replace the World Trade Center? It is proposed to stretch 1,776 feet—the tallest scraper in the world. David Childs, one of its architects, asserts, "It must be iconic. Simple and pure in its form, a memorable form, that would proclaim the resiliency and the spirit of our democracy."[89] Childs invokes the self-amending and improvisational nature of America's democracy. The skyline can self-amend with each new concrete geyser. There was no intelligent designer of the Manhattan skyline as a whole. Buildings sprang up one by one. And a composite, man-made mountain range emerged as the polished face of the continent.

In the steel chaos, Kouwenhoven contends that two things keep the skyline ordered: the (non-racially segregated) city street grid, and the architectural standards of the buildings.[90] In 1811, a New York commission proposed its plan, which included "improvements touching the layout of streets and roads in the City of New York."[91] The city grid made travel more efficient, even at the expense of increased pollution and narrower streets. The commission's intention was to "subdivide the land and lay out streets."[92] They considered embellishing the plan with circles and grand avenues, but decided that any such measure would sacrifice the utility of the city. The tangle of roads and buildings in London, for example, confuses tourists who try to navigate the city. The medieval design of London contrasts with that of New York. The New York plan demonstrated man's dominion over nature: "The landscape *had to be subdued* ... for the sake of rapid development of a commercial city whose single unit was the private building lot.[93] The plan ignored the undulations of the land, instead converting it to pure geometry.[94] One obvious drawback to the 1811 plan was the lack of horizontal space. Wood construction became hazardous as the buildings became taller, so steel cages supplanted them.

The burning steel that's needed to construct the monstrous buildings is very much the "three-dimensional variant of the gridiron street plan."[95] The efficient and monotonous steel cage structure used in one building is virtually the same as the next. Just as jazz (the popular music of the day) was mass-recorded and helped spread commercial entertainment across America (and Europe) in the first half of the twentieth century, some architectural creations were mass-produced. And when a functionally better creation came along, the new architectural form was mass-produced. The balloon frame allowed for easier wood construction and eventually made the industrialization of houses possible.[96] *Remember the exurbs—Pleasantville, Ridge Mountain, Deer Park.* The city grid and three-dimensional grid of the skyscraper order the noise of the ever-changing improvisational chaos.

The three-dimensional steel grid is a structural necessity for all skyscrapers. Without such a grid, these man-made mountains would topple. The constraints of engineering moderate the liberty of design. Similar to the call for central power found in the US Constitution, each building must have an indomitable internal strength, able to quell the insurrections of improvisation. But the power of the internal grid did not squelch architects from self-amending and deviating from the core. French writer Jean Paul Sartre noted the American city changes faster than its European counterpart: "For [Europeans], a city is, above all, a past; for [Americans], it is mainly a future; what they like in the city is everything it has not yet become and everything it can be ..."[97] The city gridiron and three-dimensional cage found in skyscrapers allow for the improvisation—art deco, modern, neoclassical, or the style of the times. The internal form is consistent, and the style is beautifully improvised.

In *Paterson*, American poet John Carlos Williams suggests the city as an extension of the inhabitant.[98] New York's skyline is an urban representation of its residents, who possess an open Kouwenhoven split mind of grid and improvisation. So, too, is a democracy a reflection of the American mind. The US Constitution and the Manhattan skyline illustrate how democracies need to reconcile the individual with the group, like in a fiery call and response jazz performance. But let's take this one level higher and look at what these things also have in common: the same process of organizing noise. The Constitution orders the interests and noise of many into a governing whole. The blooming skyscrapers may declare their individuality, but they cannot grow wild. They must respect the grid. The democratic process at work helps to reconcile security and liberty.

In his *Noise Orders*, David Brown takes us past the grid-improvisation parallel of jazz to the skyscraper. He uses the broad jazz aesthetic to help elucidate modern architecture. The "frozen music" of architecture invokes the open form and democratic spirit of the jazz jam session. He cites historian Nancy Troy to explain the motivation of artists during the interwar years: "to work through the arts to achieve an ideal future when walls that separate men would be broken down."[99] The prevalence of glass architecture summoned the spirit of the jam session, inviting the sun to shine upon all men and women. The same spirit of the jazz jam session that obliterated the rehearsed and segregated forms of music jumped into the architectural arts and helped produce an open architecture movement.

The Democratic Properties of America's Music

The parallel of jazz with democracy works for two reasons. First, jazz is music of negotiation, conversation, reconciliation, and *making.* In the 1950s, Minton's Playhouse in New York hosted many celebrated jazz jam sessions in which musicians could perform without preparation and experiment with new ideas. Successful jazz musicians like saxophonist Lester Young interfaced with younger musicians like pianist Thelonious Monk, who would become "The High Priest of Bebop."[100] The reconciliation of many voices respecting their equality, from Coltrane's ripping solos to the impressionist chords of Bill Evans, is part of this process, the making of sound and ordering of noise. The lack of preparation made for the unexpected. There is joy in *making* music together, not just reciting it to an audience. The performers, not an ancient playwright, shape the agenda both in jazz and democracy. The jazz band gives every musician their moment, organizing the performance democratically with a respect for the equality and individuality of each musician. Just as the Constitution and skyscraper require strong centers, jazz also needs the centrality of the rhythm and groove.

The free jazz movement in the 1960s and 1970s epitomized the personal declaration of independence. The music of John Coltrane, Cecil Taylor, and Eric Dolphy were criticized as "anti-jazz" by some cultural commentators.[101] I do not share the critical disdain for free jazz, but believe it's analogous to Shays' rebellion, a personal style that removes the internal strength of swing. To *make* jazz swing and evoke a finger-snapping, foot-thumping feel, there is a necessity for a grid of rhythm and the self-amending solo.

The second reason that the jazz-as-democracy metaphor is instructive is because of the invitational spirit of jazz. Jazz musicians come from all walks of life and demonstrate that power can flow in the direction of anyone. Many jazz musicians came from humble origins and their talent catapulted them to the forefront of America's first indigenous art. Though Louis Armstrong was born in a rickety house in Jane Alley in New Orleans, he "saw life from the gutter up and learned to accept it all."[102] Everyone's voice is to be heard, as anyone can participate in the musical jam session. The activist spirit found in town halls that rid the country of its blues is the same optimistic and participatory spirit found in most jazz music.

The African Tradition

Many jazz histories describe it as "American music."[103] But any true historical study shows the jazz tradition as African American. In its earliest formation, the cultural imprint of Africa can be heard. Admittedly, thousands of African cultures differ and contrast. But Professor Albert Raboteau finds that many of these African cultures share "similar modes of perception" and common values.[104] It's out of these shared values that one can trace Africa to the acoustics of jazz.

Many Africans believed in a supreme God or Higher Power to whom they show graciousness, honor, and respect. Religion was very much a personal philosophy and way of life. Africans saw little difference between the secular and the holy when it came to arts and culture. Floyd notes that there is no word for "religion" in traditional African cultures because of the pervasiveness of the deity in everyday life.[105] God was always to be honored, not just in rituals and worship ceremonies.

However, ritual served as the principal way to enact myth. In order to honor their deities, Africans performed the rituals of song and dance. To imitate and emulate a particular God through the ritual of dance enabled man to transcend his own shortcomings and live in the image of God. Perhaps the most common dance formation was the "ring." The ring is a circular formation of dancers, onlookers, and occasional participants. Floyd describes the ring as a "symbol of community, solidarity, affirmation and catharsis."[106] A ring would occur in the makeshift dance venue—a town square, courtyard, or communal garden.[107] In the Akan culture, participants moved in a circle and invited shouts of participation from the audience. The call and response blurred the lines between the performers and the audience. The *makers* of the music came from all parts of the ring. The ring was a mirror of African society, their direct democracy of culture.

The ring performance was the ritual that helped translate the raw African experience into art. The stylization of life, lest we forget Malraux, is arguably the whatness of art. The cultural memory of the ring can be found in African American music. Floyd traces the shouts of the African ring to the scat singing in jazz music.[108] Calls were common to Western African culture; they were used to announce news and meetings, and to share information. The call and response or "antiphony" was a translation of African experience into art.

In several African cultures, there is no word that matches the Western notion of "music" because there is no separation between music and daily life. Ethnomusicologist Charles Keil notes that in the Tiv language, the verb "dugh" takes on several meanings: composing music, fishing, or collecting vegetables.[109] Music is integrated into daily life and not compartmentalized into the concert venues found in Western society. In his comprehensive *Work Songs*, Ted Gioia cites the observations of a young man traveling through Africa. The young man describes the music of African life: Women sing while at work, the war drum calls men to fight, and the melodious stories and songs of raconteurs enchant their audiences. The substantial life experience of an African helps to explain the tradition of *making* music as opposed to reciting it.

In antebellum America, slaves gathered on the Sabbath to form a ring and shuffle foot-first, clapping like thunder while shouting to the sky. The West African slaves brought the cultural memories of "polyrhythms, cross-rhythms, time line, elisions, hockets, ululations, tremolos, vocables, grunts, hums, shouts, and melismatic phrasings..."[110] They brought the cultural ingredients from Africa to early African American music.

The ring structure reinforced the ensemble character of its performers: They were slaves together and shared in the horror of their circumstance. Music and dance was the collective release as the central motif of early African American music was freedom: "Because out of that peculiar experience that African Americans have had, of being un-free in a free land, has come the possibility to teach the rest of us a true battle cry of freedom. That was the anthem of the Civil War. Jazz is our battle cry of freedom," notes Burns.[111] The stylization of early African American experience was manifested in the freedom slave songs and spirituals. But the African tradition did not stop with vocal vernacular. African American music was accompanied by African instruments like the banjo, reed flutes, and drums.[112]

Musicologist Kofi Agawu argues that it can be problematic to reduce African-based music to rhythm only. Perhaps the influence of the African tradition in African American music can best be spelled out by Floyd's synthesis: (1) The rhythmic tradition incorporates hand clapping and polyrhythms; (2) the melodic tradition incorporates the shouts of the ring, grunts, moans, elisions, instrument mimicking, and pentatonic modality; (3) lastly, the textual tradition incorporates the stories of African *muthos* with a rich call and response of participation.[113]

The African and African American tradition is very much about the *making*. Unlike the recitals of Western Art music, where the centrality of the score is paramount, the liberty of emotive performance reigns. When the slaves were emancipated, they were able to express themselves, gather, and participate in the *making* of music, without encountering the disrepute and punishment of crushing slave masters. African Americans sang of freedom and valorized the bluesman whose tragic optimism was never vengeful, only heroic in declaring his freedom. The solo of the bluesman is the "manifestation of the values of the ring," an energizing and peaceful sound that connotes liberty and respect for the central rhythm.[114]

I should qualify this idea of *making* vis-à-vis Western Art music. It is certainly not a uniquely African or African American creation to *make* and improvise. Musical inventions, short contrapuntal compositions from the Renaissance and Middle Ages relied largely on improvisation.[115] Monteverdi's *L'incoronazione di Poppea* employs a figured bass and vocal line. The singers interpret and embellish the score.[116] *Accents, appoggiaturas, arpeggios.* During Beethoven's audition for Mozart, he improvised a selection. Mozart accused Beethoven of having prepared the improvisation. Beethoven improvised again, this time convincing Mozart that his musical machination was authentic.[117] Bach, Mozart, and Beethoven were fluent improvisers and believed in the beauty of spontaneity. Mozart did not write any cadenzas for his concerti.[118] But as a whole, the canon of creativity for Western art music is limited to composition. Rote performance isn't the same as *making* within a song. The tradition of *making* music represents the triumph of the verb over the noun, to make instead of a classical recitation.[119] The jam session requires proficiency but a lack of rehearsal. Playing without music is tantamount to dropping your guard. The African American tradition of *making* the blues to rid the blues is indicative of America's democratic process: Through government, our ducks are turned into swans.

The Early Rise of Freedom

However, the ring of community still dominated early jazz music. The improvisational aspect of jazz took time to develop, as early jazz music was not improvised. The all-white Original Dixieland Jazz Band (ODJB) performed Dixieland compositions minus improvisation. Their music was highly conventional; only the drummer mixed it up. King Oliver's Creole Jazz Band performed in a "controlled" manner.[120] Meanwhile, early jazz benefited from the myth of improvisation. Some bandleaders compelled their groups to memorize music in order to appear improvised. The advent of the solo represents the fusion of African to American culture. The concept of solo was unfamiliar to West African musicians.[121] The emphasis on the individual's troubles in the blues is representative of the Western world's notion of life as an individual experience or the metaphorical "life as a journey."[122] The jazz solo is a result of the American imprint on the African. Some scholars even say that African Americans improvised out of practical reasons, in part, because they weren't conversant with the European idiom or with reading music.[123]

"Collective improvisation" emerged with New Orleans jazz, the first incarnation of the music. The entire group improvises concomitantly, yet each performer asserts his or her individuality. Whitman wrote of the "lump character" of a group, and that only from it can individualism emerge.[124] Perhaps a useful analogy is a flock of birds: Each bird flies in its own way but they all head in the same direction. If an individual by himself is lonely and uninspired, an individual in a group can find what Indian poet Rabindrinath Tagore reasoned the Universal Self, and discover his definition in relation to the higher order. A trombone player can scuttle alone. With a group he may assert his ensemble individuality. In his introduction of *New Orleans Style*, Bill Russell writes that New Orleans groups must strive to help each other instead of grabbing the solo-induced spotlight.[125] New Orleans musicians never played standing up when given the choice. They sat in a single row, which elicited jeremiads from other musicians who thought their formation was reminiscent of old men. Still, today at Preservation Hall—the famous New Orleans jazz venue—the group sits in two lines because of the lack of horizontal space.[126] There is no "front" or "back" line because everyone is playing rhythm. For the final chorus, everyone stands up together. The phenomenon of the standing soloist didn't occur until later in the twentieth century.

When asked for the definition of "swing," Victor Goines, Director of Jazz Studies at The Juilliard School, describes it as "soulful participation with style and coordination." His definition invokes Whitman's "lump character" of the individual who performs with the ensemble. Soulful individuals participate in the making of jazz. Each individual has his or her own style, a freedom to improvise and create—*candy-coated, redolent, somnolent, chic.* The lion's share of rehearsal time, then, deals with coordination of the beat. Coordination is analogous to the filtration process of representative democracy. The making of coherent and harmonious music turfs out the competing styles of the musicians. The coordination of the eighth note triplets over the beat propels jazz out from the score and into the audience. The eighth notes are written as two notes of equal duration. The "swing" feel surfaces when the first note is played like a quarter note, the second as an eighth note of a triplet. It becomes second nature to interpret straight notes into a swing feel for the jazz musician. And therein we find the axiomatic city grid of jazz that Kouwenhoven imagineers: rhythm.

The Jazz Grid

French jazz musician André Hodeir endeavored to find the distinguishing feature of jazz. He dispensed with improvisation, tonality, form, and sound in favor of rhythm. One can take issue with his project, which tried to establish the "*telos*" of the music.[127] But his research magnifies the importance of rhythm and coordination in jazz. Hodeir felt that "jazz rhythmic sources are in the service of distinctive rhythmic goals of *jazz*."[128] Melodies in jazz aren't tonal concepts, when evaluated under the rules of the conservatory. Symphonies of the Classical era are dulcet and lyrical. A Lee Morgan trumpet solo cadenza, however, scatters "wrong" notes in a gust of pauses, crescendos, and modulations. Onomatopoeic buzz, squeals, and murmurs—filling the solo—aren't melodic as much as they are rhythmic. The trumpet is a *percussive* instrument that adds another car to the train tracks of rhythm. Dizzy Gillespie conceived in rhythm and gave birth with melody. It is the moment of conception—rhythm—which is the process and *telos* of jazz. With the rise of jazz, the piano became a more percussive instrument, where the pianist pressed the pedals, varied his touch, and accented the group aesthetic with a distinctly rhythmic approach.[129]

Rhythm must be constructed. Even Le Corbusier acknowledged that jazz telegraphed its times as an "era of construction."[130] The engineer determines the composition of the steel and concrete foundation. The steel and concrete "grid" is the pulsating beat that drives the song. Usually the 2/4 or 4/4 meters set the borders for the song. That is, two beats a measure or four beats per measure. Many jazz standards such as "All the Things You Are" and "I Got Rhythm" are constructed with the 4/4 grid. Hodeir refers to this rhythmic layer as the *"infrastructure."*[131] The infrastructure is the immovable city grid and Bill of Rights that must be respected. It represents the rules and the horse (not cart) of the song. When the rhythm section locks into the infrastructure, the band starts to groove. The engineer consults with the architect on the actual building's design, and how it will relate to the foundation. This *"superstructure"* is the ancillary rhythm and three-dimensional grid of the city skyscraper, laid over the primary rhythm of the foundation.[132] Dizzy Gillespie's percussive trumpet solo serves as the superstructure to the thumping "grid" beat of 4/4 that the bass player supplies. The superstructure can be magnificently brazen and declare a soloist's technical proficiency, but it cannot experiment too much with the infrastructural rhythm. When these two rhythms are out of sync, the skyscraper takes a terrible tumble, and the groove halts. Magic happens when the infrastructure and superstructure merge—not playing in unison, but when the contrasting rhythms create the intrinsic polyrhythm of swing in which jazz is born. When a jazz band is in true swing, it's like the city jiving to life, the smooth commute almost subterranean in its affect, rumbling over the grid, transporting the audience across the song in consonant comfort. It is incumbent on the jazz performer to feel the contrasting rhythm and build the *rhythmic* superstructure to respect the integrity of the groove. Only then does a concern for melody enter.

In the 1950s and 1960s, bebop became the popular form of jazz, presenting sheets of sound that befuddled the listener. Charlie Parker's solo on "Donna Lee" sounds like a tireless, unstoppable blizzard of notes. Despite the curtains of sound larding the superstructure, the infrastructure still drives the song, thanks to the steadiness of the bass and drums. Hodeir describes Parker's respect of the grid: "[He] distributed accents now on the beat, now on the off beat, now just before the beat, while still maintaining contact with indispensable points of rhythmic support."[133] To be sure, the groove may become more poly-rhythmic during a bebop tune, as jazz scholar Scott DeVeaux insists, but the underlying grid *does not* change.[134] The rhythms of jazz are a marked distinction of classical music where such rhythms—ostinatos, for example—are employed as artful embellishment.

One-part revisionism is due. The underlying grid can be tweaked. John Coltrane frequently performed with two drummers, creating an intense polyrhythm in the infrastructure. Pianist Dave Brubeck built some of his compositions with the meters of 9/8, 6/4, and 7/4.[135] Trumpeter Don Ellis's band performed songs with 9/4 and 27/16. One observer noted, "The only tune they play in 4/4 is *Take Five!*"[136] When jazz guitarist Joe Puma filled in for another guitarist, he came across time signatures 5/4, 3/8, and 7/8 while he looked through the music. He asked the bandleader, "What are these, hat sizes?"[137] Songs went back and forth between different meters, changing the sway of the superstructure but never removing its concrete. The progressive feeling of jazz's rhythm was described by trumpeter Clark Terry as the

4/4 rock rhythm jumping up and down, whereas the 4/4 jazz rhythm pushes the band forward.[138]

Chris Goddard observed in *Jazz Away from Home* that French light music incorporated meters of 2/4 and 3/4, in contrast to the American march (and jazz) music of 4/4. The French meters allowed for a fewer amount of beats within the measure, not enough room for what Gunther Schuller described as the "democratization" of the rhythm.[139] With 2/4 and 3/4, the first beat of the measure is stressed, whereas in jazz's 4/4 meter, there is more room to stress the weak beats of two and four. Tension and release are equal within the rhythm. Each beat has adequate time to demonstrate its importance to the groove, allowing for equality of voices—where the power of the grooves is vested in the four equal beats, just as a democracy vests power among its constituent people.

The seeming importance of rhythm in African American music invited the scorn of Westerners who wanted melody first, then rhythm.[140] One of my professors commented that his first impression of African drumming was purely irksome noise. Author LeRoi Jones retorts, "It did not occur to [Westerners] that Africans might have looked askance at a music as vapid, rhythmically, as the West's."[141] Moreover, Africans used drums to communicate complex ideas and phrases. Differing timbre of drums, higher inflections or lower pitches, imperceptible to Europeans, made communication via drumming more complex. For example, the African drum *atsimewu* or "talking drum" produces nine different tones. Antebellum America prohibited African drums. The African banjo and xylophone allowed Africans to adapt their rhythms. Empty cans and basins were also transformed into instruments in the African's rhythmic arsenal.[142] The African drum beats to the words of jazz musician Randy Weston: "The heart is the first instrument that man became aware of, and I'm sure that's how the drum came to be. It is as old as civilization itself, and if you look around … you'll realize that the whole world is based on rhythm."[143]

Skeptics contend that jazz's rhythm isn't its distinguishing characteristic, as Hodeir and composer Aaron Copland believed.[144] Skeptics argue that the blues tonality and improvisation are integral to jazz. And they surely are. But the grid of centrality is borne out of the jazz-specific polyrhythm that interlocks between the infrastructure and superstructure. It can be as bluesy and charismatically improvised as Dexter Gordon's tenor saxophone solos, but to borrow from Duke Ellington, "It don't mean a thing if it ain't got that swing."

My first bass instructor suggested that I listen only to the rhythm of a particular song and not the tones. It is a helpful exercise to ascertain the grid of a jazz song. You will notice the propulsion of the city grid-like infrastructure with the soloists atop. The many rhythmic expressions are melded into the greater groove of interlocking of voices; an apparent unity of purpose emerges, to make a musical conversation.

It may be helpful to the casual jazz listener to know that jazz music (and its internal rhythm) has repetitive elements. It's not all free-form and free-verse. Most standard jazz songs start with a "head" or melody which is played over a chord progression. The "head" was usually played from memory. The chord progression is usually performed by the rhythm section (piano and bass). The rhythm section repeats the chord progression for each soloist. If you are confused by the autobiographical, noodling jazz soloist, listen to the rhythm section as it will surely repeat the progression. Or sing the melody of the song when the solos begin; this will help orient your ear to the repetitive nature of most chord progressions. That's how I first learned to solo.

The grid of the Constitution, evidenced by the strict literal meaning of the document, is comparable to the rhythmic infrastructure of jazz. The Articles of Confederation were unsuccessful because of their tenor of state individuality. Jazz, too, fails to swing when it becomes exclusively focused on the individual at the expense of the group. The free jazz movement and musical experimentalism of the Association for the Advancement of Creative Musicians (AACM) certainly are known for experimental music.[145] Trumpeter Lester Bowie spoke about the AACM movement: "We're free to express ourselves in any so-called idiom ... to deny any limitation ... We could sequence it any way we felt ... It was entirely up to us."[146] I don't disparage the sophistication or complexity of the free jazz idiom. However, it does not *swing*—because that isn't its apparent mission. There is a lack of filtration or blending in much of free jazz, very little groove or centrality of the grid. The free jazz musician is able to try virtually anything in the name of creativity.

Asserting a Lump Character

The mutually antagonistic concepts of cooperation and independence (reconciliation of the individual and group interests) are evident in jazz's historical progression. New Orleans jazz was characterized by collective improvisation, whereas big band and bebop placed more emphasis on the soloist. Miles Davis stood on the left corner of the stage, back facing audience, and trumpeted for a good eleven minutes. The music became the solo, the musician the soloist. Perhaps popular entertainment is to blame for the individual-as-art metaphor: Miles Davis *was* jazz. But this line of thought is arguably anti-jazz. The Madison filtration process occurs when musicians assert their individuality with respect for the group. The whole is greater than the sum of its parts.

Many jazz bandleaders strive to create a high-level *ensemble individuality* or lump character. After the filtration process, the hope is that the group's sound will stand on its own. New Orleans drummer Baby Dodds, who joined King Oliver's Band in 1922, said flatly that no one can do anything by themselves.[147] He saw his role as the drummer as supportive in nature. When the band loses the beat, the drums roll on the snare drum without the bass drum, and the band will roll with him; then the drummer resumes the bass drum, and "everybody is right."[148] After each soloist, Dodds changes his drum pattern slightly, switching the feel from the high hat to the ride symbol, signaling to the audience and band that a new soloist is about to embark. The drummer quiets the band with brushes or helps it achieve breakneck speed. Far from being a background instrument, the drum is very much part of the melodic arc of a tune.

New Orleans guitarist Lawrence Marrero described his aversion to complex chords—9ths, 11ths, 13ths. He thought the banjo and guitar were accompanying instruments that push the polyrhythm on its merry way.[149] He didn't play banjo solos because he valued the simple yet fundamental nature of the instrument. Imperial band member and New Orleans string bassist Edward Garland only used to play two notes a measure, then four. He would thump right along listening to the melody and trying to put the right "basses" in it.[150] Duke Ellington's bassist Wellman Braud took short bass solos, rejecting the Articles of Confederation (the penchant for excessive individual liberty) so that he could recapture the propulsive pounding of the rhythm section.

Jazz musicians are our elected officials. Not everyone can play a tenor saxophone, so we live vicariously through their melismatic expressions. It's through their musical speeches that we cry and grow impassioned. These jazz legislators negotiate and make in front of us— just like we see on C-SPAN—for the direction of the song and the importance of the music. The jazz audience participates in the ring of music, clapping during the middle of a song, dancing, and singing. Come as you are, sing as you like. The rhythm section embodies the Pareto optimal solution, making the individual better off without detracting from others. That is, the soloist fiddles with the time and harmonics of the song, bettering himself, until it derails the band. The catharsis of the ring is evident in the blues. Play the blues to rid yourself of them.[151] You can't snap, crackle, pop, feel better. The *making* process is the therapy—America in motion and anew.

Observes cornetist Johnny Wiggs: "In a good band everybody contributes to the rhythm … everybody floats on top of that rhythm."[152] But what if the soloist, in an effort to be complex, loses the rhythm? The checks and balances of the band must make up for the weak soloist—the drummer rolls and resumes the bass drum to recapture the soloist to the groove. What if the drummer rushes his pattern? It's incumbent on the banjo or bass to bring him back. In jazz, the individual may blunder, but despite the mistake, the lump character prevails. The soloist may step out of the minor key, but the propulsion of the band gives the soloist an opportunity to make good.

In jazz we understand man's personal fallibility. In our fallibility is the recognition that we may engage the group system—*jazz, constitutional amendment*—to make amends for our failures. Famous radio DJ Willis Conover spoke of how musicians agree upon the form of the song, the superstructure, and can negotiate before it starts. When the terms are reached, and the compact's ink is dry, the musician is free to concoct anything within the ground rules.

Ascertaining the nature of ensemble individuality is like understanding the federalist system at work in American government. It is man's nature to create, sometimes with flamboyant effect. In the jazz system of checks and balances, the trumpet is the chief executive. The lead trumpet is the loudest, highest melodic instrument in the group and demands the most attention. When did you last watch the rebuttal to the State of the Union address? But the trumpeter can't groove without consent of the rhythm section. If the rhythm section shuts down, à la 1996 when Speaker of the House Newt Gingrich closed Congress, the trumpeter's agenda, or in this case the saxophonist, won't move.[153] Sometimes, however, the trumpeter will interpret his melodic power with unnecessary showmanship, making songs harder than they are. Louis Armstrong reminisced about the old days when the music was simpler and they just played what was on the sheet music.[154] The individual must recognize that his work is part of the greater whole: "In a typical jazz performance, each individual performer contributes his or her personal musical perspective and thereby graphically demonstrates the democratic process at work."[155]

The metaphor of divided government extends toward the reeds as the judiciary. New Orleans clarinetist Omer Simeon, who was also pianist Jelly Roll Morton's favorite clarinetist, spoke of how his instrument weaves in and out of the high trumpet line and low trombone part, connecting them melodically and rhythmically, like in the tune "High Society."[156] De Tocqueville wrote about the judiciary's duty of arbitration, and the overt political influence of the court. The judicial system resolves disputes between dueling beliefs. In 2005 the Supreme Court, for instance, resolved that government may seize the homes of people, against their consent, for economic development. The country grooves on. The reeds ornament the jazz composition and provide contrapuntal melodies that further the blues harmony. Their middle range pitch keeps the executive trumpets locked in harmony and pushes the legislative rhythm section when it's dragging.

All Aboard with Our Hero

The open invitation of the jazz jam session respects the activist democratic tradition. The alderman, city council representative, and mayor are encouraged to attend in the music-cum-government 'round midnight session. In a totalitarian regime, the power of one—Hitler, Mussolini, Stalin, Hussein—is the rule of the land. The hero is the one grand leader who lives in a stasis of power. The protagonist of the blues ballad is the American hero. Our American hero understands that improvisation is the highest of human gifts, for he can swing and "perform with grace under pressure," in the words of Murray.[157] The blues are an invitation to those who feel down, depressed, and removed: "If you don't love Blues, you gotta hole in your soul!"[158] The soulful blues of government and blues of life were answered by the *making* of democracy and jazz. Democracy is an affirmation that improving society is possible because man will ultimately participate in *making* a more perfect union, learning from legislative mistakes. The jazz hero learns from his mistakes and moves the group in the right direction, achieving harmony, the wand of compromise.

In a democracy, power is vested with local officials. Local officials are best able to represent individuals because they are keenly in touch with their constituents. The bloodlines and hereditary brew of local officials do not matter—they are elected and granted power with the democratic process. Jazz musicians often came from humble walks of life and played the music with serious talent. With only a horn, they gained attention and respect. The filtration of jazz is akin to a raw meritocracy. Power (or respect) has nothing to do with the rich or poor bubbling blood of a musician. It comes down to ability. Someone from the "wrong side" of town can partake in the democratic process of local elections and the local jam session. As Ellison wrote, "Jazz, like a country which gave it birth, is fecund in its inventiveness, swift and traumatic in its developments, and terribly wasteful of its resources … More often than not … its heroes remain local figures known only to small-town dance halls."[159] The fresh voice can become a local hero, infusing vitality into the *making* of jazz.

Cutting contests or "bucking contests" pitted players and bands against each other. One band would perform a blazing piece, and the dueling band would challenge it with a performance of its own. The audience would decide the winner. Dizzy Gillespie and Charlie Parker would often sneak into a club hiding their instruments, and during the middle of a piece they would take the bandstand and bring the house down with a solo. "This was known as an ambush," Dizzy deadpanned.[160] The process of jazz wasn't always pretty. It was a highly competitive sport just like democracy, but the road to success was paved with talent and creativity.

The open invitation of our deep democratic tradition did not come about by accident. It is because the inventors of both American democracy and jazz struggled and were once a minority voice. Both jazz and American democracy are crafted for the proverbial "little guy" so he can participate and demonstrate his pragmatic self-reliance.

American democracy arose in response to the British crown, which was steeped in the divine right of kings. New Orleans, the birthplace of jazz, smacked with discrimination, but it was an exception to the Deep South, as blacks could own and run certain locales. New Orleans is not only home to the confluence of the Mississippi River with the Gulf of Mexico, but it also has many cultures: Spanish, African, French, American, &c. The mixing of cultures could make for heightened tensions. In 1871, during Reconstruction, blacks were segregated at the Metairie Racecourse.[161] The French Opera House, once open to blacks, closed its doors in 1874.[162] Blacks sought judicial redress, but only one case found in favor of them. Political legislation like the 1868 Louisiana Constitution promised equality, but Jim Crow discrimination was difficult to circumvent. Theaters eventually allowed blacks to enter but they could only sit in segregated sections. Perhaps it was because of the segregated culture of the South that jazz musicians strived to amend civil society, making their music fertile ground for one of the first integrated American experiences. War was another integrated American experience. Colonialists (and their black slaves) went to war against the British for their independence. Their new government would be an open system (at least in words) where the democratic tradition of activism would triumph. We might not know where we are going, but we know how we are going to get there.

America's "Ultimate Skill"

An expert artist never truly masters his trade. There is always more to learn and experience. Age is often the most insightful instructor, after all. The artist's adroitness instead prepares him to "extemporize under pressure," since "improvisation … is the ultimate skill … knowledge and technique have become that which he not only performs but also plays," writes Murray.[163] To improvise is to fuse proficiency and style, creating an unmatched personal force. To improvise in a jam session is to assert one's musical liberty and also to respect the grid of rhythm.

American (and international) artists have taken the liberty of expression found in jazz to heart. Just as the Constitution has been the progenitor of new laws and amendments, so, too, has jazz inspired new art forms. To "jazz" has in some sense become a modern style. This jazz style has changed over the years from representing freedom in the 1960s to intellectual high culture at the turn of the twenty-first century. But the importance of improvisation seems to be consistent with the jazz style. We detect the jazz style in prose and poetry. Remember French novelists such as Albert Camus, who wrote with a newer style, and F. Scott Fitzgerald's stream of consciousness narrators. Jack Kerouac's writings, such as *On the Road*, were inspired by jazz improvisation; he wrote it on one scroll of paper.[164] One critic noted that Kerouac's improvisation was evident in his use of loose language, which catapulted him to literary liondom. Kerouac often refers to "blowing" and the space between breaths of a musician.[165] The spontaneity of his writings is meant to reflect the inner emotions and true voice. Kerouac even penned jazz poems in his *Book of Blues*.[166] Jazz inspired writers of the Harlem Renaissance, too. The "jive and jazz" of the street spawned new words for writers Langston Hughes and Rudolph Fisher to use.[167] Some writers even affixed their works with "Harlemese" glossaries.[168] The paintings of Matisse depicted visual jazz. The brilliant splotches of color in his *View of Collioure* and *Luxe, Calme, et Volupté* resemble a poly-chromaticism of hues that emerge from each other, like cascading solos in a swing tune. Abstract expressionist painter Jackson Pollock admired jazz as "the only other creative thing happening in this country."[169] He was presumably referring to his work as equally creative. Actors such as Marlon Brando brought jazz inspiration to their characters, as he did not learn lines. He improvised speeches in the early 1970's *Last Tango in Paris*.[170]

To improvise is to survey the frontier and explore the wilderness of the unknown—a musical manifest destiny. Once the unknown has become colonized with enough settlements, a new form is born. The African tradition gave birth to ragtime, dixieland, jazz, bebop, and free jazz, among other forms. Giving birth to improvised (yet ordered) art and improvised (yet ordered) legislation illustrates how jazz and democracy are infinitely extensible. Improvisation does not mean free-for-all performance. The soloist must play within the key and rhythm. It can take years to learn the proper soloing techniques and tonalities. The student soloist starts by flouting technique (performance as fire). It is when the student learns to perform with simple mastery (performance as water) that the student becomes the musician. The greatest musicians are able to master the technique and think nothing of it while they perform, allowing the infinite extensibility of the music. Charlie Parker was once blowing on the up tempo tune "Koko" with classical Russian composer Igor Stravinsky in the audience. During his solo he quoted Stravinsky's *Firebird Suite*, enthusing Stravinsky, and continued on with his solo, melding shreds of ideas together into his man-made Sierra.[171]

To "jazz" is to create a story. Iyer cites John Coltrane's comments during the outtakes of his recording "Giant Steps." Coltrane says to his fellow musicians, "I ain't goin' be tellin' no *story* ... tellin' them *black* stories."[172] Iyer posits that Coltrane wasn't speaking of his personal story. Instead, Coltrane insinuates that his solo could tell the black narrative. One man could speak to a group of people and represent them through his audacious individuality. He could conjure the lump character of the African and African American tradition. Perhaps that better explains Coltrane's declaration, "It's a sharing process—playing—for people."[173]

Charlie Parker's intentional "raucous and uncultivated" sound was the instrumental extension of himself.[174] He did not detach himself from the instrument or the process of *making* jazz. He merged with his instrument. There need not be separation between instrument and performer. This allows for the most efficient means to express oneself. To perform in a detached manner, there is an extra step of translating emotions onto the device. The musical masters saw *themselves* as the instrument. The heroism of the jazz musician exhibits what's expressly American about America: a dogged self-reliance.

Rugged self-reliance is at the heart of Rafi Zabor's *The Bear Comes Home*, in which the saxophone-playing English-speaking bear protagonist relies on jazz to discover himself. The Bear (Bear's name is Bear) leaves his apartment to play at a jazz club, gets arrested, escapes jail, falls in love, goes into hibernation in the wilderness, yet plays jazz all throughout. The Bear grows paralyzed by believing perfection existed as a product, an attainable end. He grows disgusted with himself when he cannot attain it: Why can't he express himself and why is he castigated? His odyssey teaches him that the process of self-discovery is the product of perfection. There is no beginning or end, simply a cycle of awareness. "He saw the tremulous rainbow, the iris tremoureux, whose delicacy eased their passage between worlds," during his culminating solo. He realized he was capable of greatness.[175]

Instead of spouting notes, the music acted as a spiritual geyser. The Bear's self was hidden from him at first. The musical quest of The Bear and John Coltrane was one of self-discovery that enabled them to explore distant worlds of knowledge: Indian classical music, Albert Einstein's theories, *The Charterhouse of Parma*. Their musical quest eventually brought them back to themselves. The end is the beginning, just as with Joyce's modernist tale *Finnegans Wake*, which alludes to the "commodius vicus." This theory of cyclical history was propagated by Philosopher Giambattista Vico, who believed there were three eras of the world: the era of divinity, the era of heroes, and the age of mankind. He believed that the dawn of a new cycle was upon us.

The performances of Coltrane and saxophonist Sonny Rollins certainly fill "the boundaries of the world as normally recognized."[176] These jazz luminaries provide the spiritual affirmation of *making*: Not only is jazz about rhythm changes and shout choruses, it's about flying gloriously towards the heights of feeling. Mythologist Joseph Campbell describes how he ambles from a busy street into a cathedral. He feels a heightened "cathedral consciousness" with the stained glass windows, mystery, symbols, and clues.[177] When he returns to the street, however, he's back in the real world. Taking the "cathedral consciousness" found in a church or music to the street is the key to harmonizing inner beliefs with the outer world. Bringing the lessons of improvisation from jazz to our civil society can arguably help us harmonize. All told, when music is soft and lights are low, improvisation trains the light of knowledge on us.

Walt Whitman's Wish, Technology-As-Art, and the Spirit of Jazz

It is the activist spirit of democracy codified in art for which nineteenth century thinkers yearned. Whitman lamented, "America has yet morally and artistically originated nothing."[178] Even poet Henry Wadsworth Longfellow hungered for an American poetry in the 1820s. European arts were imported to nascent America. Whitman went on to say that America possessed legions of newspapers but few literary forms and models. It bothered him that America had not achieved its own artistic style, because national art is a collective remembering of society. It is the gateway to his third stage of American evolution: (1) the organization of the nation found in the Declaration of Independence and Constitution; (2) the economic prosperity evidenced in labor, produce, and mining; and (3) a "native expression-spirit" that is full and extensive, evidenced by indigenous songs, literature, and art.[179] Progression can be wrought by the democratic process, but a deeper form of progression must be wrought by the democratic spirit.

Whitman spoke of how the shared democratic spirit could nudge America to see its purpose. Indigenous art would offer shreds of perfection to emulate: "Not but in one sense, and a very grand one, good theology, good art, or good literature has certain features shared in common. The combination ... appeals to emotions, pride, love, and spirituality common to humankind."[180] America would be truly great, reasoned Whitman, if its art brought about the blossoming of the individual. America is capable of creating a unique art because of the jam session spirit of the American experience. The translation of such an experience would codify the aspirations and ideals of the proverbial melting pot, a group of people that had never come together in the history of mankind. If each citizen contributes his artistic style, a grand American style will emerge, deporting Western art music back to Europe and ushering in an era of Americana. If America should decay and grow wary of internal or external threats, an American art will offer cultural regeneration. Draw strength from the collective memory of the American people who painted and sang with their intuition, God's alphabet.

Some say that Whitman's cry was answered by America's technical language. Jay Hubbell, founding editor of *American Literature*, said America's literature "has always been less American than our history."[181] America's indigenous art has been technology from the beginning, reasoned Kouwenhoven. George Washington's troops fought with long guns during the Revolutionary War that could kill a rabbit in the hinterland, demonstrating a functional advantage. Eli Whitney's cotton gin provided a functional advantage that allowed the South to generate mass wealth. Bridges, roads, highways, even technological infrastructure like the Internet have given America the functional advantage in trade and commerce. Perhaps our technology really is our art and our scientists our artists. One could argue, like one cognitive scientist, that there are scientific aspects of art. In creating art, one must explore and inquire, experiment and be comfortable with an ever-changing result. Technology as art may be a revealing theory, but was this really the "native expression-spirit" for which Whitman yearned?

While it's true that technology is part of the American vernacular, I believe Whitman's cry was answered some fifty years later with jazz. Technology may be a collective memory of a time. The "Information Age," Internet, and iPod may be how we remember the early twenty-first century. But America's purpose isn't technology or maximizing efficiency. Technology is like blood to the American economy. We need it to live, but it isn't the point of life. Jazz is the indigenous art that would have appeased Whitman because of its democratic tendencies, for he believed that democracy was not just manifest in political democracy but in the arts and literature.

To be culturally free is to climb the summit of liberty. Even James Joyce recognized this, yearning for Irish cultural independence through the mask of Stephen Dedalus, the protagonist in his well-known novels. There is a well-defined path towards political and economic freedom, but cultural freedom takes time to emerge. Tagore recognized freedom as "not the mere negation of bondage, in the bareness of our belongings, but in some positive realization which gives pure joy to our being."[182] Jazz is a positive realization of the American experience. If we do not like the tune, there's no need to lament. Simply invent a new melody, a punchy solo for change. The extensibility of jazz invites us to renew and amend our native art to fit the relevancy of our cultural conversation. Every solo, each note, is more than it lets on. The notes of jazz are just veneers and facades. Each note represents an emotion and feeling, the cultural freedom of mixing. Beneath the veneer we discover the *making* of America, the city grid of rhythm, and the extensibility of improvised possibility. Jazz awakes the democratic spirit in its music—and the making of the raw American experience.

The self-reliance of the jazz solo epitomizes the very blossoming of the individual into self-awareness. Paradoxically, a heightened self-awareness makes us more aware of the group and our position in the group. It is through improvisation—and the aesthetic arrest of an awakened art—that we learn about ourselves and escape the rhymes of banality. "The soul unfolds itself, like a lotus of countless petals," says Lebanese poet Kahlil Gibran.[183] Jazz allows for self-discovery. It is a path, not the end answer. The path will provide us answers for perpetuity. The lantern of jazz shifts the nomadic shadows with us along our journey. Gibran continues, "The musician may sing to you of the rhythm which is in all space, but he cannot give you the ear which arrests the rhythm nor the voice that echoes it."[184] We can find our voice through an improvised style. The Bear and Coltrane engaged in a musical journey, but the fruits of their journey are virtually impossible to describe: They gained wisdom, for sure, but of what kind? It doesn't have to be music; religion provides a personal path, pushing humanity towards Leo Tolstoy's "new theory of life."[185] But in our tireless jazz-as-democracy metaphor, we see that jazz has taught us to realize ourselves, assert our individuality, and escape from the preparation of cultural decline.

Chapter 2
The International (Sonic) Bomb

"We drive into the future using only our rearview mirror."
—Marshall McLuhan

The jazz-as-democracy metaphor is a self-portrait. Both jazz and (American) democracy share certain properties like the tradition of making, constructing a grid of security, and allowing for improvisational liberty. But the entire metaphor is that of Americans describing America or constituent parts of the whole discussing the whole. This is not a setback to our understanding, but sometimes it's difficult for an individual to address its greater group. I'm not exactly an impartial commentator.

The lessons of exploring jazz from the view of foreign nations can shed more light on the true nature of American democracy and our native self-expression. As Erik von Kuehnelt-Leddihn writes, "A great book on a given country *has never been written* by a native. It *has* to come from an alien. The self-portrait is always biased."[186] Frenchman De Tocqueville's *Democracy in America* is perhaps the most insightful commentary of American democracy because he was an impartial observer.

It might help, for once, to look at ourselves from a distance. American author Ralph Ellison contends that African Americans are on the outside, looking in at America's democracy.[187] To look outside-in at America and its native music can help to understand why foreign nations held America in esteem during the twentieth century. Such an outside-in approach provides an honest reality check: We can see what America once represented, and whether the US has lost its cultural influence or "soft power." There was a time when the world was in love with our music and mythology—it did not scoff at our cultural rupture. To explore jazz abroad is to study our cultural condition. Does our art still reflect the *making* spirit of democracy? Does the music of today speak to who we truly are?

Drummer Eddie Allen, channeling the spirit of American author Henry James, moved to France in 1989 and ironically discovered his American identity: "I had to come to France to find out I'm an American. I miss America; it's my country. I appreciate my culture much more now that I'm here. [So] now I'm an American outside of America; it gives me a different perspective."[188] Allen recognized the value of an outside-in approach, that observing America through a foreign lens would shed light on the nature of America.

To examine the European story of jazz before overtly creating a Jazzocracy (see next chapter) is consistent with the arc of jazz history. Americans did not recognize the value of jazz until Europeans flashed a conspicuous thumbs up. My university professor describes his experience exiting a California jazz hall as a child in the 1950s. His father whined about the primitive "black" music. But now jazz is not associated with the primitive and puerile antics of Uncle Tom—it is a prestigious symbol with a buffed and polished place in the pantheon of American music. Musicologist David Ake explains, "The privileged position jazz now enjoys in such an august institution as Lincoln Center demonstrates that a steady swing feel ... no longer denotes the primitive."[189] In many ways, the Europeans elevated jazz to a higher status, signaling the go-ahead for mainstream American acceptance. That Czech composer Antonín Dvořák borrowed from black spirituals in his Ninth Symphony of *From the New World*, exemplifies the Old World approving of the new. With a short-scripted history, America up until the mid twentieth century took its cultural cues from Europe.

Many countries saw America through the kaleidoscope of jazz; polychromatic, unhinged, improvisational and desperately alive. For a singular music to represent an entire country speaks to the potency of jazz during the early twentieth century. Foreign listeners heard more than just America in the music; jazz represented liberty and equality; it was the juxtaposed and syncopated marriage of primitivism and modernity. It was perhaps the first time in history that a particular type of music had such a global following. With the rise of broadcast technology and the improvisational nature of the music, jazz became the world's liberty bell. As Gutenberg made liquid the written word, democratizing God and unseating the Catholic hierarchy, so, too, did the radio swing of emerging technology unleash a common rhythm across waves and planes of distant lands. Individuals didn't need democratic government to understand jazz, they didn't need courts and congresses; they just needed ears and a sweet, sweet yearning for the mechanics of maybe, the potential of consonant possibility.

Democracy's positive connotation is a relatively new happening. Mandelbaum observes that "democracy" once had as low a reputation as "dictatorship."[190] Critics of democracy felt that to vest power in the people would lead to violence and corruption. Democracy was synonymous with anarchy. Early democratic examples of Greece and the Roman republic devolved into tyranny and cruelty. Adolf Hitler assumed power through an electoral process. At the turn of the twentieth century, there were only ten democracies in the world. By turn of the twenty-first century, there were over one hundred democracies.

Jazz music and democracy went from a lowly and unappreciated connotation to a respected and worthy one. Jazz music and democracy grew up and learned to swing together.

In 1958, pianist Dave Brubeck wrote in the *New York Times*: "The fact is that jazz, our single native art form, is welcomed—not simply accepted—without reservation throughout the world, and is felt to be the most authentic example of American culture."[191] And yes, Mr. Brubeck, you're correct to say that "[Jazz] arouses a kinship among peoples; it affords them flashes of recognition of common origins because of its basic relationship to folk idioms; and the forthrightness and directness of its appeal are grasped alike by the naïve and the sophisticated."[192] Could one say the same of modern music?

But what of the bans and purges? If jazz is as Brubeck writes, a musical language strengthening our bonds and integrating our differences, why then the demonization of the music in some foreign countries? Is the directness too direct? Is jazz a tablespoon too honest? Too bitter—no—too sweet a pill to swallow for Stalin, Hitler, and their ilk? Foreign governments recognized the cultural message of freedom found in jazz. "Culture" (read propaganda) tsars of the Soviet Union fiercely enforced anti-jazz measures. It is surprising, however, that the US government didn't officially integrate jazz into its cultural arsenal until the 1950s with Willis Conover's Voice of America radio show, which broadcasted jazz to the Soviet Bloc. Decades later, in 1993, Congress honored Conover by passing a resolution which referred to him as "one of the country's greatest foreign policy tools."[193]

God left music as the one communal language after the unraveling at the Tower of Babel. Music speaks to humanity; there is no need to translate or decode, decipher or discern. Jazz music spoke to the humanity of those in the Soviet Union and Nazi Germany, floating the Western world, if only for a moment, back to Pangea because of the promise of freedom and solidarity of expressive sensibility and sentiment. At a time when nation states stifled free speech, jazz allowed folks to speak freely in the common tongue of music. Oppressed people could escape *La Condition Humaine*, or, as Malraux describes "man's fate," and take part in a participatory and democratic music, throwing off the screws of serfdom. To solo off the grid of rhythm is to jump off the precipice of musical recitation. Without a score or musical chart, folks could create and extemporize under pressure, learning more about their individual creativity.

Critics may crow that to study jazz abroad can disprove the jazz-as-democracy metaphor. After all, the Soviets weren't beckoning for "democracy in sound" or a democratic government (at least initially). They clamored for *part* of the democratic process that they heard in the jazz compositions: the improvisational freedom of the jazz solo. The music allowed the Soviets to be free. But while they enjoyed the freeing nature of jazz, they heard the grid of rhythm. Jazz music to the Soviets was an indirect promotion of democracy: Musical freedom would eventually make way for freedom of speech. The reconciliation of individual and group interests was absent in the Soviet Union. There was no process of *making* in Soviet music or political affairs. The little guy had no recourse. He did, however, own a radio.

Improvisation has always been an allure of jazz. At the first big band jazz concert that I attended, I couldn't believe that the musicians were making up their solos. While the jazz solo is representative of cultural freedom, it is still inexorably linked to the centrality of the grid. The jazz solo swings because it deviates from the central rhythm. But without the infrastructure of the groove, the jazz solo would stand alone (without accompaniment). What makes the jazz solo truly sing is its conversation with the greater group. While the Soviets listened to the wailing soloist spouting his brassy free verse, the musical democracy of jazz was indirectly promoting cultural and political democracy.

There is no immediate need to update or amend the jazz-as-democracy metaphor. Freedom is very much part of the democratic promise. Security is, too. It is understandable why jazz was known as the language of freedom. Humans clamor for more liberty; there is a trenchant disdain for governmental or cultural oppression. To see America only as the land of the free (and not also the grid of the Constitution) occurs even today. In *Imperial Life in the Emerald City: Inside Iraq's Green Zone*, Rajiv Chandrasekaran relays his conversation with an Iraqi taxi driver after the toppling of Saddam Hussein's regime. The driver, who used to observe the rule of law, was blatantly running red lights and breaking the law. Chandrasekaran asked the driver why he was flouting the law. His driver responded, " ... democracy is wonderful. Now we can do whatever we want."[194] Sometimes observers see only the cultural freedom of America and not the rich conversation between improvisation and the grid. "Even ... freedom becomes a matter involving security measures and thus a justification for restrictions which exceed those that generated the thrust toward liberation," notes Murray. Let's not confuse liberty with what America's music truly represented. Murray continues, "The world... should be... all too familiar with totalitarian systems which began as freedom movements."[194]

The Cold War was won for a variety of reasons. America's military muscle and the adept leadership of President Ronald Reagan played a significant role, of course. "Mr. Gorbachev, tear down this wall!" declared Reagan. Some historians posit that the Soviet Union collapsed from within. It wasn't the specter of nuclear crisis that broke the red nation. It was in part simply the hope and desire for freedom. The Soviets yearned to be culturally (and eventually politically) free like Americans.

Forget the academic observations for a moment. Jazz music simply made folks feel good. Former President Bill Clinton described the role jazz played on a trip to Russia when the saxophonist Igor Butman performed for Clinton and President Vladimir Putin of Russia: "All those people liked us that day ... because they saw us through the eyes of jazz."[196] Jazz serves as a willing ambassador that represents the best of America. Jazz was and continues to be an honest reflection of American values, and answered the Whitman-wish for cultural democracy.

The Jazz Weapon

"Domestic policy can only defeat us; foreign policy can kill us," said President John F. Kennedy.[197] Violence is antithetical to the democratic process of crafting domestic policy. One's opponent is seen not as a warring enemy but an actor with a different interest. To incite violence with an opponent is to escape the democratic process altogether. Kennedy recognized that foreign policy calls for peace and war. Peace is a struggle. "True peace is based on mutual confidence...not concealed hostility," wrote Tolstoy.[198] Prussian military philosopher Carl von Clausewitz considered war to be an extension of politics, another arrow in the quiver of political strategy. Clausewitz lived during the Napoleonic Wars (1799-1815) and saw how war was used as a political means to an end (the submission of an enemy). He did not live to see the rise of technology and broadcast, and the effect on state politics and conflict.

American foreign policy is not just predicated on military might or "hard power." Cultural influence or "soft power" is another way to compel and coerce an enemy. Political scientist Joseph Nye refers to diplomacy and culture as "soft power."[199] Persuasion via values, culture, institutions, and music account for soft power: "If I can get you to *want* to do what I want, then I do not have to force you to do what you do *not* want to do."[200] In other words, if the US could infiltrate Soviet culture, it could possibly speak directly to the Soviets. There is probably some truth that soft power is based on hard power, but soft power can certainly augment the impact of hard power.

Psychological warfare, arguably an early tactic of soft power, started to gain recognition as an ancillary part of the military's arsenal during the 1940s.[201] During World War II, the British dropped propaganda leaflets over Germany, part of their so called "truth raids."[202] Later, President Dwight Eisenhower touted psychological warfare and pushed for a single office to execute psychological warfare operations.[203] Psychological operations (PSYOP) included Central Intelligence Agency (CIA)-led coups and goodwill jazz missions to win hearts and minds. The United States Information Agency (USIA) executed most of the covert-cultural operations. The agency later became part of the State Department and CIA. In the 1950s, a State Department report described how foreign policy wasn't solely determined by diplomats. Public opinion, playing a more significant role, determined how diplomats and state heads acted towards other countries. If the US could positively affect the masses in foreign nations, it would bring about pro-American policies.[204] Strike the masses and influence public policy, from the ground up.

Though jazz was very much part of the psychological warfare mission, it is important to remember the difference between propaganda and art. In the words of President Kennedy: "We must not forget that art is not a form of propaganda; it is a form of truth." The artist who overtly politicizes his art degrades his work, turning it into an advertising program. The artist who politicizes his work eschews personal integrity. Murray notes that "no truly serious ... writer can afford to enlist in any movement except on his own terms."[205] Jazz was able to escape overt politicization because it emphasized instrumentals over vocals. Indeed, there are many distinguished jazz vocalists, but the attention to instrumental voice is unsurpassed. Popular music today emphasizes vocal lyrics, which makes it more susceptible to explicit didactical politicization. Think Green Day's "American Idiot": "Don't wanna be an American idiot / One nation controlled by the media / Information nation of hysteria / It's calling out to idiot America." Joyce believes that didactic artwork, evidenced in music with obvious messages such as Rolling Stones anti-war lyrics of "Sweet Neo Con"

("You say you are a patriot / I think that you're a crock of shit"), are devoid of radiance. Joyce felt that a "simple beholding" of an object can make one aware of the interrelationships of parts, "the harmonious rhythm of relationships."[206] An aesthetic arrest occurs when the audience loses itself and the artwork instead beholds the observer. Comparative mythologist Joseph Campbell caps Joyce's belief: "The aesthetic experience transcends ethics and didactics."[207]

There was little need for Americans to propagandize the music of jazz with political lyrics. Jazz already represented the very best of America. The jazz bandstand was integrated with blacks playing alongside whites. The security of the grid-rhythm and the improvisational freedom of the jazz solo were the makings of democracy in sound. The United States deployed the weapon of jazz to execute its cultural war abroad. Where planes and tanks were restricted, the missiles of jazz were launched. America was engaged in a metaphorical war, the Cold War, and attacked its enemy with hot jazz. America's weapon was truth against Soviet cultural restrictions and lies.

The USIA recognized the importance of cultural influence: "We are in competition with Soviet Communism primarily for the opinion of the free world."[208] The covert cultural operations of the USIA were not limited to those countries behind the Iron Curtain. Certain nations were indifferent or hesitant to join sides during the Cold War. The USIA operated in some ninety-one countries not part of the Soviet bloc.[209] The largest operations were in Germany and Austria. It also had operations in India, Pakistan, Yugoslavia, and Iran, for instance. Jazz musicians were eventually dispatched around the world. Pianist Erroll Garner's manager arranged an appointment for Garner to receive a smallpox shot before an international tour. It was required by the government, she told him. "So how come you send me places where I can get sick?" he quipped. [210]

On January 27, 1958, a cultural agreement between the US and the Soviet Union was reached: "Agreement between the United States of America and the Union of Soviet Socialist Republics on Exchanges in the Cultural, Technical, and Educational Fields."²¹¹ Both countries were criticized from within. American critics feared Soviet spies. Soviet critics feared an increased American cultural dominance already evidenced by large crowds at jazz concerts.

The 1958 cultural agreement allowed for some transmissions to be broadcast into the Soviet Union. The Voice of America (VOA), which is still the official international broadcasting unit of the US government, came into being in 1942 as part of the Office of War Information. The US government had a thirty-year vision for VOA to eventually foment pro-American opinion in distant lands. VOA began to broadcast into the Soviet Union in 1947, as the USIA distributed thousands of radios. Soviets tuned into America in order to tune out the Reds. The initial programming was to feature Negro spirituals and jazz. Short segments of narrated American history were to fill the non-musical airtime. The history of the Tennessee Valley Authority, for example, was to be aired.²¹² Five weeks after going on air, VOA found initial success with Soviets chattering about the radio content in the streets and shops. One Soviet who was buying a new radio was overheard asking whether it would receive VOA broadcasts.²¹³ The USIA became the operator of VOA during the Cold War. A publicly funded media broadcast, it drew the ire of conservatives like Senator Joseph McCarthy, who assailed the USIA and VOA for being (*what else?*) communist.²¹⁴ VOA remains on the chopping block even today because of concerns among some conservatives.

The late VOA DJ Willis Conover was "thronged by eager crowds" when he visited Moscow, whereas in America he was relatively unknown.²¹⁵ Conover's show was broadcasted six nights a week into the red nation. His voice rumbled, "This is Willis Conover in Washington, D.C., with the Voice of America Jazz Hour."²¹⁶ He played the music of pianist Oscar Peterson and composer (and pianist) Duke Ellington. His voice found over thirty million listeners in the Soviet bloc and one hundred million around the globe. Conover was well aware of the similarities between jazz and democracy: The tradition of *making* was alive in the jazz combo and political discussion. He observed that performers can consent to the chord changes, tempo, meter, and the key of each composition. After the terms are signed (and a melodious introductory piano preamble), the individual can solo and self-amend, always respecting the centrality of the rhythm grid.

It was the jazz on Conover's program that helped Europeans think "American jazz as necessary as the seasons."[217] Europeans had a propensity to analyze and scrutinize the music according to conservatory rules. Whilst analyzing the musical theory of jazz, they grew more familiar with the originators of the music, African Americans. The burning curiosity and yearning for the American sound compelled some folks to risk their lives by smuggling jazz records into Communist countries. Soviet children could easily recite the names of jazz performers better than their American counterparts.[218] *Veni, Vedi, Velcro: the music came, saw, and stuck around.* One European observer asserted, "Jazz is not just an art ... it is a way of life."[219] Felix Belair Jr. of *The New York Times* described the jazz phenomenon in 1955: "American jazz has now become a universal language. It knows no national boundaries, but everybody knows where it comes from and where to look for more."[220]

The Soviets fought back by tightening press restrictions, a sign of VOA's growing influence: "The Moscow newspaper is so much on the defensive in its tone that one might almost detect a certain amount of worry concerning the 'Voice of America' broadcasts."[221] Feeling threatened, the Kremlin jammed VOA transmissions; the Soviet intelligentsia assailed and ridiculed the VOA with bile.[222] But VOA broadcast transmissions were incessant. After the death of Joseph Stalin, the enigmatic jazz bans of Nikita Khrushchev were reversed and the radio transmissions were allowed.

American Ambassadors

America's cultural warfare was not limited to the radio transmissions of the VOA and Willis Conover. Three notable global nomads, among others, helped to trumpet the jazz gospel in person. These American Ambassadors of Goodwill were Louis Armstrong (nicknamed Satchmo), Dizzy Gillespie, and Duke Ellington. In her *Satchmo Blows Up the World*, Penny M. Von Eschen chronicles the contributions of each Ambassador: Armstrong, the Real McCoy; Gillespie, the orator; and Ellington, the statesman.

Louis Armstrong recognized the paradox of promoting American democracy abroad while the democratic promise at home remained unfulfilled. When Arkansas Governor Orval Faubus forbade African American students to enter a Little Rock high school, Armstrong snapped, "The Government can go to hell."[223] He unnerved state department officials with his candid remarks, especially since "Ambassador Satch," had the ears of millions around the world. The Soviets even recognized the contradiction, lampooning America for its racist and divided society. American music was more democratic than American civil society. President Eisenhower was aware of America's democratic shortcomings and government officials likely wanted grinning black man Louis Armstrong to put a smile on American democracy. Racist attitudes weren't confined to the Jim Crow South. Some officials in the State Department were notorious for their racist attitudes. Nevertheless, President Eisenhower promoted jazz tours to represent that which was good in America.

Armstrong's only State Department-sponsored trip occurred in 1960, when he performed in the Belgian Congo. Unbeknownst to him, the CIA was plotting to assassinate the prime minister (the US sought natural resources in Congo). Ambassador Satch was the goodwill advance man. His international tour took him to twenty-seven cities. Von Eschen describes how Armstrong was easily shuttled from East to West Berlin with little difficulty. His famous face transcended walls and borders. When the American Ambassador to Germany learned of Armstrong's Berlin travels, he was surprised because not even he could travel the city with such ease.[224]

Dizzy Gillespie led the first state-sponsored international jazz tour in 1956, at the request of President Eisenhower. His eighteen-piece group was to perform in Pakistan, Turkey, Greece, and Syria, among other countries.[225] Dizzy's "stealth weapon" of jazz propagated America's position as a "benevolent supremacy."[226] Despite the on-going Civil Rights struggles, or perhaps *because* of the Civil Rights struggles, Dizzy played his horn with fervent optimism. Though Dizzy joked that if someone gave him a gun on the battlefield, he might shoot the wrong enemy (he perceived white Americans to be the immediate obstacles for African Americans, not Germans). Even though America was an imperfect nation, or as Tagore might reason, an incomplete nation, he believed that America would rise to fill its democratic charge. In Greece, Dizzy performed for students who were recently part of an anti-American demonstration. After his performance, Dizzy was feted and carried through the streets.[227] The cultural exchange of musical ideas influenced Dizzy perhaps as much as he influenced others. He learned new musical ideas from instrumentalists in Africa, Asia, and Latin America. International musicians helped Dizzy discover and create Afro-Cuban music. He would later integrate aspects of Afro-Cuban music in his jazz compositions. Years later, | Nelson Mandela told Dizzy how much Dizzy's music helped him during his twenty-six years in prison.[228] Good for Dizzy for launching his "Dizzy For President!" campaign for the 1964 election. Initially started as a joke, the campaign gained some legs. Dizzy's ticket included appointees Miles Davis as Director of the CIA, and Duke Ellington as Secretary of State.[229]

The refined and cosmopolitan statesman of jazz, Duke Ellington performed his cultivated music to the world in an era of rock and roll. Born "Edward Kennedy Ellington" in 1899, he received his nickname from teenage friend Edgar McEntree who labeled him "Duke" because of his kind manners and sartorial style. To the chagrin of State Department officials, Ellington told audiences the world over that jazz was a misnomer. For him the music was "America's classical music," something to be lauded—for it took Americans decades to realize the cultural and international significance of *their* music. Ellington's orchestra toured Syria only days after a coup. His band traveled as far away as India.[230] Duke played the role of advance diplomat (a true Secretary of State) when he toured the Eastern bloc after President Richard Nixon's impending visit was announced. In the Soviet Union, Duke's orchestra played with local musicians and encouraged exchanges of musical expression. Ellington's international role as an American Ambassador of Goodwill, not to mention a cultural creator within the United States, did not go unnoticed. President Richard Nixon recognized Ellington with the Congressional Medal of Freedom, the highest civilian honor, on Ellington's seventieth birthday. The *New York Times* heralded the White House ceremony: "Last night the Duke was King."[231] President Nixon even played "Happy Birthday" on the piano for the Duke, though we must question Nixon's authenticity when he greeted bandleader Cab Calloway in the reception line by saying "Mr. Ellington, it's so good you're here."[232]

The international jazz tours were not without controversy. When the State Department tapped clarinetist Benny Goodman to tour the Soviet Union in 1962, it caused concern among several black musicians. Why was a white man playing and representing black music? The tour was born out of a cultural agreement between the US and Soviets. As early as 1955, the State Department had asked Goodman for a sampling of his records.[233] In exchange, the Soviets sent the Ukrainian Dance Ensemble to the United States.[234] The Soviets ached to throw the albatross of racism around America with a white man playing black melodies, but the US successfully negotiated for an integrated band to play with Goodman. Some argued in favor of including American spies in Goodman's band.[235] Surprisingly, the Soviet Ministry of Culture officially approved Goodman and his music.[236] Upon arriving in the Soviet Union, the president of one of Moscow's jazz clubs invited Goodman to a jam session with local musicians.[237] Goodman very much enjoyed meeting local musicians and not necessarily adhering to the official schedule, which irked state department officials. Goodman and his band met informally with citizens and played in late night jam sessions with Soviet swingers—sharing the same language of jazz. In his global travels, Goodman also jammed with King Bhumibol Adulyadej of Thailand, a saxophonist, pianist, guitarist, and clarinetist.[238] *The King of Swing could have no less.*

Armstrong, Gillespie, and Ellington spread their music, the music of cultural democracy, to foreign lands even while circumstances at home were grim. Their fight may not have been with guns and missiles, but their performances taught the world about America and reminded Americans of their incomplete mission at home. The world learned that jazz was a modern music that brought folks together: Think Dave Brubeck in Turkey or Ellington in Syria. Jazz indirectly taught other countries about the American way of life, how individuals can sing their freedom and still remain stitched to the grid of rhythm. The integrated bands demonstrated the activist, invitational, and democratic spirit of jazz—it was the democratic ideal wrapped in the jazz aesthetic. To Americans, jazz abroad meant a cultural affirmation of optimism. These jazz ambassadors hoped to change the very worst of America by celebrating the best. These jazz ambassadors reminded America that it wasn't a mosaic but a melting pot. African American music became *American* music when performed abroad.

Pioneers they certainly were. These jazz musicians provided the first burst of American music on the global stage, later to be followed by the rock and roll craze. The Beach Boys, for instance, were invited to the Soviet Union to perform in 1978.[239]

Though they were not Americans, the Beatles helped to bring Western music and ideas to the Soviet bloc: they "borrowed" from the African American tradition. They were the white face that made black music more palatable for the mainstream. Remember the words of (gasp) rapper Mos Def: "You may dig on the Rolling Stones, but they ain't come up with that style on they own." The Rolling Stones performed "imitation black blues."[240] Let's not forget the true originators.

Perhaps jazz was just in the right place at the right time. But that can be said for almost any influential idea or music. Jazz was the first melting music. It incorporated the *making* tradition of America's call and response democracy. The music also changed with the times. The collectivist jazz performance occurred at a time when workers were unionizing. The complexity of bebop solos and the affirmation of the individual solo came a few short years before the Civil Rights protests. The notes weren't the only things the Europeans could hear. They heard the meaning of the notes, the context of the times, the interplay between dissonance and harmony, and the dynamics of an integrated band.

Jazz musicians played their role in transcending American democracy and pushing the democratic ideal on foreigners. When foreigners and the American mainstream looked at the integrated jazz band, they saw a projection of what America would become. Whitman's wish to culturally regenerate according to a native art was indeed answered by the musical democracy of jazz. To some it may be difficult to grasp how jazz music could have represented more than music, or habituated foreigners to democratic tendencies. To study the musical democracy of jazz in non-democratic countries helps to explain how the music won the hearts and minds of foreigners and familiarized them with democratic precepts.

The twentieth century saw the rise of three types of government: communism, fascism, and democracy. All three types rejected monarchy and the divine right of kings. All three claimed to rule in the name of the people, but democracy was the only form of government that actually delivered on its promise. Both communist and fascist states considered war an essential strategy in dealing with other nations, and both pushed to expand their borders with war.[241] Both subordinated personal liberty and popular sovereignty in order to achieve state objectives. The jam session spirit found in American (and French) culture could not be found in fascist regimes, for instance, as fascists saw those that they had conquered as inferior and unequal.[242] The communists of the Soviet Union, fascists of Nazi Germany, and democrats of France reacted to jazz in contrasting and telling ways.

The Red Path

The history of jazz in the Soviet Union is one of indecisiveness and resiliency. Soviet officials banned jazz music (and reversed the bans) several times, but Soviets citizens continued to listen. Jazz was like the Road Runner from the Looney Tunes cartoon. It couldn't be killed. The Soviet government instituted jazz bans and detained jazz musicians, claiming that the Soviet Union must purge their streets of Western decadence. But try as they did, the music just wouldn't die.

Jazz was the popular music of the day. It wasn't the music of prestige, intelligence, or elitism. It did not have its "museum music" connotation of today. Instead of springing from the European conservatory, the music came from below with a grassroots under-the-carpet sound. In *Red & Hot*, possibly the most comprehensive history of jazz in the Soviet Union, S. Frederick Starr mentions the mass acceptance of jazz because it was a "second revolution on 1917 ... of spontaneity, individual expression, the liberation of the human body from state-imposed prudery, and the possibility of culture ... being shaped 'from below.'"[243] Because of its bottom-up swell of popularity, jazz was seen as anti-establishment music. And the Soviet regime reacted in a predictable way. Soviet officials denounced jazz for its connotation of being an overly sexual and promiscuous art. It was decadent music that would lead citizens to engage in louche and lewd behavior.

The Russian Revolution of 1917 was a freedom movement to overthrow the tsar and Romanov dynasty after it had been severely weakened by World War I. After the Russians toppled the resulting Provisional Government, the Bolsheviks moved in with their Marxist political philosophy and communist agenda. With the creation of the Soviet Union in 1922, citizens would soon grow accustomed to collectivist policies, some of which called for top-down cultural programs.

The communists discouraged democratic institutions of civil society from forming. With a government that required absolute social control, there was no room for autonomous organizations or voluntary groups.[244] In the communist Soviet regime, power was not based in the people or popular sovereignty but in the ruling cabal that claims it knew the interest of the people. In reality, the communist programs of the Soviet Union were not informed by the reality on the ground, since there were no democratic elections. For instance, the Soviet government seized private property by force: "[communism] involved a war waged by the government against the society it governed."[245]

For the citizens of the newly created Soviet Union the gust of jazz was more than fresh air. Jazz allowed Soviets musical freedom of expression. Couched in the songful solo, jazz taught of the necessity to balance the collective interest of the Soviet state with the moxie of individual expression. It was the freedom of expression and thought that worried Soviet officials: without the moral compass of collective policies, New World music would lead to the mass adoption of brow-furrowing vice. Would the culture of the newly established Soviet Union come from below, or drip from the tower of tyranny? The Soviet debate between top-down and bottom-up culture would take five decades to resolve. The cultural wars had begun in earnest.

A hodgepodge of American music had already gained a small following: music from vaudeville entertainment, Dixie-lite, and non-improvised jazz. American music grew from the bottom-up, from the masses. It was, to borrow a cliché, music of the people and for the people. The directors of Soviet conservatories (and for that matter, European conservatories) and centers of learning remained aloof from the music. The postwar isolation of the Soviet Union initially inhibited the spread of jazz. From 1918 to 1920 Russians were engaged in a civil war that made it difficult for American music to spread. There was a lack of records, instruments, and sheet music. It wasn't until 1922 that jazz reached a wide enough audience to cause concern among the cultural overlords.

After the Revolution and implementation of the Bolshevik New Economic Policy, native son Valentin Parnakh broke the cultural isolation. He first encountered jazz music in Paris and later in Berlin. When he returned to his motherland, he brought instruments and music. Parnakh not only brought the tools of jazz but a bevy of fresh ideas—freedom in music and the harmonics of blues tonality. Parnakh's band performed several compositions without improvisation. At that time, the individual solo was not an integral part of the jazz song. The Soviets, however, fell in love with the syncopation and rainbow timbres of the different sections of the band. That the trumpet, a military instrument, could spurt a newfangled sound showcased how the old could become the new. The instruments of the European conservatory spoke in another tongue, the American vernacular. *A bent note? A cut note? A muted riff? Hesitate not.*

In a theatrical production, artistic director Vsevolod Meyerhold featured Parnakh's band. Meyerhold intended to contrast the appropriate Russian style with the decadent American music. Staccato march music blared with Russian dancers marching in lockstep with the beat, like wind-up prim and proper dolls. After the march, Parnakh and his band took the stage. Parnakh's European instruments squealed and howled. Sexy dancers sashayed across the stage, suggesting their (sexual) freedom. The audience voted with their feet, crunching the floor with boots. Meyerhold had succeeded in contrasting the Russian and American styles. And jazz had won.

With Western music came Western musicians. Pianist Sam Wooding brought his band into the red nation. Though Wooding's band toured many countries, including Holland, Belgium, Turkey, Romania, and Switzerland, he described his performances in the Soviet Union as some of the best.[246] However, many in the red nation yearned for a more authentic jazz sound. Yet Wooding wouldn't exactly play the part. A black man and an artistic connoisseur of Western art or "classical" music, who listened to symphonies and choirs, he brought the music of the conservatory to his jazz compositions. His "classical" or "symphonic" jazz was not hot enough for some. It's not that Wooding's musicians were not accomplished. Trumpeter Tommy Ladnier, who performed with Wooding's band in the 1920s, went on to perform with acclaimed clarinetist Sidney Bechet and Fletcher Henderson's orchestra.[247] Wooding's symphonic jazz called for musical arrangements that blended tones, even including string instruments. The audience wanted to dance, and Wooding's music was far removed from the bustling New Orleans sound.

Benny Peyton and The Jazz Kings gave the audience what it wanted. Peyton led a fiery group of instrumentalists who belted finger-popping, toe-tapping tunes. Starr describes Wooding's and Peyton's impact on the Soviet Union as "enormous … The jeunesse dorée took jazz to its heart, seeing it in the uninhibited behavior of Peyton's bandsmen, in particular, a living model for elegant rebellion."[248] *Elegant rebellion?* Wooding's "symphonic jazz" pleased the critics, whereas Peyton's down-home music cajoled the masses.

The Soviets wanted it harder, racier, and freer. Native son Leopold Teplitsky traveled to America (funded by jazz-loving Soviet officials) to return with instruments, recordings, and knowledge on how to perform jazz. He organized a jazz band full of conservatory-bred instrumentalists. Initial reviews were mixed. *Could Soviet jazz ever rival the real deal?* Teplitsky's band inspired other bands to organize. The initial burst of Soviet jazz groups was a case of quantity over quality. One group toyed with Hawaiian guitars; another band mastered the works of composer George Gershwin.[249] Many Soviets enjoyed jazz because they could experiment and tinker with a new art form, making it their own: "The brisk tempo, spontaneity, physicality, and individualism of the twentieth century, which found their expression in jazz, were quite at home in post-revolutionary Russia."[250]

It is worthy to note that music didn't just flow from West to East. Russian composer Joseph Schillinger brought his music to America, for example. Many intellectually curious musicians, like George Gershwin, Benny Goodman, Earle Brown, and Quincy Jones, have studied Schillinger's music and method. Born in 1895, Schillinger immigrated to the US in 1928 and created a mathematical technique of studying art. The Schillinger Method sometimes calls for the musician to examine his or her music with graphs and visual representations of the music.[251] After a piano performance, Schillinger challenged the audience to name the composer of a particular song. *Mozart? Mendelssohn?* Schillinger wrote the piece based on a graph that appeared in the *New York Times* that showed the vacillations of wholesale prices of agricultural goods.[252] To open a cultural door is to create an exchange of ideas. The US-Soviet cultural exchange allowed both nations to learn more about each other.

The open exchange to and fro soured. Stalin's Five Year Plan, launched in 1928, pushed the country to industrialize, doubling coal and iron production. Civil War again gripped the country as farmers refused to cede their private land to the state to establish communal farms. The crisis was mostly concentrated in the countryside, away from urbanites who relished their jazz music. In order to build solidarity, Stalin sounded the alarm against jazz music and jazz musicians. He whipped many Soviets into a xenophobic white heat against foreigners, creating a difficult climate for foreign jazz bands. Stalin threatened to purge those who associated with decadent capitalists of the West. It was only a matter of time until the Soviet Union instituted jazz bans; the first of which occurred in 1930. The Association of Proletarian Musicians acted as the quasi-official censorship arm of the Communist Party and attacked jazz for tainting the mass market.

Soviet Author Maxim Gorky wrote an essay entitled "On the Music of the Gross," in which he railed against the chaos of jazz music. He blamed modern musicians for playing sexually suggestive music, as it foretold of the West's imminent cultural and perhaps political decline. Gorky even tenuously linked jazz to homosexuality (man can only view women as sexual tools and not real romantic partners). The sex-obsessed Western elitist was the Bolshevik bogeyman.

But Gorky should have held his ink. Though his faith in the Bolshevik movement wavered, he still traveled abroad to raise money for it.[253] In 1906, Gorky toured the United States and met luminaries like authors Mark Twain and Upton Sinclair. *The New York World* published a story about Gorky staying at his hotel with a mistress. The hotel evicted him, and Gorky's famous American supporters withdrew support: President Theodore Roosevelt nixed his White House invitation.[254] Though Gorky was known in the West for his mischief, he continued to assail Western society for its debased values. He even spun a palm full of conspiracy theories: "Jazz and the foxtrot were now the dominant religion, manipulated by the new capitalist masters in order to secure and extend their dominion," notes Starr.[255] When Gorky's essay appeared in *Pravda*, the propaganda publication of Stalin, the Association of Proletarian Musicians took it as their marching orders.

The gathering squall of jazz critics in the Soviet Union was quickly reaching its zenith. Soviet officials and the culture tsars pointed to black Americans to illustrate the decadence of jazz: blacks were still slaves, but this time to the American dollar. Soviet officials argued that if jazz was not banned, their nation would fall off the precipice and into Western decay: For these critics, jazz acted like a parasite, leeching off the base instincts of its audience and ruining the country from the inside (years later jazz was seen as a parasite, notably in Czechoslovakia before the 1989 Velvet Revolution).[256] The anti-jazz decrees required schools to expel students who professed a love for jazz. Teplitsky was exiled. Possession of a jazz record could lead to fines and jail time.

The jazz ban probably made sense in theory. The problem, however, is that controlling culture by fiat, especially sonic culture, is terribly difficult. Music is the warp and weft of a country's cultural fabric. To call for a jazz ban is one thing. To enforce it is another. Rid the listeners of their music, and what shall the audience listen to? What shall the masses dance to? How would Soviet culture replace it? The Association of Proletarian Musicians piped insipid melodies over the radio waves, but the public wasn't having any. The jazz bans prohibited not only jazz, but music derived from jazz. The widespread effect of jazz's pulsating rhythms and colorful harmonies made composers question the ban because composing without borrowing or developing from jazz was nigh upon impossible. Jazz music went the only place it could. Underground.

Soviet officials weren't always knowledgeable about jazz music, which made it more difficult to enforce jazz-bans. An American journalist who traveled to Moscow had his luggage inspected by a Soviet guard. In the luggage, the guard found several recordings with self-descriptive labels. *Foxtrot.* The guard considerately informed the American of the jazz ban. The guard found a recording with "Charleston" written on the label. He asked the American what it meant. "Oh, that's a new form of American light operatic music," said the journalist, fibbing through politeness.[257] The guard permitted the American to leave with his "operatic" music in tow. It's no wonder why the American journalist's residence in Moscow became a meeting place for under-ground animated dancers.

Enforcing the jazz bans was increasingly difficult. Instead of banning the music, the Soviets would try to reframe it. Cultural commentators rushed to re-brand jazz music as the music of the proletariat: Jazz was primitive and folksy, the music of the working people. Others labeled it the music of the bourgeoisie since wealthy citizens patronized the art, providing musicians with a recurring and steady source of revenue.

A series of unusual events led to the Soviet about-face on the jazz-ban. Suffice it to say that it was far too difficult to replace jazz with a Slim-Fast alternative. In addition, Stalin's Five Year Plan had been finished in four. Time to celebrate. *The New York Times* spelled it out: "For years the Communist party frowned on jazz as being bourgeois and non-proletarian. Now they admit it is an authentic and valuable form of music."[258] The question of whether jazz could jive with communism was discussed widely. "At one such debate a jazz orchestra played selections for an hour so that the club members could form a judgment on good evidence. The result was an overwhelming vote of 'Yes.'"[259]

The government's acceptance of jazz prompted singer Vera Dmitrievna Dneprova to declare the dawn of the "Red Jazz Age."[260] More natives, like the legendary jazz singer Leonid Utesov and pianist-composer Alexander Tsfasman, hit the jazz scene (American jazz artists were reluctant to visit). The early 1930s was a good time to be a Soviet jazz musician. The largest salary of the day went to a jazz bandleader.[261]

But lightning struck again. In the late 1930s, jazz was the target of the government. The inroads of jazz during the early 1930s led to a backlash among Soviet officials. Jazz had infiltrated the cinema, theater, Moscow hotel, and even the corner café. A new jazz ban was instituted. Bans were, in effect, the perpetual alter egos to the disturbing pervasiveness of the music. This ban was different, however. It smacked with violence. Stalin arrested jazz musicians and sent them to hard labor camps.

In 1936, a long debate over how to handle jazz gripped cultural commentators. The debate pitted the official megaphone of the Communist Party *Pravda* against *Izvestiia*, the official publication of the Soviet government. Pravda claimed that jazz had a growing number of supporters and railed against the b-word (bourgeois). It endeavored to re-brand jazz as proletarian music (though *Pravda* suggested that messier forms of jazz and symphonies should be banned). The classical musicians writing for *Izvestiia* urged Soviet officials to act. Point-Counterpoint-Rebuttal. *Pravda* criticized its literary opponent for espousing poor morals. *Ad hominem* attacks were leveled at jazz musicians in *Izvestiia*.

Pravda won the debate as many Soviets thoroughly enjoyed jazz, but *Izvestiia* won the policy. A purge of several jazz-loving Soviet officials ensued. Jazz musicians were also purged, and many were sent back to hard labor. Starr tells of jazz pianist Alexander Sotnikov and his tribulations. Sotnikov was exiled to a distant mining town and asked permission to form a jazz group. The police reluctantly allowed him. *Ban the music we love, too?* Sotinov's group saw up to fifty members during his stint in the labor camps. Sotinov served as a bright star in jazz's dark night.

Volte-face, yet again. The debate of 1936 confirmed the intensity of feelings in favor and in protest of jazz. The Soviet government struggled to quell the cultural rift, and it settled on an awkward solution: to nationalize the music. Restated, the government created a state jazz band. The group performed banal, filtered, watered-down jazz music. Stalin quietly approved, but the public knew a bogus concoction when they heard one. The Soviet government played its usual game, recasting jazz music as its own, a Soviet music of the people.

World War II ensnared the Soviet Union in 1941. The morale of the country sank and jazz was brought to the front lines to boost the spirits. On many an occasion, military band members died alongside soldiers. *Band of Brothers warring for political and cultural freedom. Onward ho!* Bands performed jazz-infused *dzhaz* for soldiers, reminding them of the "glorious" times back home, Nostalgia in Red Square. The US-Soviet alliance during the war proved a boon for jazz lovers; it was more hip to listen to American music. Recordings, sheet music, and "jazz knowledge" trickled into the hands of Soviet military band members who entertained the troops. And when the allies won, the Soviets celebrated the victory with a performance of the State Jazz Orchestra in Sverdlovsk Square. *Remember President Clinton's words: "All of those people liked us that day."*

Victory in hand, sacrifices to boot, the Soviet Union was ready for another jazz ban. The third ban resulted because the Soviet Union and USA were no longer allies but emerging and staunchly opposed enemies. The Cold War had dawned. Hot jazz chilled to a deep freeze. Stalin appealed to xenophobia, blaming the resulting economic malaise of World War II on decadent capitalists. And western music once again irked cultural commentators. For example, jazz-bashing publication *Izvestiia* assailed jazz bandleader Eddie Rosner "The White Louis Armstrong" because he played "rampant trifles set to jazz."[262]

While the Soviets invented legions of enigmatic conspiracy theories, the lessons from previous jazz bans were not learned. It was thought that President Harry Truman and his capitalist cohorts in the West were the puppeteers of the colorful jazz marionette. The country closed its borders to the west. But that darn dilemma exploded again. What was to replace jazz? The officials who were charged to enforce the anti-jazz decree were jazz fans themselves. *Everyone wants to dance, right?* An underground bazaar complete with jazz recordings emerged. The counterculture, the irksome "decadent" art, still operated at the margins and below the surface. The government not only exiled jazzmen but banned VOA and Willis Conover's jazz broadcast. (Later, a Russian jazz enthusiast said of Conover, "He was like a saint to us."[263]). The inconsistent ban was apparent. US Ambassador to the Soviet Union Alan G. Kirk hosted a ball to celebrate the Fourth of July, festooning the party with American regalia and inviting a top-notch jazz group to perform (diplomats tried to ignore the music, instead conferring in a corner about matters involving the Korean peninsula).[264] But the third jazz ban was short lived and faded away after Stalin died in 1953.

Jazz cafés dotted the streets of Moscow.[265] They were beacons of freedom where young folks could express themselves musically. Young Soviets admired the jazz solo. It was the ultimate form of self-expression, without immediate punishment. Youth festivals fed the jazz craze. The post-war enthusiasm for bebop finally spread to the Soviet Union. Young Soviets yearned for the freedom of expression of the bebop solo. The virtuosity and technical proficiency of the bebop solo symbolized the brilliance of an individual when he stands alone. The Soviet government reacted to bebop by issuing *diktats* on what types of jazz were permissible: "The American type of jazz, formerly frowned upon in the Soviet Union, received the qualified blessing of the Communist newspaper for youth groups today ... the newspaper ... cautioned that instruments in jazz bands should not scream in strange voices."[266] Bootlegged recordings fed a "deep hunger" of Soviets.[267] Mrs. Thomas Whitey, wife of a former Associated Press reporter in Moscow, confessed her knowledge of the underground bootlegging scene in 1953. She pointed out that Soviets found American music in anti-American films. "American music is permitted for that, and Russian composers can write jazz for that. So the people, while they are supposedly learning to hate America, are really loving its music and learning it."[268] *Meyerhold Redux.*

Soviet Premier Nikita Khrushchev briefly banned jazz when he took office in 1964. Khrushchev targeted the music because of escalating Sino-Soviet tensions. The Chinese assailed Khrushchev for being softhearted towards capitalists. Mighty Khrushchev fought back by attacking jazz, that convenient, erstwhile scapegoat. But Khrushchev's intermittent and ephemeral efforts ended after his reign. Moderate Soviet officials eased his anti-jazz measures in 1965, and with that, clubs reopened. The music of Miles Davis and John Coltrane was at its peak.

However, the young generation aged with jazz, creating an elitist and obsolete aura for jazz, much like what happened in America. Rock signified a changing of the guard in popular culture. Rock was banned, notably because it goaded listeners into violence, and because of its inherent unrestrained nature.[269] Starr relates the story of a concert in Kaunas, Lithuania, in which a rock group's concert culminated with an intense fight and broken windows. At another performance, listeners attacked the musicians: "Not even jazz had produced such a scandal."[270] *Too free? Rather, rock provoked rather than freed?*

In the late 1970s, the Soviets built academies to study jazz music. Alex Kan of the BBC writes, "Jazz … a complete outcast barely two decades earlier, in the minds of many it still indiscriminately bore an image of a liberating spirit, with improvisation—a musical metaphor for freedom—at the heart of it."[271] A tumultuous path, indeed. In the 1980s, free and avant-garde jazz became the anthem of the counterculture or "second culture." Such experimental music lacked the indomitable swing found during the interwar years.[272]

The Soviets never succeeded in engineering a "mass culture." As one writer put it, "In no other field of endeavor is the restrictive character of the Soviet regime so evident as in literature and the arts."[273] "[Communism] can be halted only by force from without or by disintegration from within," wrote Aleksandr Solzhenitsyn clairvoyantly in 1980.[274] The disintegration of the Soviet bloc came from within and culminated decades later. The musical democracy was one outlet of free expression. In a country that eviscerated property rights, the jazz listener still owned his or her voice. No government could restrict the inner voice that becomes auditory through jazz improvisation.

Weimar & The Third Reich

Jazz in Germany was a case of Dr. Jekyll and Mr. Hyde. During the Weimar Republic (1919-1933), there was no greater joy than to visit a cabaret club or swing performance. The Weimar Republic had a reputation of being a modern state, friendly to painters, writers, and musicians. The Nazis, however, viewed jazz music in much the same way as did the cultural engineers of the Soviet Union. But the Nazi's motivation for criticizing the music was more than a fear of Western capitalist decadence. Negrophobia obsessed the Nazis in a way that rarely, if ever, occurred in the Soviet Union.

Fresh from its loss in World War I, the Weimar Republic was the first German attempt to create a liberal democracy. The German economy was in shambles, suffering from a decline in pre-war exports. Despite economic malaise, the Weimar Republic boasted a vivacious and modern nightlife with flocks of visitors and scintillating cabarets, which led one columnist to write, "Art as a whole is cultivated and enjoyed in Germany as nowhere else."[275] The thirst for cultural modernity and cultural exchange was not new to Germans. During World War I, Germans were known for watching performances of Shakespearean plays "even under the thunder of English guns."[276] Berliners even adopted the British tradition of four o'clock tea.

The Weimar Republic provided fertile ground for artists. Expressionist painters conveyed differing emotional and psychological states in their works, helping to lift German spirits from the traumatic effects and bitterness of World War I. Poet and writer Dr. Richard Huelsenbeck moved to Berlin and helped to start the German Dadaism movement, which also helped to renew the German spirit with the child-like and seemingly innocent portraits.[277] A modern art institution, "The Bauhaus" called for Germans to create art that would reflect the future, where representation would be obliterated in favor of abstraction. It was open to avant-garde painters and designers.

Dance artist Rudolf Laban helped to introduce the German Ausdruckstanz, or "expressive dance."[278] He explained expressive dancing by citing the philosophy found in Nietzsche's *Thus Spoke Zarathustra*: "And we should consider every day lost on which we have not danced at least once."[279] Nietzsche frequently wrote of Apollo and Dionysus. In his *Birth of Tragedy*, Nietzsche explains that Dionysus shows that we are not limited to individual occurrences and experiences. We can break away from the fate of death by entering rapture now. While Dionysus may free ourselves, we require Apollo to temper the ecstasy of Dionysus. The unification of Dionysus and Apollo creates the tragedy found in expressive art. For Laban, Apollo and Dionysus represented the opposite forces in German dance: Apollo was a "reasoned, consciously ordered form of the physical world."[280] Dionysus, however, represented the "inner reality that symbolized 'blissful ecstasy,' which 'pays no heed to the individual, but even seeks to destroy individuality and redeem it with a mystical sense of unity.'"[281] Perhaps the most influential words of Nietzsche for Laban were that man had become a work of art.[282] Expressionist dance in the Weimar Republic honored man as art, and not just its intelligent designer.

Weimar jazz bubbled with steamy sounds. Bandleader Sam Wooding toured the country and was well received. He pleasantly remembered one of his performances: "When we finished, everything was still for about two seconds ... then, like a clap of thunder, the audience started banging their feet and shouting, 'Bis, noch'mal, Hoch, Bravo!'" or "again, high, bravo!"[283] British jazzman Jack Hylton visited Germany with a flamboyant act, serving as a hot Dionysian release to Wooding's symphonic and cultivated Apolline sound. African American entertainers like Josephine Baker and Louis Douglas led dance troupes into Germany as well. Despite their high prices, early recordings of Louis Armstrong, singer Mamie Smith, and cornetist Bix Beiderbecke were in circulation because German record companies distributed American labels such as Oden and Columbia.[284] To dance the Charleston, foxtrot, and two-step to the popular jazz tunes of the era all but signaled your hipness. The Weimar years gave jazz an aura of style and sophistication. Most German jazz listeners were middle-class and upper-middle-class.[285] Cocktail-drinking youngsters frequented expensive night clubs to hear jazz performances.[286] They listened to jazz to feel better and attain social advantage (over other classes) by understanding the modern and new.

Some German musicians took to jazz with difficulty. In *Different Drummers: Jazz in the Culture of Nazi Germany*, Michael Kater explains the difficulty of grasping the rhythm-grid of jazz. A distinct departure from the German march beat, German musicians misinterpreted the role of the drum, beating it loudly as to overshadow the instruments. The drum was called "the jazz."[287] Jazz writer Hans Siemsen notes the contrasting German and jazz styles: "[Jazz] knocks down every hint of dignity, correct posture, and starched collars. Whoever fears making himself laughable cannot dance it. The German high-school teacher cannot dance it. The Prussian reserve officer cannot dance it."[288]

German musicians quickly learned and started to mesh old classical tunes with jazz tonalities and rhythms. The cultural exchange went both ways. Wooding incorporated quotes from European productions such as "Ach, du lieber Augustine" and "The Lorelei" in his arrangements.[289] Many German schools integrated jazz into their curricula. These were the first institutions to teach jazz in Europe or the United States. Bernhard Sekles, Director of the Hoch Conservatory in Frankfurt, announced that the institution would, as of January 1928, offer instruction in saxophone, drums, and other jazz instruments.[290] German academics reasoned that the rhythmic properties of jazz helped students develop better rhythmic precision.[291] The Hoch program was in existence for five years (the Nazis pressured the conservatory to nix jazz teachings). The freedom found in the jazz performance was an indirect promotion of democracy: " ... many creative spirits of the Weimar Republic saw in jazz the essence of the era's modernism, an influence toward greater quality and emancipation—in short, democracy for Germans."[292] The struggling liberal democracy of the Weimar Republic could use jazz as a model for cultural regeneration after World War I. The integrating force of the music signaled a cultural democracy that honored the *making* of music—an artistic forerunner to which Germans could aspire. One observer joked, "If only the Kaiser had danced jazz, then all of [World War I] never would have come to pass!"[293]

Despite the popularity of jazz, the seeds of discontent were soon to flower. To some, the popularity of jazz was a reminder of the American victory of World War I. The Americans were back again, this time colonizing German culture. *Stars and Stripes Forever.* A critic compared jazz to "American tanks in the spiritual assault against European culture."[294] One only had to look to the Eldorado Club in Berlin where homosexuals, transvestites, and modernists gathered.[295] The mixing of vice was corrosive to German culture, argued the critics. Historian William Manchester described Berlin as "conspicuous for its lack of virtue whatever. It had become the new Babylon."[296]

Negrophobia lurked in the Rhineland. Blacks in Germany were few in number, whereas France hosted a vibrant African scene. The detest of blacks, among some Germans, stemmed in part to the Great War in which Africans fought alongside the French army (and African Americans with the American army)—and they had won. The French dispatched blacks to occupy the Rhineland, known to Germans as the "Black Horror on the Rhine."[297] With American black jazz musicians trumpeting their music into Germany's culture, right-wing ideologues grew embittered and despised the "savage-like" blacks.

The tide of modernity was beginning to ebb. The fractious political climate of the Weimar Republic pitted those who argued for the "politics of liberty" against those who supported absolute power of a central governing figure. It should have caused more alarm to Weimar officials that the first eugenics office opened in 1926 in order to provide advice to couples on their "physical fitness for wedded life and parenthood."[298] With the fall of the Weimar Republic and establishment of the Third Reich in 1933, modernist art suffered a near fatal blow. In 1926, movie theatres jettisoned live musicians for less costly audio equipment, creating a jobless class of musicians. And in 1929 the Weimar economy soured. Musicians found fewer gigs. With less disposable income, German citizens were less wont to visit the theater or club. A nettlesome row between German musicians and foreign musicians occurred over the limited gig opportunities. Many foreign musicians left, wary of German xenophobia. Foreign art was blamed for ruining German culture. Cultural modernity had been checked, but not mated.

Both blacks and Jews were the Nazi scapegoats for the loss of World War I. The Nazis had particular disdain for jazz because it signaled a Negro-Jew alliance. Jewish tunesmiths like George Gershwin wrote jazz compositions for black musicians to perform. Jewish arrangers and distributors wielded cultural influence in the Weimar years. "Without Jews there would have been no 'Weimar culture'," notes American writer Walter Laqueur.[299] The Negro-Jew alliance scared the Nazis like turkeys in November. A knee jerk reaction would have been for the Nazis to ban jazz outright. That happened in some instances, and modern artists certainly felt the pressure: Laban's expressive dance was banned when he produced *Ibm Tauwind und der Neuen Freude* (Off the Spring Wind and the New Joy).[300] But the Nazis enacted a series of often contradictory policies, from tentatively banning the music to curiously promoting it.

Though Hitler rarely spoke on the record about his feelings toward modern music, he made his feelings of its purveyors well known.

To Hitler, Germany had suffered from the "black shame." Hitler admired the music of German composer Richard Wagner who often made derogatory comments about Jews. But Hitler was wise to the difficulty of controlling culture by fiat. In 1938, Hitler noted: "Without the loudspeaker, we would never have conquered Germany."[301]

Hitler left his henchmen to mop up the dirt of cultural liberalism. Propaganda Minister Dr. Joseph Goebbels—who received his doctorate in 18th century European opera—led the anti-jazz efforts for the Nazi regime. He reasoned that birds of a feather flock together: Transvestites, blacks, Jews, gays, and prostitutes frequented jazz halls. Goebbels wouldn't have his German culture commandeered by the Negro-Jew alliance. But the Nazis took issue with more than jazz musicians. They took exception to the music itself: Jazz was like "democracy itself ... The democratic manner in which jazz musicians were wont to improvise among themselves—all being essentially equal members of the group—spawned more suspicion.[302] Goebbels scorned the democratic spirit of the music. He turned the jam session inclusiveness of jazz into cause for alarm. Goebbels affirmed that the individual did not matter; rather, the collective good of the fascist state (not suffering a second "black shame") was paramount. [303] "Whoever eats of it," said Goebbels of jazz, "will die."[304]

Fresh from Hitler's ascendance to power, the Nazis took their first steps to curb the American "rot." The German Broadcasting Authority announced it would ban jazz in radio transmissions. And two short years later, the authority did just that.[305] They even proudly claimed, "As of today, ni**er jazz is finally switched off on German radio."[306] Musicologists debate whether the Nazi regime ever officially banned jazz music, but Hitler's henchmen made their disapproval known: The Nazis prohibited Louis Armstrong and Duke Ellington from performing. But German citizens traded bootleg copies of the latest jazz recordings. The thirst for jazz was so strong that the Nazis tweaked their policies and even engaged in a bit of revisionist history, claiming that a German by the name of "Adolf Sax" invented the saxophone (an egregious falsehood).[307] Despite having to recant the story, Air Minister General Hermann Goering incorporated the saxophone into several bands.[308]

Ms. Beeke Sell Tower at the Goethe-Institute in Boston describes how Europeans, particularly Germans, felt towards the music: "Jazz was metaphorically burdened with all the ills of an America that seemed too fast, too mechanized, too uncultured, too alien to European minds. Conversely, it served as a manifesto of modernity and progress, especially among the young members of the post-war avant-garde."[309] I know of no better analysis and summary that explains the Nazi aversion to jazz than the arguments put forward in Kater's paper "Forbidden Fruit? Jazz in the Third Reich."

> Since jazz quintessentially represented the principle of improvisation, equaling musical freedom, it was anathema to a dictatorial system intent on robbing its subjects of their free will and manipulating them toward its imperialistic goals ... Second, in the Nazis' racial terms, the originators and disseminators of jazz music were degenerate blacks and Jews ... Third, the syncopated rhythm of jazz, too complex for a steady marching beat, did not lend itself to the transmission of (repetitive) propaganda messages ... Fourth, jazz was so individualistic as to be trivial compared to the racial-communal, lofty objectives of the Nazi rulers. In its essence, jazz flew in the face of the collectivist ideals of the Nazi party.[310]

For the Nazis, German culture needed to be purged. In 1933, they recruited the nation's youth to enlist in their efforts by introducing a law that created a student union at each university called *Deutsche Studentenschaft*.[311] All student unions consisted of Aryans and Nazis. Students ratted on professors, who were then replaced with loyalists to the Nazi agenda. The purge also involved musicians. Many German musicians would not perform with foreign musicians for fear of reprisal. The invitational and democratic spirit of the jam session had been surrendered. The Nazis badgered Jewish musicians, yelling "Down with the Jews" during some performances.[312] After the Night of Broken Glass or *Kristallnacht* on November 9, 1938, the purge of Jews and dissidents was in full effect.

As in the Soviet Union, jazz thrived beneath the surface. Goebbels recognized his dilemma: How could one justify a ban on a music that many enjoyed, and not cause a backlash? Even many of Goebbels's deputies had professed their love for jazz music. By the 1930s, the European radio audience had increased by millions, and German radio stations competed with those in France, Britain, and Luxembourg.[313] Goebbels tried to strike a happy medium by creating the "Golden Seven" jazz band that was to perform light jazz under the supervision of a Nazi director.[314] Radio transmissions broadcast the Golden Seven, going against the position of the German Broadcasting Association. The German public, however, did not take to the light derivative music of the Golden Seven. They voted with their radio dials, tuning in to the music of Ellington and Armstrong on foreign stations. *Can't beat the real thing.*

The underground market for bootlegged and authentic jazz recordings was searing hot. Bandleader Benny Goodman (a Jew) and bandleader Benny Carter (a black) were among the artists whose albums were coveted commodities. Hotels still hosted jazz troupes and all white European big bands occasionally performed in Germany. A handful of blacks courageously performed in Nazi Germany, avoiding the Nazi dustpan. The Nazi policy towards jazz was precarious. It was almost as if the Nazis would decide whether a certain jazz performance was acceptable post facto. The Nazis stomached jazz for fear of a backlash. In fact, in 1937 the *New York Times* declared that "Swing is the Thing in Germany."[315] Young men and women danced to the rhythms of "Harlem hoofers" and syncopated beats. The Nazis argued that they allowed some jazz performances as a concession to American tourists. But the truth is that jazz was a necessary evil.[316]

Still, the quality of the music suffered. Academies were not allowed to teach it, and American musicians were largely prohibited to perform alongside Germans. But German musicians were less inclined to play modern tunes. A few jazz clubs remained open, one of the last vestiges of the Weimar Republic. During World War II, however, these clubs suffered at the expense of the anti-air raid measures and lights-out decree. The air raids killed indiscriminately—jazz musicians and the audience.

In 1939, the Nazis asked German citizens for the whole hog, totus porcus. The nation went to war. The ranks of musicians thinned and jazz patrons disappeared. Goebbels still allowed some jazz and dance performances to give the impression to the Allied forces that life in Germany was normal. Goebbels had an astute antenna. He deftly juggled the Golden Seven, anti-jazz decrees, and hot jazz performances. He improvised. When times got tough for Germans citizens during World War II, Goebbels would ease his cultural diktats. He did not want to upset those in the trenches, which led Kater to observe: "Something so hated as jazz survived in large part because it was needed to humor those who were assigned to destroy its originators: the Jews, Americans, and English."[317] One Nazi soldier who decoded German transmissions surreptitiously listened to jazz on the radio—America on tap.[318] Because German jazz artists were increasingly difficult to find, Goebbels turned to Belgian and Dutch bands to broadcast. In 1941, Goebbels contemplated a ban on jazz that might have led to increased jingoism, but he couldn't pull the trigger. The Nazis had staged an offensive in the Soviet Union: The German blitz signaled a watershed moment in the war because Germany and the Soviet Union were allies from the Molotov-Ribbentrop Pact of August 1939.

The British realized their sonic advantage. They attracted German listeners with radio transmissions and interspersed the music with anti-Nazi messages, both in English and German. Goebbels was not to be outdone. He distributed more radios to the troops, allowed more "jazz-like" (he wouldn't call it "jazz") songs, and hoped that the troops would tune in to German jazz. One Nazi pilot fortuitously tuned in to the BBC before he was supposed to bomb it.[319] *Whoops!* Goebbels created a German big band that played light jazz, sans improvisation, on the radio. And some jazz tunes were rewritten with anti-British lyrics. The German "jazz" broadcasts carried pro-Reich messages interspersed in the transmission. The battle of the broadcast was in full swing.

The tempest for the Germans was still gathering. America entered the war and sent troops overseas in January 1942. Goebbels needed to explain the American motivations to the German citizenry. The Nazis tried to convince their citizenry that President Franklin D. Roosevelt was forced into the war against his will because of intense lobbying from the "Jewish, plutocratic, democratic, bolshevik, imperialistic clique."[320] Hearing the siren voices of his party, Goebbels attacked American culture, describing it as "a cheap and materialistic conglomeration of jazz bands, canned goods, and three-in-one apartments, which … Mr. Roosevelt is seeking to force on Europe."[321] He criticized American culture for being unoriginal, mooching from blacks and Jews.

The paternal palms of Goebbels crafted a new pet project, the "Debunk" radio station. Broadcasted from Germany, the voices on Debunk claimed they were broadcasting from the American Midwest. The radio station played jazz music and interspersed commentary that criticized President Roosevelt and General Douglas MacArthur. Debunk illuminated and manufactured a mirage of American dissent, distorting reality for German citizens.[322]

Goebbels oversaw the creation of movies meant to portray America in a negative light—but many moviegoers went just to hear the American music. Goebbels's ministry created a German jazz band, "Charlie and his Orchestra," that played American swing. This time, however, the Nazis broadcast the jazz performances to American and British troops in the hopes that the Allies would become nostalgic for their motherlands. Through jazz music, Nazi propagandists hoped the American forces would lay down their arms to dance.[323] Charlie and his Orchestra changed American lyrics into Nazi propaganda. The lyrics of Cole Porter's "You're the Top" were changed to Nazi propaganda:

[American Version]

> *You're the top!*
> *You're the Coliseum.*
> *You're the top!*
> *You're the Louvre Museum*
> *You're a melody from a symphony by Strauss.*
> *You're a Bendel bonnet,*
> *A Shakespeare sonnet,*
> *You're Mickey Mouse.[324]*

[Nazi Version]

> *You're the top,*
> *You're a German flyer.*
> *You're the top,*
> *You're machine-gun fire,*
> *You're a U-Boat chap*
> *With a lot of pep.*
> *You're grand,*
> *You're a German Blitz,*
> *The Paris Ritz,*
> *An army van.[325]*

Nazis dropped hundreds of bombs on their opponents: the Allied Forces relatiated, and the American forces even dropped patriotic phonographs on Germany.[326] President Roosevelt boosted the fighting will of the American GI by citing Nazi contempt of American culture. He claimed that the Nazis felt that "people in the United States are decadent, weaklings, playboys, spoiled by jazz music … "[327] He spoke to the hearts of soliders: "Neither your own fathers in 1918, nor your father's fathers in 1863 or 1776 fought with greater gallantry or with more selfish devotion to duty and country than you are now displaying on the battlefield."[328] The fight of the generation was for the American way of life. Already prevalent in the Rhineland, the grid of America's music would soon be accompanied by the military— part of the American security grid.

While the ferocious fracas raged, jazz flourished in other European countries. In Holland and Nazi-controlled France, one could find the latest jazz compositions. Many Nazi troops enjoyed jazz music, the *ne plus ultra* of French modernism, and rollicked in Parisian vice. In addition, jazz albums produced in foreign countries were taxed and sold in dozens of markets, generating much-needed revenue for the Nazi war machine. But citizens in jazz havens still went about listening to the music in furtive manner: The prevalence of hidden jazz clubs would have pleased Jay Gatsby. Song titles and lyrics were rewritten, and a youth subculture was born.

Youth subcultures had different monikers in each locale: "Swing Boys" in Hamburg, "Schlurfs" in Vienna, "Zazous" in Paris, and "Potápki" in Prague.[329] Collectively known as the "Swings," these youngsters resembled a jazz-infused protest movement in the the United States. The Swings made sartorial statements with dark, long jackets and long hair. They spoke in jargon with "hip" and "hot."[330] Women were not fully integrated into subculture, tagging along as girlfriends. Fitted with proper brown trousers, the Hitler Youth attacked the Swings. In Vienna, fifty Schlurfs banded together to attack the home of a Hitler Youth.[331] The Hitler Youth received help from the Nazi regime—Swings were forced to cut their hair and forced into labor and concentration camps. Music historians debate the seriousness of the Swing movement. Teenagers joined the counterculture arguably because they simply enjoyed the style and anti-fascist message.[332] Jazz was newer and freer. They saluted and shouted "Jazz Heil!" instead of "Zeig Heil." The Swings might not have known why they liked the music, but they flocked to it in droves.[333]

The end was near. At Stalingrad the Nazis were trampled and defeated. Smoke covered Berlin after the Allied assault. Goebbels started to spin. He shut down performance venues and movie halls, but Nazi troops needed some form of leisure, so he quickly reversed his decision. German business spiraled downward, as did the regime ... but not the music. The continued popularity of jazz was thanks in part to the foreign-born musicians now supplying Nazi troops with an Esprit de Corps. "But because their work was classified as being important to the war effort," said singer Evelyn Künneke, "they sat at music stands in Berlin, and not behind barbed wire, and made swing." Goebbels fed the songful beast of mass culture by creating the Deutsche Tanzund Unterhaltungsorchester (DTU), a Nazi-backed German jazz band that played more "hip" jazz.[334] Although individual solos were prohibited, the DTU encountered mild success but was quickly nixed because Goebbels couldn't bear the blunt, swinging music. The Allied Forces continued their sonic assault, broadcasting the music of bandleader Major Glenn Miller, an able trombonist who enlisted in the US Army at an age too old for combat, so he entertained the troops.[335] His rendition of "American Patrol" regaled the GIs. The day after D-Day, Americans broadcast jazz on their radio transmissions. Germans tuned in, searching for the truth. Germans were losing the war but were asking for more jazz, more America.

The Nazis surrendered on May 8, 1945. Courageous Allied troops won the war. But do the music men deserve a jasmine garland

and place in the winner's circle, too? American writer Herbert Mit-gang cut to the heart of the case of jazz in Nazi Germany: "Can words and music be weapons of war?"[336] The allied hard power won the war, but the power of jazz shows the influence of soft power. The Nazis attacked jazz music because it represented the American way of life. In his anthology *Jazz and the Germans*, Michael Budds notes, "The notion that a relatively young nation, an upstart such as the United States, might 'teach an old dog new tricks'—especially in matters of music—is nothing less than historic."[337] The *making* tradition of jazz, democracy of notes, collective harmony, and self-reliant solo were new tricks to the Germans.

The fall of the Third Reich ushered in a new era of liberalism. In 1949, German director Rudolf Jugert created the musical *Hallo, Fräulein!* that fused German and American culture. Actors spoke Ger-man and English. German folk songs and jazz music were performed, an overt attempt to Americanize the Rhineland. Maria the heroine learned jazz by listening to the BBC during the war.[338] An American officer named Tom, a devoted jazz lover, falls into raptures with Maria. African American troops enter and exit the stage. The love triangle is completed by Walter, a former German POW. Tom and Walter both attend the same college, share an interest in Maria, and possess similar underclothes. Maria cannot decide which suitor to marry. Eventually, Tom allows Walter to have Maria, a symbol of American permis-sion for German self-determination. Maria's contemplation of Tom as a serious lover illustrates her acceptance of the American, and the German acceptance of democracy.[339] The musical received little atten-tion because of its "elusive pedagogical mission," but shows the overt attempts to liberalize German culture.[340]

Modernism & France

Unlike the Soviet Union and Nazi Germany, France was a beacon for cultural liberalism. Instead of beating and buffooning modern art, the French encouraged the expressionism of the jazz jam session and solo. Unlike in Nazi Germany, the French Prime Minister did not exile jazz musicians. The French were much more tolerant of different cultures, and decried blatant racism. Prince Kojo Tovalou Houénou, grandson of the king of Dahomey (now known as the African country Benin), visited France and a white American assaulted him for dancing with a white woman. French Prime Minister Aristide Briand responded, "Discrimination against people because of their color will not be tolerated in France … France does not want the dollars of those who cannot respect her laws and customs."[341] Rampant Negrophobia did not cross the Rhine into France. "Paris was where I understood that all white people weren't the same, that some weren't prejudiced and others were," wrote Miles Davis in his autobiography.[342]

Actually the modern democratic principle of popular sovereignty originates from France. Brought about by the French Revolution of 1789, *La Déclaration des droits de l'Homme* or the Declaration of the Rights of Man states that "no office and no individual can exercise an authority not expressly emanating from it."[343] In other words, power is vested in the people. Not the landlords, elite, or three-fifths of the populace but *all* people. Popular sovereignty ensures government as the property of the people. The recognition that all government is owned by the people is the great equalizer in democratic government. The modern concept of "nationalism," the right for a nation to constitute an autonomous political community, is said to spring from the French Revolution. Paine felt America and France shared similar ideals: "The revolutions of America and France have thrown a beam of light over the world, which reaches into man."[344]

After the Franco-Prussian War in 1870, the French established the Third Republic, which was a republican democracy with a bicameral parliament. But democracy is more than elections and speeches: "Genuine, robust democracy must be brought to life through democratic individuality, democratic community, and democratic society," writes an American author.[345] The success of jazz in France can be attributed in part to the call and response conversations among the French citizenry. There was almost no repercussion for expressing personal beliefs and participating in the *making* of law, allowing freedom of speech and creativity for artists. The tradition of *making* (and cultural democracy) had been established long before the sounds of jazz washed onto the shores of France.

The French were familiar with resonant debates over the merits and nature of art. During the Enlightenment, philosophers Jean-Philippe Rameau, Jean-Jacques Rousseau, Jean le Rond d'Alembert, and Denis Diderot exchanged a series of missives that discussed the distinguishing characteristics of music. In his *Treatise on Harmony* (1722), Rameau claimed that harmony was the foundation for music. A music theorist, Rameau crafted the fundamental bass method that explained the structure of chords and chord progression.[346] His inquiries form the basis of modern music theory. Rousseau disagreed with Rameau and felt that harmony was, "the same for all nations."[347] In his *Lettre sur la musique française* (1753), Rameau identified melody as the whatness of music. Diderot argued in favor of treating music as a science, scrutinizing the acoustics of a performance. A mathematician, d'Alembert analyzed music with a scientific perspective steeped in Cartesian rationalism. He also recognized the nexus of art and politics. D'Alembert observed that essayists often wrote about traditional freedoms of trade, marriage, and the press. But what of freedom in art? "Freedom in music implies freedom to feel, freedom to feel implies freedom to think, and freedom to think implies freedom to act."[348] French philosophers sought freedom in music and prepared the intellectual circles for the arrival of the jazz jam session several decades later.

The vitality of debate had not dissipated at the dawn of the twentieth century. The Dreyfus Affair, the Peter Pan of French politics, exemplifies the call and response conversation over French identity that swept (and divided) the nation. In 1894, Franco-Jew Alfred Dreyfus, a captain in the French army, was found guilty and sentenced to life in prison for conspiring with the Germans. Dreyfus was demonized as a traitor, and anti-Semites argued that Jews shouldn't hold positions of high rank. In 1896, the French Director of Intelligence discovered evidence that proved the innocence of Dreyfus (who was later exonerated in 1906). French writer Émile Zola elevated the Dreyfus Affair to a fierce national debate when he wrote an open letter addressed to the president beginning with the words "J'accuse" or "I accuse."[349] The tumultuous Dreyfus Affair divided the French between conservatives who opposed Dreyfus and liberal-socialists who supported him. The Dreyfus Affair was a struggle between those who espoused strong national authority of the French state and those who believed in egalitarian culture and the ideas of the French revolution. It took decades for the intensity unearthed by the Dreyfus Affair to dissipate. The cultural factions were in pitched battle over what constituted French identity. The battlegrounds would be politics, literature, and art.

Modernists not only craved the freedom of expression in jazz, but shaped the music into a statement on French culture. They felt jazz was not just American but French. Good feelings are to be shared, *n'est pas?* It was Ernest Hemingway's categorical imperative at work: what feels good becomes The Good.[350] The French traced jazz to 1844 when black minstrels visited Paris; the French pointed to a dubious sixteenth century picture that included a *"jazz-nègre"* participating in a marriage as evidence of the French origin of jazz. Jazz was a "racial expression," not necessarily an American expression.[351] The French endeavored to find the *ancien régime* of the music, the Africa hidden in the acoustics.

Already familiar with *l'art nègre*, the French saw jazz as a creative and improvisational art, a departure from the overly polished music of the conservatory.

The story of jazz in France, however, starts in Black Manhattan— in Harlem. During World War I, military officials called on aptly named James Reese Europe, an African American orchestra leader who was slated to become a lieutenant, to organize an army band. Europe had founded the Tempo Club in 1914, and a year later, his booking agency made upwards of one hundred thousand dollars. Europe's superiors sought to inspire their fighters with tunes of Europe's band. The musical 15th Infantry, later nicknamed "The Harlem Hellfighters" and part of the 369th Infantry Regiment, came together as Europe found local musicians and traveled to Puerto Rico to recruit others.[352] Eventual jazz luminaries such as drummer Buddy Gilmore and trumpeter Arthur Briggs joined the group.[353]

Lieutenant Europe's band encountered resistance. One US politician criticized the War Department's decision to create a black unit. The Hellfighters were prohibited from marching down Fifth Avenue with their white compatriots in a military send-off parade. After the Allied victory in World War I, however, a newspaper warned about the "throngs" of people waiting to welcome the troops, including the Harlem Hellfighters.[354] More welcomed the 15th at Carnegie Hall, and Lieutenant Europe addressed the crowd.[355]

The Hellfighters were sent to France to perform for General John Pershing at his headquarters. Pershing's underlings criticized the black regiment and forbade them from socializing with French citizens.[356] Pershing sidestepped his underlings and placed the Hellfighters under French command. Napoleon Bonaparte transformed warfare by relying upon patriots to fight his battles, instead of mercenaries or professionals.

During the Napoleonic wars, these patriots "believed they were fighting *for* something."[357] The French did not divide their regiments by race. They did not let internal division destroy their solidarity against the common and real enemy. African Americans were aware of France's commitment to equality and increasingly saw France as the "true land of liberty."[358] The French disparaged the Americans for separating military units by race. The French weren't perfect but took their racial tolerance from literature to action—from Racine to reality.

The Hellfighters traveled over two thousand miles and toured the battlefront with dozens of musical performances.[359] Drum major Noble Sissle, who performed with Europe's band, noted how the "jazz germ" continued to spread.[360] Europe and Sissle wrote "On Patrol in No Man's Land," which eventually became a favorite of American veterans.[361] Europe was in the hospital recovering from a gas attack while he co-wrote it.[362] The song's melody made the mundane military tasks easier to bear. Europe's band inspired other bands such as Lt. Tim Brymn's 350th Artillery Band "Seven Black Devils" that performed for President Woodrow Wilson at a peace conference.

Eventually the Hellfighters' music sent them to the Rhineland, becoming the first Allied unit to reach the Rhine with the French. In fact, one member of the unit earned France's first war medal for an American private.[363] The French fell in love with the Hellfighters' music, and after the war, many black American expatriates remained in Paris (over two million US soldiers were in France during the war—200,000 of which were black). *J'adore le jazz. J'adore la France.* Over 135,000 soldiers from French West Africa were in France during the war, and many brought recordings back to Africa.[364] The froth and spray of France's first wave of jazz signaled the go-ahead for the oncoming tide: Channeling the spirit of Alexis de Tocqueville, African Americans would be the impartial foreign observers of French democracy and equality.

Jazz spread almost as quickly in France as it did in America in the early 1920s. In France, jazz meant more than music. It meant freedom in music, a precept of d'Alembert and a modern way of life.

Le jazz, for instance, could mean a style, performance, musician, or tune.[365] The French could indeed claim a small role in the invention of the saxophone: Belgian Adolphe Sax moved to Paris and created the sax in 1844 and performed at Salle Herz in Paris.[366] In 1846 the patent for the sax was awarded.

"Jazz is a French invention!" screamed one newspaper.[367] Fortunat Strowski, a member of the Institute of France, went to great lengths to establish the French heritage of jazz music: "Jazz is old French music on which Mississippi Negroes grafted their African tom-tom rhythm. America is merely the place where it was incubated … [Strowski] recalled that the Mississippi basin, cradle of scores of moaning saxophone melodies, was once all French."[368] Why the typical pout, prance, and pirouette over who invented jazz? Modern music had eclipsed romanticism, and the French adapted to the new music. French modernists believed that jazz would reinvigorate songs from a previous era with lively African beats. To adapt jazz to French songs— to *jazz* jazz—would result in the French version of an American music. *La France* held up the jazz mirror and saw its reflection—a nation of makers imbued with a spirit of a modern democracy.

Criticism remained a minority sport. Some complained that jazz compositions were too similar. Others oddly complained of its detrimental affect on the nervous system.[369] *C'est domage.* The most common criticism was that jazz embodied Fordism, which signaled the loss of indigenous French culture. Named after automaker Henry Ford, Fordism was a system of mass production and consumption in the early part of the twentieth century. The assembly line increased efficiency of the production process, which led to sustained economic growth. The mass production and consumption of jazz (e.g., radio, phonographs, performances, and films—including advertisements) was a musical extension of Fordism.[370] In some ways, jazz arguably helped to usher Fordism into France during, as one Parisian called the times, "the cocktail epoch" because of the intoxicating effect of many cultures mixing. Jazz was the Fordist mass-production system for making French citizens feel good.[371] The standardization of the jazz big band ensemble occurred during the cocktail epoch. All bands were to have brass, reed, and rhythm sections.

In the early twentieth century, the musical democracy of jazz was fastened to the commercial Fordism of the era. Free markets, part and parcel of Fordism, are essential for democracy to take root. Each market transaction is a compromise between the buyer and seller. The tendency to negotiate and compromise habituates the citizen to political deliberation. The consumer grows accustomed to choice not just in the marketplace but also in government. The triumph of choice over discrimination has resulted (and I mean the denotation of "discrimination," to exercise wise judgment, as Oxford Professor Julian Johnson posits). Madison observed that men are not angels. A government curbed by checks and balances was needed to channel the ambition of each actor. The democratic promise of liberty extends to economics. In the free market, a citizen can pursue his or her self-interest with no (or minimal) government intervention.

Free markets make democracies more appealing. Citizens of undemocratic countries most likely want to emulate rich countries. With the exception of oil-rich states or petro-states, Mandelbaum notes that countries with a higher per capita output are more likely to defend freedom and promote elections.[372] The affluence of America brightens the halo of American political democracy. The jazz recording and performance were profitable ventures, which helped to brighten the aura of jazz, which in turn habituated the foreigner to freedom of musical expression and democratic tendency.

But to the French—in foreign policy parlance: Was Fordism continuing the game or ending it? The game, in this sense, is the ability of America to command and control the dynamics of world culture and politics. After all, the Americanization of France, critics rolled their eyes, led to American ideals, language, and music shaping French culture. If France became an American cultural outpost, would the US effectively control it? Game over. French cultural nabobs worried that Jazz Fordism would result in a homogenized mass culture or "mass-cult."

Although he was a German philosopher, Theodor Adorno's criticisms of jazz were echoed by some among French intellectuals. He dismissed jazz as mechanical sounding and fascist.[373] The metallic saxophone and sizzling cymbals were wholly different sounds next to soft orchestral music. Adorno conflated the new sound of jazz with the technology of the instruments. There were few wood instruments in the jazz band, and the very look of the music was technologically advanced. Moreover, he railed against the use of technology (new instruments, phonographs) in the production of sound, and lamented the commoditization of art.

Despite the criticisms, many authors and artists infused the jazz aesthetic into their works. Literature and the visual arts were influenced by jazz expressionism. Jazz era novelists like American F. Scott Fitzgerald introduced a "new sensuality in the language" and replaced "the omniscient narrator by the unconscious."[374] In 1932, French novelist Céline published *Voyage au bout de la nuit* that drew on fluid prose that didn't conform to traditional French norms; his language bent the rules. A decade later, Albert Camus wrote his famous *L'étranger* entirely in the imperfect tense instead of the traditional *passé composé* verb tense. Novelists *jazzed* the French language, leading some to call this new form "Americanese."[375] Novelists incorporated tragic expressiveness and sympathy in their stories: A criminal could be sympathetic hero, for example.[376] Pablo Picasso lived in Paris during the jazz era. His cubist portraits flattened the multidimensional jazz solo. Picasso's *Le guitariste* (1910) shatters standard and form with orange and brown hues, translating the cocktail epoch onto mural. Henri Matisse's Fauvism drew simple lines and exaggerated perspectives to accent message and context. Matisse published *Jazz*, a collection of his works, in 1947.

Though not a French song, the 1923 jazz-cum-pop song "Yes! We Have No Bananas" typifies the bending of language to wring maximum emotion from towel-dried words. The lyrics are about a Greek storekeeper trying to cope with street life. The song started as an ethnic joke, providing an "optimistic take on ethnic dissonance ... [It] sounded global production and consumption, the urban concentration of an ethnically diverse population, the Fordizing of entertainment, and other hallmarks of American modernity—as opportunities for linguistic and national reinvention."[377] Bandleader Paul Whiteman and his band performed the song, which became a worldwide hit. Bassist George "Pops" Foster played a gig at Local 44 in Illinois in 1923. A large rugged man walked in with a pistol ordering the band to play "Yes! We Have No Bananas" all night long, occasionally pointing the gun at the musicians.[378] The band consented. Foster had trouble playing the song ever again. Notice the crooked pronunciation:

> *YES! we have no bananas; we have no bananas today.*
> *We've string beans, and HON–ions,*
> *Ca–BAH–ges, and scallions,*
> *And all kinds of fruit and say,*
> *We have an old fashioned to–MAH–to,*
> *Long Island po–TAH–to*
> *But, YES! we have no bananas; we have no bananas to-*
> *day.*[379]

Parisian neighborhoods Montmartre and Montparnasse were havens for aspiring and influential artists. Montmartre hosted the Parisian-bohemian art scene in the late nineteenth century. In 1924, Eugene Bullard opened Le Grande Duc, a jazz nightclub, at 52 rue Pigalle.[380] Le Grande Duc, the first home of jazz in Montmartre, was the hotspot for blacks to gossip, perform, and "jive."[381] With performances of jazz singer Florence Embry Jones, the nightclub attracted a coterie of celebrities (another venue attracted the Prince of Wales, who was an amateur jazz drummer).[382] The moniker given to the Harlem Renaissance in Montmartre was *le tumulte noir*, the title of Paul Colin's book on the Parisian jazz age.[383]

The din and tumult of jazz rolled down the Montmartre hill, as most evenings were "American Nights."[384] It was rare to hear French spoken at some locales:

> One hears a single French voice among the guests, the bulk of whom are Americans, with a scattering of English. It seems inappropriate that the announcements of the entertainers should be made in French; it is almost the only French spoken in the room. At least some of the entertainers, and probably most of the audience, know scarcely anything of the language.[385]

Josephine Baker, jazz singer and biggest star of the day, performed at several Montmartre hot spots. Born in 1906 to a St. Louis drummer, Baker moved into the home of a fifty-year-old man after her father deserted the family. She later left him when complaints of impropriety arose and joined the dance group Dixie Steppers, which toured the southern states and later toured France with the vaudeville show *La Revue Nègre*.[386] Her nearly nude dancing, gaudy costumes, and gold fingernails encouraged the French to believe "black is beautiful."[387] Once a white American tourist asked a restaurant manager to refuse to serve Baker, who was eating at the same place. The manager asked the insolent American to leave. *Chantez!* Baker won over the French with her fey ability to entertain. She occasionally sang in French and became a French citizen in 1937. Baker performed at magnificent theatres like the Théâtre des Champs-Élysées, not jazzy nightclubs like Le Grande Duc, and she attracted white and black audiences alike. Baker eventually opened her own place, "Chez Joséphine."[388] At her funeral in Paris in 1975, Baker became the first woman honored with the twenty-one-gun salute.[389]

On the opposite bank of the river Seine was the Left Bank of Montparnasse. The name came from the nickname "Mount Parnassus," the home of the Greek goddesses of the arts and sciences.[390] Some artists moved from Montmartre to Montparnasse just to avoid the growing crowd of tourists. Hemingway frequented La Coupole on Boulevard du Montparnasse.[391] One writer observed, "the Montparnassian risks forgetting his own language."[392] The French police noticed that Montparnasse was becoming overly raucous, a musical kerfuffle. In 1927, Police Officer Jean Chiappe created a decree that banned jazz.[393] The pianos were padlocked in order to acquiesce to the decree. Many bohemians in Montparnasse mourned the decree. The artists of Montparnasse and Montmartre danced to the residual debate of the Dreyfus Affair: Both represented the old and new France. What was French? And where was France going? Hot jazz or indigenous bohemianism?

The French government recognized potential revenue and taxed jazz recordings heavily at the tune of 25 percent.[394] Despite the taxes, after the carnage of the war, Parisians wanted to enjoy the levity of life. And to them, jazz was a "pleasure commodity" that helped them achieve a vivacious end.[395] But heavy taxation also drove cabarets into the red. Ten cabarets went out of business in early 1927.[396] The 1930's financial depression hit the jazz scene. With the "10 percent law," clubs were to limit their acts so that only ten percent of musicians were foreign, creating more opportunities for French musicians.[397] The summer of 1933 was particularly difficult for Montmartre because of the dearth of black musicians and patrons.[398] Clubs tried to find loopholes, but efforts resulted in little. Black musicians traveled elsewhere—to other European countries, Africa, and even Asia. Nevertheless, in the words of Manchester, "The City of Light, the nation's capital, still glowed."[399]

In April 1934 officials nixed the ten percent rule when saxophonist Willie Lewis, who was once part of Sam Wooding's orchestra, performed at Chez Florence.[400] A new breed of hot jazz clubs opened attracting new artists and proven talents. Created by jazz lovers, The Hot Club of France enhanced the public's understanding of hot jazz. Hugues Panassié became well known for stewarding the club. The Hot Club attracted the likes of Django Reinhardt, the gypsy guitarist who burned part of his hand in a fire. What started as a jam session at the Hotel Claridge became the Quintet of the Hot Club of France, the first European group to "compete on favourable terms" with Americans.[401] In December 1934, the group recorded on the Ultraphone label, which shot the quintet to stratospheric success in Europe.[402] Django helped to create a new sound of music by fusing American jazz with gypsy music; he *jazzed* jazz, making it his. Django became the most celebrated European jazz artist of the era.[403] He played the guitar in a percussive manner and was largely influenced by Duke Ellington and guitarist Eddie Lang.[404] He introduced the "lead" and "rhythm" guitar concept to the band, where one guitarist plays the grid of rhythm while the other improvises and reconciles his individuality with the group. Django's group split up in 1939 as the specter of World War II neared, but it showed that a European could self-amend an American music, making it truly his. His quintet concerts converted critics into astute observers. The group's success attracted even Duke Ellington to accompany the group.

Music halls provided a broader audience. Jazz in music halls tended to be more melodic and symphonic, like the music of Paul Whiteman. Hiding jazz with a "white face" masked the music with a less exotic visage.[405] During the interwar years, music halls became well known for flamboyant acts unlike any appearing in other nightclubs or cabarets. Blacks performed at music halls, as did bands led by white bandleader Jack Hylton.[406] Critics argued that white musicians weren't the real thing: jazz required soul-searching black musicians.

But the white face added legitimacy to the music, according to Paul Whiteman. His opinion is a *baguette* of contention.

France inspired blacks in a way that America did not. African American leaders like Booker T. Washington and W.E.B. Du Bois spoke favorably of their French experiences. Du Bois saw France as a model democracy, and during the war years he galvanized the readers with his editorials in *Crisis* magazine to learn from France and bring the fight for democracy to America:

> By the God of Heaven, we are cowards and jackasses if
> now that the war is over, we do not marshal every ounce
> of our brain and brawn to fight the forces of hell in
> our own land. We return. We return from fighting. We
> return fighting! Make way for Democracy! We saved it
> in France, and by the great Jehovah, we will save it in the
> United States of America.[407]

Did the French feel indebted to blacks for fighting on their behalf during the Great War? Africa was a staging ground where the French could fend off the Germans. Supposedly, this made the French treat blacks "with marked consideration and indulgence."[408] Or were the French remorseful to blacks for their acts of imperialism in Africa several decades earlier? Those restaurants that did not serve black customers were forced to close. Such stories crossed the Atlantic and inspired black Americans to immigrate to France, a paragon of human equality.

Despite the trenchant call for equality, the French were not blind to foreigners. From 1919 to 1939, some 20,000 articles about foreigners appeared in eight newspapers and over three hundred books.[409] Anti-African American groups tried to recruit followers but their efforts were stymied as the French government strived for racial equality. Anthropologist William Shack writes in *Harlem in Montmartre*, "French citizens' belief in human rights explained their interest in

Booker T. Washington's account of the fate of former slaves in America."[410] The French were genuinely interested in blacks and struggled to treat them right by the *Déclaration des droits de l'homme*.[411] Detractors kebabbed France over its colonialist record in Africa as a nation not concerned with human rights. French history was not perfect, and citizens recognized the imperfection of French culture. With jazz, the French could turn their foibles into marks of character—a nation that had learned to honor the dignity of man.

The French commiserated with the primitive, nostalgic abstraction of the African vernacular in jazz. Many were nostalgic for their own past: a once-dominant global power with a refined bohemian culture. To traditionalists, French culture was slipping away to an American way of life. But the music ironically helped France self-amend and discover itself.[412]

The egalitarian nature of French society was extended to Jews, as seen in Captain Dreyfus's ascension to high military rank. Many French citizens reasoned that because Jews could relate to the struggle of African Americans, they could help to translate the music. Jews straddled the line between modern Western Europe and more traditional Eastern Europe, just as blacks coped with a duel identity of being an American and African American.[413]

During World War II, many musicians left for America. French violinist Zino Francescatti was one of the first French musicians allowed to leave. With the musical exodus, concerts were increasingly rare in France, noted Francescatti.[414] Over a million people left in exodus during the German occupation.[415] Some weren't that lucky. Trumpeter Arthur Briggs was sent to a camp until France's liberation.[416] The French bemoaned Nazi occupation and criticized the British for the lack of support.[417] The Nazis ordered blackouts in Paris from 10 p.m. to 5:30 a.m. in 1941, a blow to Parisian nightlife.[418] Shack writes of the musical exodus, "If Harlem had invaded Montmartre before

America's engagement in World War I...now Montmartre came to Harlem..."[419]

The Nazi bans and blackouts were haphazard. The Inspector Javert of cultural liberalism, Goebbels did not want to turn cultural oppression into a rallying point for the French, so the Nazis banned American cultural exports but allowed French jazz. The Nazis banned black performances in Paris, but blacks still courageously performed (with a wink from jazz-loving Nazi soldiers). In fact, ever more nightclubs opened during the occupation: almost 125 cabarets in downtown Paris opened after 1940.[420] The Nazis relished Paris and basked in its nightlife.

Music helped the French to escape the brutal reality of occupation. Jazz music was indeed "a reminder of a different time and different place."[421] Jazz symbolized freedom and resistance. Jazz magazine *Down Beat* described the sentiment: "The French seized upon hot music as upon a floating straw in a sea of doom."[422] The music flew in the face of Nazi fascist orthodoxy. To play jazz openly meant to flout the fascist authority with the self-reliant solo of freedom. While the First World War introduced jazz to the French, the Second World War *made* jazz French. During the occupation, jazz concerts that normally attracted audiences of four hundred now lured thousands.[423] The public bought more jazz records that featured French musicians. With fewer American musicians, French musicians brought local sensibility and color to jazz. The French used the word "jazz" instead of "swing" to avoid Nazi condemnation. And song titles were renamed: "I Got Rhythm" was renamed "Agate Rhythm."[424] The Hot Club camouflaged Louis Armstrong's recordings with the name Jean Sablon. The Hot Club of France brazenly stirred the pot with a jazz concert in protest to the Nazi occupation that sold out immediately.[425]

The music of Django perhaps best explains the phenomenon of fusing jazz rhyhtm with French sensibility. Django started a new group with saxophonist and clarinetist Hubert Rostang. Zazou youths coalesced around the music of Django and danced the jitterbug. The Zazous rallied around their chant, "*Je suis swing.*"[426] Already a household name in France, Django lived in the center of Nazi-occupied Paris, a particular affront since Jews and gypsies were targeted by the Nazis.

African American soldiers rushed to the frontlines of the war. They marched in de Gaulle's parade, drawing on the spirit of the Harlem Hellfighters, who were not allowed to march in the French parade of American troops some twenty years earlier. After the liberation of France, academies to study jazz were established. American musicians like saxophonist Dexter Gordon traveled to Paris, but the war had arguably made jazz French, as citizens could claim the music as their own. For the French, the musical democracy was a reflection of their democratic traditions. The vigorous debates surrounding the making of music resumed with the emergence of bebop. The Hot Club of France was divided into two groups: Panassié's group supported traditional swing, whereas French author Charles Delaunay's group enjoyed bebop in its existentialist abstract form.[427] A handful of American musicians questioned French critics. Guitarist Albert "Eddie" Condon said of Panassié: "I don't see why we need a Frenchman to come over here and tell us how to play American music. I wouldn't think of going to France and telling him how to jump on a grape."[428]

"France woke America up to jazz," said saxophonist Garvin Bushell.[429] The most important French contribution was the affirmation of jazz, which added legitimacy for the America mainstream. *Jazz Hot* magazine wrote, "Long before the Yankees realized its interest, intellectuals of the Old Continent became interested in the new music."[430] Miles Davis held France in high esteem: "In Paris—shit, whatever we played over there, right or wrong, was cheered, was accepted."[431] The 1950s and 60s brought American boppers to France. Free jazz players Don Cherry and Archie Shepp traveled to France with their "free" and creative jazz.[432] The jazz scene in France today is largely dominated by

"Euro-jazz," a European abstraction of an American music.[433] That jazz was once an American creation glides towards an *oubli*.

International Lessons

This chapter could have focused on jazz in countries as far away as China. Jazz singer Coco Zhao says that Chinese jazz went underground during the Cultural Revolution with the rise of the propaganda song: "[Jazz] was never really gone, but just never really anyone talked about it. Many professional jazz musicians swear by audiences in Japan, as they are attentive and appreciative of the music."[434] The music also gained a strong following in Latin America, and was greatly influenced by Latino music. Afro-Cuban music and Latin jazz is a rich vein in the history of jazz music. The US is the fifth largest Spanish-speaking nation in the world. The tales of Dizzy Gillespie and Cuban percussionist Chano Pozo are particularly amusing. I suggest reading Raul Fernandez's *Latin Jazz*.

But this chapter is limited to European countries and the Soviet Union because it was the Old World that elevated the New World music and added to the music's legitimacy. European traditionalists venerated the novel American music. The inventiveness of the self-reliant and pragmatic jazz solo stood affirmed by the so-called European traditionalists. Before the US State Department jazz tours, Felix Belair of the *New York Times* wrote, "What many thoughtful Europeans can't understand is why the United States Government ... does not use more of [its money] to subsidize the continental travels of jazz bands."[435] Americans came late to the realization that jazz could be weaponized and deployed during the Cold War. The soft power of the music helped to foment favorable world opinion and affirm auditory American values.

Jazz away from its native land creates an honest outside-in view of the music. We can draw two main lessons from jazz in the Soviet Union, Weimar and Nazi Germany, and France. First, jazz was a language of freedom. While freedom of speech was restricted in Nazi Germany and the Soviet Union, the jazz solo was freedom in music, a tuneful protest. Second, jazz was a sonic abstraction of America the beautiful: the freedom in music, a self-amending spirit, a concrete grid of central rhythm, the romantic lyricism of the blues ballad, the sizzle of the swing band, and the dialogical *making* of the jam session.

Not every Soviet went cock-a-hoop for jazz, but the music made many just *feel* better, princely or poor, communist or capitalist. It made them recast their blues into buoyancy. Freedom of expression in music was the life preserver in the ocean of discontent. In Germany one sees the inevitability of swing. Peace is not the absence of war— peace is also a struggle. The peace of the Weimar years demonstrated the struggle of Negro-Jew music and ideas against intractable fascist doctrines. The inevitability of swing helped conquer the Nazi regime, as many Nazi soldiers fought against something they secretly enjoyed: freedom in music packed into the accordion folds of a single solo. The *making* of democracy and the spirit of the jam session were already integrated forces in French culture. The French freed themselves from recited tradition by self-amending via an auditory abstraction. The French placed a premium on the individual's interpretation and élan, allowing the self-reliant jazz solo to orbit freely around the grid of rhythm.

The Soviet debate over the nature of jazz illustrates the length to which many went to claim the music as theirs. Would jazz be "high brow" or "proletarian"? Soviet officials hankered to reach for their future with a foray into their past, hoping peasants would listen anew to aged folk songs, romanticizing a pure "Russian" culture and heritage.[436] They wanted to make jazz theirs. The oppressed can escape the prison of collectivism and solo over a freedom verse. Turkish mystic philosopher Gurdjieff defines an objective art as a work with mathematical precision strong enough to tear down the walls of Jericho. The fecundity of the jazz solo encourages freedom of expression and helped jazz to play its small role in tearing down the Berlin Wall. Did it not?

In *Policy Review*, Lee Harris writes that tradition can be a "useful fiction."[437] Tradition, in other words, acts as a gilding agent that allows the "uneducated masses" to accept a new idea.[438] The democratic tradition found within jazz served as an artistic forerunner of civil society in each country. With the tradition of jazz firmly ensconced in the cultural liberalism of the time, many started to value the concept of dialogical albeit musical freedom. That a music could teach a continent how to *make* again is no small feat.

Jazz abroad was a case of American possibility and the beauty of American resiliency. Author Penny M. Von Eschen notes, " ... the US promoted black musicians as symbols of the triumph of American democracy when America was still a Jim Crow nation."[439] Jazz music was more democratic than American democracy. Fresh from the military victory of World War II, Americans clamored for democratic victory at home: equality, civil rights, human rights. Not only were Americans longing to make good on the democratic promise, but so were decolonized areas in Latin America, Asia, and Africa.[440] The promise of democracy remained unfulfilled at home and abroad.

"Life is a sea," wrote Ellison, "art a ship in which man conquers life's crushing formlessness, reducing it to a course, a series of swells, tides and wind currents inscribed on a chart."[441] Jazz taught the world about a democratic spirit and making tradition. Where is our ship headed? If our culture is our guide, America is wandering without a meaningful map of oral tradition. Whitman reminded us that our indigenous expression can help regenerate our culture. Jazz music helped to inspire the world. Can it inspire us again?

Chapter 3
Rhythm Saves the World

"Though I speak with the tongues of men and of angels, and have not charity, I am become as sounding brass, or a tinkling cymbal."
—I Corinthians 13:1

I suspect that two hundred years from now, the end of the twentieth century and dawn of the twenty-first will be remembered for the personal computer and the Internet. These inventions have fundamentally reshaped the bricolage of communication. Economic historians will study the "new globalization" of our era and how private equity groups and venture capital firms financed the next wave of successful corporations. Political historians will no doubt evaluate America's reaction to September 11, 2001, and how foreign policy was reshaped to combat Islamic terrorism. There will be many worthwhile political and economic events for social scientists to consider. Sometimes I wonder what cultural historians will say of our modern culture.

During summer break, a schoolchild visits Washington, DC with her family. She and her family visit the National Gallery of

Art. She wanders through the East Building that hosts the artworks of Henri Matisse. The splotchy saturated canvas of *Open Window, Collioure* connotes the serene expressiveness of Matisse's brush. A crooked line of museumgoers trickles into the new special exhibit called "Early Twenty-first Century Art and Music." In the expansive hall, turquoise drapes stretch from ceiling to floor. On the welcoming wall of the exhibit are printed the words in heavy Arial font: "My black g-unit hoody just reek of marijuana, Cocaine comin out my pores in the sauna." On the opposite wall, another twenty-first century entertainment salvo: "Now I don't like fake t****** but I'll f*** lil kim," from Kanye West's classic. "Early twenty-first century artistic music is reminiscent of the barbarism of Attila the Hun," whispers the tour guide. The tour group shuffles forward. The schoolchild stares at the ominous visage of rapper 50 Cent. "Don't fall behind," her mom whips.

To compare the music of Kanye West and 50 Cent to the barbarism of Attila the Hun is unfair, but I offer this example to exaggerate and provoke the question: How will our culture be remembered? Will the museums of the future crown the CDs of Eminem in a glass exhibit case? Will Britannica and Encarta suggest that *American Idol*, Jay-Z, and T.I. are the collective expressions of our time? Will our collective cultural legacy be that of venting explicit brutality and overt wretchedness?

[While it may seem that I take issue with these popular rappers and entertainers, my displeasure is not aimed at them. Kanye West is free to entertain and promote his scoop. And I (gasp) acknowledge his perspicuity. My displeasure springs from the mainstream's cultural failing to encourage beauty in our art and popular entertainment.]When was the last time we listened to a popular song today—and thought enough about its beauty to consider it timeless? Art can be difficult to understand and appreciate. It takes work to comprehend. Art, Dana Gioia reminds us, challenges us with visions of the future, not pleasing payola representations of the present.

Forget our eventual cultural legacy for a moment; consider our past and present. During the Cold War, America the Beautiful was broadcast around the world to win the hearts and minds of allies and enemies. The jazz bomb helped to increase American soft power in a time of intense international conflict. What music should the VOA broadcast into the Middle East to teach American values? Do we want our Billboard Top 10 broadcast in full, unedited, and uncensored brazenness around the world? Or does the thought of vapid melody and brutal lyrics representing America make you (like me) cringe?

Tagore wrote that musicians are the designers of paradise; and jazz is America's paradisiacal art. But somehow, somewhere, our cultural liberalism took a turn toward the brutal, crass, and absurd. Maybe in order to understand mankind, we have to look at the word itself: 'Mankind.' Basically, it's made up of two separate words—'mank' and 'ind,'" so joked comedian Jack Handey. It's mysterious why American culture has become devoid of modern (and epic) poets, sculptors, musicians (who play instruments, not program computers), and writers. What once was the glorious stomping ground for Frost, Twain, Ellington, and Armstrong is fallow with rhyme. Are our best (artistic) days behind us?

America's modern music speaks not of America the beautiful, nor of the quintessential values of Americana. Beauty does not equate to happiness: The auburn glow of the kneeling figure in Rembrandt's *The Return of the Prodigal Son* is drowned out by the gloomy darkness. Beauty to me is a simulacrum of meaning. Our modern music has lost its beauty because it has lost meaning. It has lost its meaning because art has become divorced from that which gives meaning to our artistic cultural expression: mythology.

This chapter ventures into a utopian province of a jazz-inflected society or Jazzocracy. It is my hope that the jazz-as-democracy trope can not only explain Americana, but channel the spirit of Whitman who reminds us that if we lose our way, we need only to remember our

native self-expression and heritage. [We can and must culturally regenerate with an eternally optimistic and pragmatic democratic spirit to
re-center American music back to myth. We can return (and advance)
to *making* music and opening our arts to the jam session of contradiction and reconciliation.] Before mapping out how exactly, however, it
may prove worthwhile to explore the components of myth and mythic music. And so I humbly present to you (with apologies to Joseph
Campbell and Robert Graves).

A Primer on Myth

Myths are fantasy. They are creations of another world, a parallel
universe that suggest a level of potentiality not found in the human
world. Myth and its meaning have made for perennial debate. The
Greeks viewed discourse in terms of rational dialogue, *logos*, and its
opposite, myth, or *muthos*.[442] Those who defined *logos* in terms of ra-
tionality saw *muthos* as irrationality. *Logos*, like a mathematical proof
or systematic algorithm, brought one to truth. How could truth be
unreasoned? Yet others during the Greek Enlightenment interpreted
myths as allegorical clues to morality and truth. Yeats remembered the
Greek saying, "Myths are the activities of Daimons."[443] In the modern
era, those who seek knowledge of the present and future in Western
society seemingly prefer to use the compass and telescope rather than
kill the turkey and read the entrails.

Some in the West see myth as antithetical to the scientific process, echoing the beliefs of Aristotle and Plato. However, one could
argue that scientific thought has been governed by the prevailing non-
scientific paradigm of an era. If it weren't for Copernicus's heliocentric
system of the universe, we may still believe in Earth as the center of the
universe. Einstein theorized that space is curved, and removed New-
ton's theory of inflexible space from common conception. General

relativity is at odds with quantum mechanics—born from Heisenberg's uncertainty principle that states that the more accurately you measure a particle's position, the less you can track the speed.[444] Modern physics is apparently built on contradictory theories. The pursuit of a unified field theory such as string theory teaches us that even science can contradict. Theories are not laws.

Consider the Sumerian myth of Tammuz and Ishtar from two to three millennia before Christ. The demon imprisons Tammuz in the underworld. Ishtar the female consort of Tammuz descends to the underworld to rescue Tammuz. Ishtar returns to a grand feast and celebration.[445] In the yearly Festival of Tammuz, reenactments of the myth were performed with great celebration. Is this myth true? One could argue that the veracity of the myth doesn't matter because it serves as parcel of an oral tradition and an agent of societal cohesion. Sumerians shared certain myths and narratives that generated a group identity and sense of community.

For Westerners to consider another culture's myth as untrue misses the point. Similarly, those in the East might consider the story of a great deluge, an ark, and two creatures of every kind as a falsehood. The point is to see that most (if not all) cultures believe in certain stories that give meaning and shape to a community. Perhaps a lesson we can draw from looking at other cultures is to be careful to not think of myths as pejoratives, resurrecting Plato and Aristotle's dismissal of *muthos*: "My beliefs are a strong conviction, yours a dogma, his a myth."[446] One person's myth is another person's reality.

Anthropologist Joanna Overing discovered that while "civilized society" may dismiss myths as untrue, the Piaroa people in the Venezuelan rainforest think metaphors are false.[447] To say "it's raining cats and dogs" would be a lie to the Piaroas, yet metaphors are poetic devices for us, sometimes offering shreds of truth. Myths are not necessarily kooky ideas and phantasmagorical schemes. Myths may be "phantom realities." Just as political democracy is the ordering of human nature into a governing and self-amending system, myths are crucial in ordering societies.[448]

Renowned comparative mythologist Joseph Campbell bemoaned that Greek mythology was no longer taught to students.[449] To study and understand mythologies is to comprehend the values of a particular society. Myths are instructive in nature, just like the rich literary works of James Joyce and Thomas Mann. Many novels require the reader to make sense and draw meaning from the work. The author produces the pieces of the puzzle, whereas the reader assembles them into a composite form. Similarly, myths order the world so that we can make sense of it. Most often myths give us clues to our world and the human condition. Quite simply, "We are trying to tell the stories to harmonize our lives with reality."[450]

How do we personally relate to a greater mythological story, a public dream? Many Americans subscribe to the potentiality of the "American Dream." The American Dream is not a scientifically proven fact, despite the attempts of very many social scientists. Nor can one induce *logos* to explain the deeply seated American belief. It is a belief that Americans can shoot for the sky and avoid the nimbus clouds of failure. Many an entrepreneur has harmonized effectively with a particularly harsh business climate by seeing himself through the lens of the American Dream. We may not see ourselves as reenacting a mythological story like Tammuz and Ishtar, and thereby living in the image of God, but millions of Americans arguably harmonize their economic misfortune with the public dream found in Horatio Alger's dime novels. Travails comes triumph. Tom Joad didn't want a free ride. He went West looking for work. The American Dream is an instructive and generative myth that helps us cope and relate with cruel reality. The $700 million self-help book market testifies to the American yen to improve and achieve.[451] To understand the American Dream is to comprehend part of the American psyche—a burning and eternal optimism that through self-amendment, the blues of life can be transcended. Taken to a higher level, to understand any culture, one must understand its myths.[452] Myths make up a shadow-history of the world. As historian James Oliver Robertson put it, "they *explain* the world."[453]

Myths, like language, are part of our oral tradition. When stories aren't written down, there is a higher probability of alterations, embellishment, and amendment to a narrative over time. To *burn* a CD meant something different in the early 1990s than it does now. MTV updates its jargon from "shake your booty" to "drop it like it's hot." Words may change, but the new phrase may still evoke the same meaning. Similarly, myths may take on new personages and heroes, but the basic message may not change.

Myths provide original patterns, life models, and archetypes to which individuals can relate. "Archetypes are born of the collective soul, but they are enacted by individual souls."[454] Are Madonna or Marilyn Monroe the modern personification of Aphrodite, the Greek goddess of beauty? Is cornetist Joe "King" Oliver the personification of Apollo, the Greek God of music? A variety of life models have filled world history: Zeus, Athena, Jesus Christ, Buddha, Mother Theresa. Not everyone aspires to the same life model; each archetype encapsulates a different value set. The archetype that I propose we emulate and re-introduce to American society is that of the rugged jazz musician.

Another way to conceptualize myth is to consider its two dimensions: (1) the archetype or infrastructure; and (2) the narrative or superstructure. The infrastructure of myth means the "ethical obviousness" of a certain concept or the "moral of the story."[455] The infrastructure is the societal grid—the core beliefs and attitudes. America's infrastructural belief in individualism can find its roots in Puritan belief: self-reliant American colonists. The superstructure, according to Lee Harris, is "the system of myths and statements and arguments that are used by the community to justify obedience to the commandments, injunctions, and prohibitions."[456] The superstructure involves stories and anecdotes such as Davy Crockett and Billy the Kid that build on the ethical obviousness of the infrastructure or archetype. The superstructure of Luke Skywalker trusting the force in *Star Wars* can be peeled away to infer the deeper meaning of the infrastructure. Skywalker's trust of the force is a reincarnation of the *infrastructural* belief in Goethe's Faust that technology isn't going to save us.[457] *The Economist* notes that several American myths are "variations on the Odyssey—wagon trails to the west, the Lewis and Clark expedition, Huckleberry Finn."[458] Peeled away, Huck Finn is our American Odysseus, exploring the unknown and awakened to curiosity. These are superstructural stories built atop the grid of ethical obviousness and infrastructure.

The superstructures of symbols, crests, and mottos can be peeled away to expose myths at work.[459] The fifty stars on the American flag represent each state of the union. The thirteen stripes stand for the original thirteen colonies. These symbols are grounded in mythology. Campbell points out the mythological significance of twelve: Jesus Christ was surrounded by twelve disciples. Campbell claims that the number thirteen signifies resurrection. Professor Mark Gabriel notes that Muhammad surrounded himself with twelve key followers as well, not to mention twelve wives.[460] Muhammad spent thirteen years preaching in Mecca.[461] The eagle, the bird of Zeus, fashions nine feathers in its tail: nine representing the number of the divine power when descending from the heavens. The pyramid on the dollar bill is topped with the "eye of reason," and in the background, the desert of Europe or the Old Continent.[462]

The eye of reason is that of modernity and invention. Americans will self-amend and improvise in the *making* of a new democratic tradition. The US has been called the world's greatest experiment. We are a nation of self-amenders and discoverers. Americans following in the folklore of Columbus who sailed west and against all odds found the "New World." Americans identify with Columbus because he is us:

"We are on those ships."[463] With the discovery of the new world came a mentality of invention and self-discovery. Colonial nomenclature reflected the New World—New York, New Jersey, New Hampshire, New England. The New World was a fresh chance to re-make society for the colonialists and answer the problems of the "old world." The Great Seal that affixes American currency says "Novus Ordo Seclorum," or "a new order of the world."[464]

Columbus himself became synonymous with infrastructural concepts of discovery and courage. In 1784, King's College was renamed "Columbia" to show "both the rejection of England and the glorification of America."[465] Washington, DC (District of Columbia) married George Washington to Christopher Columbus, the father to the discoverer. On the ship *Columbia*, Captain Robert Gray named the Columbia River while exploring the western "New World." The Columbia spaceship was named after Gray's vessel. Some even suggested changing "United States of America" to "United States of Columbia."[466] Columbia became a mythic figure, dressed with a helmet and holding a spear. American textbooks lauded Columbus for being America incarnate, a champion who tamed the "old world" by discovering the new one. In 1844, Congress allowed a group of marble sculptures to don the eastern porch of the Capitol. A sculpture of Columbus wearing armor and carrying an orb inscribed with "America," while historically incorrect, symbolized his heroic nature.[467] Musicians even incorporated the myth of Columbus. Jazz legend Fats Waller sang:

> Mister Christopher Columbus
> He used rhythm as his compass!
> Music ended all the rumpus
> Wise Old Christopher Columbus![468]

A young George Washington cut down a cherry tree, did not lie to his father, and was forgiven. The mythical inference is that the honesty of American intention may trump the purity of the destroyed.[469]

The George Washington myth never really occurred; it is pedantic lore, instructive legend. Yet it occurs every day. To invade Iraq with the honest intention of stopping Islamic terrorism justifies the pureness of that which is destroyed. The usable cherry tree myth suggests that the civilians that America kills are collateral because of the grandness of intentions. The manifest destiny foray into the frontier is justified by honest exploration, nary a worry of Native American destruction. Another myth is that of Thanksgiving, America's secular Christmas.[470] Strange men, the Native Americans, brought gifts of food (and survival) to the pilgrims. November is the wrong month to hold a harvest festival, but Americans recognize the myth's meaning: Thanksgiving was America's birth. American myths also extend to the Holy Trinity: George Washington, the nation's father; Ben Franklin, the son of virtue and individualism; and Thomas Jefferson, the Democratic spirit.[471] The Declaration of Independence, Constitution, and Bill of Rights make up the holy trinity of scripture. Changing domains, some consider Coltrane, Pharoah, and Aylers to be the post-bop jazz trinity.[472]

Some jazz luminaries have reached mythological heights in America. Jazz writer Neil Leonard contends that Charlie Parker took on a mythological characterization after his death. Hooked to narcotics, he was the inimitable hipster, trying to shortcut his path into *inner* space. He was often in his own world, walking off the bandstand, urinating in a nearby telephone booth, and laughing about it. But like America's Paul Bunyan, Bird was a hyperbolic figure, a founding father of bebop. He was an artistic and inventive genius on the level of Picasso, and embodied creativity and the escapist mentality that could only lead to personal and societal transcendence, a new day in America. After his death, graffiti covered New York with the phrase "Bird Lives."[473] Writer Hunter S. Thompson said that John F. Kennedy would always be remembered as a young man. Charlie Parker, who died a young man at 34, will long be remembered for his immortal genius. He lived and died his epic.[474] But it's not genius we must strive for in adopting a new mythology. Geniuses are individuals who have a spark that can rarely be replicated. Indeed, modern musicians can replicate Parker's bebop solos, but never, as a society, duplicate his creative talent.

Taxonomy of Myth

Perhaps the most basic way to classify mythical interpretations is with the functionalist and structuralist systems. David Emile Durkheim, one of the founders of modern sociology, stressed the value of the myth to society, the *function* of a myth in society. The content of a myth can be untrue and irrational, but myths bring "social cohesion" and "functional unity" to a group.[475] Narratives like Tammuz and Ishtar or Paul Revere's midnight ride act as cohesive agents for a people. Shared stories help to encourage shared identity. Functionalists see myths as a functional ingredient to society: Myths operate in the daily lives of citizens even if they don't recognize it. Structuralist Claude Lévi-Strauss felt that the underlying meaning, the infrastructure of myth, should be evaluated. Instead of studying the narrative of myth and the function they serve in society, myths must be read for deeper, analogical, and semiological meaning. Structuralists examine rituals, rites, and traditions of a society in order to grasp the embedded structure of how meaning is produced. Some scholars say that structuralists remove myth from every day society and delve into the abstract.[476]

I am hardly a qualified mythologist, but suspect that both functionalism and structuralism can help explain the role of myth in society. Brought to our times, what is the function of myth in America's oral tradition? Music and myth are part of our oral tradition. Does mythic music help to unite Americans and create a shared purpose? Can Americans listen to popular music and hear America? Or is our mythic music helping to divide and vulgarize? Structuralists can look at our mythic music and question the deeper semiotic meaning:

Popular entertainment reflects the excess and indulgency of the .
American psyche. It is by listening to our current popular music and
the lack of ritual-infused performance that the structuralist may con-
clude that America is rife with vapidity.

Instead of rushing pell-mell to describe a jazz-inflected mythology, I hope to ground the journey in an appropriate framework.
My improvisation requires a grid of reality. Professor George Schöpflin posits that myths overlap, contradict, and support each other. He
groups myths with a loose taxonomy: redemption and suffering, kinship, unjust treatment, valor, and antiquity, among various others.[477]
A functionalist could say Schöpflin's mythopoeias show that myths
serve many functional purposes: communicating facts, simplifying the
complex, encouraging shared identity, and suggesting an appropriate
archetype to emulate.

To recognize a myth at work in society is to distinguish the proverbial "big picture." Astute politicians, advertising professionals, and
those who need to tap the collective conscience of a group often invoke
myth. The Nazis went to great lengths to paint jazz as a Negro-Jewish
art, invoking a myth of kinship: Germans are to be pure with shared
ancestry. Negroes and Jews, they believed, were not part of their kin.
In Nazi ideology, German music such as Wagner's operas was superior
to foreign degenerate music. The Nazi right-looking eagle connotes
an image of power and military valor. The French assimilated jazz and
were arguably participating in a ritual of rebirth, stretching bohemian
culture into the twentieth century. Structuralism teaches us to find
the deeper and hidden meaning of our narratives and oral tradition.

America's Rupture

Aesthetic theory distinguishes between art and entertainment as each serves different purposes in society. I wince at my reductionism but proceed for the sake of brevity: Entertainment pleases and amuses. Entertainment succeeds because it is *expected* to. Art, however, presents us with a challenging depiction of ourselves and who we could become. The tenor solos of John Coltrane tell a story, but not in a traditional beginning-to-end arc. Instead, he obliterates traditional form and splinters plot by jettisoning notes on the audience. His solo is half the battle. It requires *us* to make sense and decode. Like a classic novel, we can come back to Coltrane's solos time after time and infer different meaning. Art speaks to us in a deep and meaningful manner each time we revisit it.

Where do you turn for art? Tune to the radio. Awake to independent promoters paying radio stations to broadcast songs—a profitable payola.[478] Adjust the television dial. Awake to vacuous Paris Hilton glamorized for promiscuity (she earned $6.5 million in 2005).[479] Install the svelte Playstation 3 adjacent to your small screen. Awake to ten-year-olds playing "Grand Theft Auto San Andreas" with its hidden pornography.[480] Laugh with Conan O'Brien and Jon Stewart. Awake to their special guests hawking a new movie or (smile) book. Awake to modern entertainment. Awake to America the bootylicious.

I am a supporter of economic liberalism. I understand that CNN, Comedy Central, and Playstation 3 are parts of greater businesses. Their operating companies need profit to thrive. We need not blame outlets of popular entertainment for providing amusing images. Instead of presenting challenging and enigmatic work, entertainment companies entertain with pleasing postures. I am a frequent viewer of *The Daily Show* and enjoy the occasional *FIFA Soccer (or Madden)* grudge match—and appreciate the P.T. Barnum circus acts of entertainment.

In the name of cultural liberalism, the sharp rise of entertainment has arguably led to a decline of the role and importance of art in American culture. I don't decry the prevalence of entertainment. Instead, I bemoan the lack of pushback—the shortage of (popular) art in modern America. Is it possible to have an abundance of entertainment and art in a culture? I think so. But our oral tradition has divorced myth from music and has been nearly consumed by popular entertainment. Our modern music suffers from a loss of beauty and meaning, a rupture of mythology.

Marsalis calls this rupture a "conformity to the absurd."[481] He relates a story of an elementary school student who performs a rap song for him in class. The child grabs his crotch because, as the teacher explains, "That's what they do nowadays."[482] The seven-year-old children that I worked with at a neighborhood homework help organization could recite 50 Cent's lyrics from memory. One eight-year-old was scolded for talking about his teacher in a blatantly sexual manner. An enlightened education is a necessary defense to fight the absurd. That is, those who do not unquestionably grab their crotches recognize the bizarreness of such an artistic act, as they have been educated and understand how to act in a society.

But isn't rap just a new art form? After all, the US government banned *Ulysses*. The Catholic Church came out against polyphony. It even considered the tritone (an interval spanning three whole tones or an augmented forth) as a creation of the devil. The Church labeled the inharmonious interval *Diabolus in musica*. Violent acts are a result of the demythologization of culture, notes Campbell. Gangs, for instance, invent myths because greater society does not teach these stories:

> This is why we have graffiti all over the city. These kids
> have their own gangs and their own initiations and their
> own morality, and they're doing the best they can. But

they're dangerous because their own laws are not those of the city. They have not been initiated into our society.[483]

Commentator Bill Moyers responds to Campbell by paraphrasing psychologist Rollo May: "There is so much violence in American society because there are no more great myths to help young men and women relate to the world."[484] Where have all the heroes gone? Channels of calm have trouble competing with the semi-pornographic flicks of popular entertainment. And a case could be made that the lack of balance in popular entertainment shares in responsibility for societal trouble.

Rules and laws can compel individuals to act in a certain way. While rugby is hardly mythical, it shows how rules and norms govern the way folks act. Once a group of Americans tried to play rugby with British chaps and threw a forward pass, prohibited by the rules of rugby. The British chaps stopped the game. Similarly, the norms of a society can often be inferred from its composite mythology. In America, our foundational beliefs are based upon a written law. But the downside, Campbell contends, is that "Lawyers and law are what hold us together. There is no ethos."[485] Laws don't make for mythologies because they lack the story-like narrative grip on citizens. Laws are topical. But it's hard to make a case that the Clean Water Act, for example, is mythological. Laws and myths both help to organize society. Laws are rules. Myths help to create identity.

The rupture of America's mythology is a case of the superstructure of story deviating from the infrastructure of a society's core belief. Usually, societies become more learned and adopt new conceptions and myths like Maxwell's equations or the scientific reason for not eating uncooked meat. But the conflict between ideal and actual can tilt the entire structure: Myths may become unrepresentative or gross misrepresentations of a nation's core beliefs. The 1950s' and 1960s' "rebel without a cause" superstructure myths of Billy the Kid and James

Dean misrepresented the "rugged individualism" infrastructural belief borne out of the puritan ethic. Gangsta Rap portrays angry black men who glamorize the violence of ghetto life, rebelling against … what is their cause? Violence is antithetical to the democratic tradition. The peaceful transfer of power or spotlight is echoed in the jazz tune. The pervasiveness of popular rap music, from coast to crib, speaks to our collective acceptance of an oral tradition that does not reflect American infrastructural beliefs. In the name of entertainment, Americans accept a vulgarization of America's oral tradition.

The rupture of America's mythology cannot be pinned on one particular genre of music. Much of Don Byron's spoken word compositions, with his landscape of imagery and poetry slams, tell meaningful stories and challenge the listener with a vision of potentiality. The Sugarhill Gang and GrandMaster Flash entertained without odious froth at the mouth. The rupture of America's mythology, however, can be placed at those forms of entertainment that talk loud but don't say much. The escalation of noise is a rarely checked force in the perpetuation of modern mythology, which keeps the musicians of today busking at the vanity fair.

Attali writes of the four musical "networks": sacrificial ritual, representation, repetition, and composition. Each network can be mapped to the history of music over the last five hundred years. Music was part of ritual when the primary patron of the arts was the church in the sixteenth and seventeenth centuries. The hymnody of the church incorporated the teachings, myths, and narratives of the Bible. Coltrane tried to bring American music back to Attali's first network, acting as a musical shaman, for instance.[486] He was an inspired and soul-searching musician: "[Coltrane] was all the way into music, and if a woman was standing right in front of him naked, he wouldn't have even seen her," observed Miles.[487] Music entered the network of representation during the era of concert performances when audiences gathered to hear the ordering of noise. Franz Joseph Haydn's works for the princes of

Esterházy are a prime example of such representation as these compositions represented the sensibilities of the Austrian Empire.

Franz Joseph Haydn enjoyed one of the best working conditions known to any composer or musician. Haydn focused on his passion without financial worry. Princes Paul Anton Esterházy and Nikolaus "the Magnificent" Esterházy fully funded Haydn. Prince Nikolaus appointed him to the position of Kapellmeister in which he composed church music. Perhaps Haydn's most memorable composition, Symphony No. 45 also known as Farewell Symphony, represented and communicated the true feelings of the musicians. Prince Nikolaus Esterházy spent the entire summer living in his new palace with Haydn and his musicians. These young musicians left their families for six months in order to entertain the Prince. In Farewell, all the musicians leave the stage one by one extinguishing their respective lights, quieting the beautiful music. At the finish, only Tomasini's solo violin remains audible. Prince Nikolaus understood the hint that the musicians wanted to return home, and he decided to return as well. Attali's network of representation is exemplified by those communicative performances that express emotion and affection that would otherwise be tacit. Attali contends that increasingly music finds itself in the network of repetition.

In what may be the most dangerous of networks, repetition means to freeze human invention and trap our identity.[488] It's the cold calculation of what will sell, arriving at the absence of meaning. The mass production of music ensures that most will listen to the same music instead of discovering and creating art for themselves. Attali's last network is that of composition—to invent music (on the fly) and discover one's artistic identity. To jump from repetition to composition requires a cultural awakening to possibility.

Neophobia, Realizing the Past and the Spirit of Collage

Does neophobia threaten innovation? It is one thing for popular entertainment to spout Vicodin-venerating rappers, but quite another when we have little escape. Americans are long on popular entertainment (and its popular and humorous yet absurd antics), but short on the timeless abstractions of art. The DJ and his beat machine supplanted the virtuosity of the instrumentalist. Computer technology is integral not only to the mixing of music but the entire production of certain modern compositions. Isn't technically sampling music analogous to editing music via word processor?[489] The new instrument has become the computer, the valves the keyboard, and the horn the speakers. Studio-recorded music is filtered to remove imperfections. But the bond of humanity is imperfection: to filter blemish down to the microtone is akin to deleting the human out of the sound. Levitin says recording engineers can readily exploit neural circuits of the brain to create special auditory effects that stimulate the mind and tickle the ear. This isn't necessarily bad, but it shows the length to which scientists and musicians will go to attract the ear.

To think linearly about art is problematic because art is not a progression. Art is not technology. Schoenberg is not an improvement over Strauss because his works are more recent; his twelve-tone method is not superior to Erik Satie's impressionistic harmonies because it came later. Fast turnover of stars and celebrities is indicative that newness has been confused with hipness, and entertainment confused as art. Entertainment is a fleeting and passing fashion. Many of my peers look back with horror that they danced to the Macarena or primped a giant pompadour in the 1980s. On the contrary, art is a static symbol of beauty. Music is meant to touch the human and radiate emotion: "Styles of art change, but the technology of the human soul doesn't. How are you going to move past the touching of the soul?"[490] We don't need to explore the outer world anymore. Philosopher Arthur Danto acknowledges that all continents have been discovered: "The time for next things is past. The end of art coincides with the end of a history of art that has that kind of structure … this means returning to art to the serving of largely human ends."[491]

"But wasn't R&B inspired by jazz and the blues?" You may learn from different types of art and adopt its lessons. But this isn't "progress." If it were, what are we progressing to? A more perfect art? A collage of sound that speaks so directly to the human soul that all previous forms will be forgotten? Malraux writes in *Picasso's Mask* that painters aped other paintings not to improve on them. "Was it because [Van Gogh] wanted to 'paint better' than Delacroix? And did Cézanne want to paint better than Sebastian? No."[492] He continues, "They didn't want to paint better; they wanted to paint differently. They had no intention of trying to improve upon the model in its own domain."[493] Artists saw themselves as contributing to a particular domain or questioning it, but never improving on it. The ancient artists of Egypt and Greece created masks, but it wasn't until the Italians that expression-filled eyes brought sculptures to life. Yet it wasn't an "improvement."[494] They wanted to assert their own individuality, like the tall skyscrapers of the Manhattan skyline, and if an emergent style or "lump character" emerges, then a new form is borne. Nor did these artists fall prey to neophobia, an artistic paralysis where they felt that recreating the works of masters was the highest form of art: "You can keep an old tradition going only by renewing it in terms of current circumstances."[495] Some American television shows feature contestants who are "made over" to become handsome, successful, and accepted—a plot reminiscent of Shaw's *Pygmalion*. The characters change but not the infrastructural core.

Similarly, some see jazz and classical music as obsolete. Consequently, I have known some peers who will not perform works in these genres because they see the newer forms, from rock to rap, as more recent and more hip. Professor Olly Wilson offers a compelling distinction: "Entertainment, while engaging our aesthetic sensibilities, is immediately gratifying, less concentrated in content, and tends not to make a lasting impact on us. Art ... requires concentrated active participation."[496] He believes that we can return to art because it speaks to us differently each time. There is a need to return and reinterpret. The invitation to reinterpret is what Joyce thought as the best characteristic of art, *claritas*, the whatness of the art, its radiance. Shelley refers to it as "enchantment of the heart."[497] Such radiance speaks to every human, as Gibran describes "an image you see though you close your eyes, and a song you hear though you shut your ears."[498] Art is soul made plastic, idea made visible.

Consider the process of inventing new art as adding to a collage. Instead of replacing one form with another, there exists a vast American mural-cum-collage on which artists Scotch tape their creation. The American collage represents the aesthetic stasis of music, recognizing that artists *contribute* and respect *models*. We may learn new lessons from listening, but music doesn't progress. It just is. Jazz learned from the blues and African tradition: The metrical contrast, soloing in a percussive way, call and response forms, replicating vocal sounds on instruments, and body movement during a performance.[499] White Americans didn't improve on African tradition. "How can I invent something new?" should change to "How can I contribute to the American collage?" Jazz music teaches the importance of collage and respecting forms. In most of my gigs, I play standards written by jazz legends, honoring the forms and traditions of jazz. Recognizing the beauty of musical models—Bach, Beethoven, Bird, and Basie— helps us to venerate the standards and forms of the past, instead of blatantly obliterating them. Models like the twelve bar blues are "standards" for a reason. They are the collective standardization of an era. The twelve bar blues was a condensed format of a blues song, limited by the short recording time available in the early 1920s. The I-IV-V chord progression gives abbreviated tension and release in every chorus.

It was the standard on which the boogie-woogie and early jazz music was built.[500]

Louis Armstrong was an avid collagist. He would cut newspapers and magazines (sometimes in the middle of gigs) and paste images onto his collage. His collages were patchworks that included advertising slogans, pictures of himself, stationary, and scotch tape. Professor Jorge Daniel Veneciano considers Armstrong's collages a prism for the critique of the artistic output of the jazz pioneer. Armstrong's collages reflect clippings from the "stuff of life," and show that he drew upon a multitude of narratives to express himself. His "equipmental" outlook on his surroundings helped him integrate the prosaic and refined into his collages and musical compositions. He did not look with disdain to previous forms and standards. His equipmental outlook convinced him to travel with a dictionary and tape recorder. Veneciano paints Armstrong as the bricoleur—one who gathers objects and ideas, storing them until he can make use of them.[501] The pragmatism of the bricoleur is at odds with the engineer who requires the appropriate tools for construction. Picasso frequently interrupted his conversations to collect a stone or tree branch. Malraux writes, "He was in search of what he 'could make of it.'"[502] What can we make with what we have?

Contributing to the American collage isn't just a musical mindset. American legislators should continually think of *contributing* with a patchwork of ideas and legislation. The Progressive Era contributed anti-trust legislation. Are the US Congresses of the early twenty-first century contributing to the American collage with anti-terrorism legislation or healthcare reform? To contribute (rather than "improve") is to recognize the importance of one's predecessors and successors. It's to understand the forms and traditions of the past and integrate these works into our own bricolage and collage. We are temporary stewards of our music and government. Let us make good on our inheritance and bequeath legislative items and our own expressions of music. Contribution is participatory in nature and recommits us to the *making* (and reinterpretation) of democracy. To contribute means to participate in the great American experiment. Such a mindset has perceptible benefits. Professor of Economics Richard Layard writes on happiness, "We need to feel we are contributing to the wider society."[503]

Survival of Myth and the Rise of a Jazzocracy

Unless the narrative of popular entertainment actually speaks to our true nature, then our oral tradition has deviated from core American beliefs. Many rap lyrics brutally describe degenerate life and destroy any semblance of hope. But didn't jazz signify the erotic and allude to the sexual? The freedom in jazz music enabled culturally oppressed Soviets to dance and the French to steal a glance at the scantily clad Josephine Baker. Admittedly, some jazz music has a checkered history: part and parcel of Fordism, an erstwhile synonym for sex, and a stimulant for hedonism. The moniker "Jazz Age" had more to do with publicity than New Orleans-style music.[504] There is, however, a difference between the romanticizing of love and brutalizing acts of love. The real abuse of sex, posits Gurjdieff, is the association of the sex center of the mind with negative emotions. When sex becomes associated with only materialism, or worse, rape and derogatory acts, then the romanticism of sex is eviscerated.

I have yet to come across the vulgarization of modernity in the tunes of jazz. The lyrics of a Jay-Z composition blatantly enflame a racial stereotype before our very eyes: "Three things n***** love ... money, p****, and drugs."[505] When these words enter our oral tradition, how do we collectively codify them? When Louis Armstrong was accused of his Uncle Tom act, he still commanded respect with his talent and virtuosity. The superstructure of our popular entertainment narratives and oral tradition is at odds with America the beautiful. We speak not of American brilliance but of warped meaninglessness.

The self-amending individual determinism of our American hero does not push him to discard the myths of yore. He does not confuse the fickleness of narrative with the deeper meaning of core belief. He recognizes the tradition of America's democracy and the beauty of cultural liberalism. Philosopher Friedrich Hayek defends tradition and myths of yesteryear because they function as fossils of survival.[506] As our coping mechanisms of a troubled past, strains of our mythology have survived and can instruct again. These fossils congealed in an era of optimism and self-amendment. Hayek provides a way out: "We can ask ourselves as individuals whether we like ourselves the way we are today, or whether we liked ourselves better in the past."[507] To be sure, there are fewer incidents of overt discrimination and greater tolerance for diversity in America. So why is it that American art does not reflect the increased societal progress made in the last fifty years? The superstructure narratives of the past were more reflective of America's core beliefs.

In its heyday, jazz was *the* popular entertainment. It pleased and amused swing dancers. It also presented a challenging vision of the future with integrated bands and a discernable melting sound. It accented the jam session of American life and the making of conversation and democracy. The liquidness of the jazz solo invites the listener to return for additional inference. The blues tonality helps us to harmonize with our major problems in a minor key.

In response to the rupture of America's mythology and influx of the infomercial, I suggest we swerve towards the usable history of jazz. The music of jazz abstracts the American oral tradition into a new and non-traditional form. We can look into the mirror of jazz, however daunting, and write our own script. Re-mythologizing a culture can be dangerous. To question our current narratives leads to further questions about core American beliefs and whether they are threatened. To question the narrative of Davy Crockett is arguably to doubt the American frontier spirit. But I feel that jazzing our culture and civil society will not result in what author Thomas Bailey calls a "traumatic shock."[508] Thankfully, jazz allows us to reach back into our usable history, our tradition, and harmonize accordingly.

But what exactly would a Jazzocracy look like? The balance of this chapter presents a collage of ideas, myths, and perspectives that can help to marry music with meaning and myth. Not all suggestions are mythical or narrative in form, but showcase a jazz perspective brought to an American culture and government. If Chapter 1 was a comparison of jazz with democracy, and an explanation of metaphor, this section is an application of metaphor and tropological thought to foment an artistic and cultural renaissance. A Jazzocracy is a workshop in how we may culturally regenerate with the spirit of Whitman. In such a society, there need not be a demise of popular entertainment. And modern music need not *sound* like jazz. A Jazzocracy reflects a value set that the genius of tomorrow can incorporate in order to abstract new form and to conceive the next American tradition. After all, jazz has been reputed as an inventor of new languages and expressions.[509]

Myths of Redemption and Suffering

These types of myth involve stories that help nations cope with painful histories. After suffering a tragic loss or painful episode, a nation goes through a period of atonement and redemption to cleanse the past. In order to heal, however, the nation needs healers. Too often social scientists and pundits decry the problems with society: urban violence in Philadelphia and the trafficking of narcotics across the US-Mexican border. Healers not only commiserate with those who suffer, but provide solutions. In *The Omni-Americans*, Albert Murray affirms that "the time for accentuating the positive and eliminating the negative is long overdue."[510] To focus on the negative just to be negative doesn't achieve anything. Suffering without redemption is endless tragedy.

The Myth of Blind Lemon Jefferson

Born in the 1890s to Texas sharecropper parents, Blind Lemon Jefferson busked with his guitar on street corners, in barber-shops, and hustler parties.[511] His family were members of the Shiloh Baptist Church, so Jefferson became well versed in church spirituals and blues.[512] Jefferson had his shortcomings, mixing alcohol and violence. He was eventually discovered and signed with the OKeh label. He died relatively young, in 1929.[513] Despite living in the Jim Crow south, his music was not one that sought pity. Jefferson's songs spoke about his woes: blindness, suffering, and failure, but also of redemption and hope. Author Alan Govenar observes that Jefferson's lyrics in "Hangman's Blues" sympathized with his audience: "Jurymen heard my case and said my hands was red. And judge, he sentenced me to be hangin' till I'm dead."[514] Though there is no record of Jefferson spending time in jail, he personalized the human plight, but he wasn't down and out. As Albert Murray says in *Stomping the Blues*, "The blues as such are synonymous with low spirits. Blues music is not."[515] What Blind Lemon Jefferson sang was low in lyrics but affirmative in spirit. Blues music cancels out the blues of life. Blues music takes its ring of listeners and performers from suffering to redemption. Blues music accomplishes its intended effect by employing the pentatonic, five-tone scale that derives from the minor scale. By changing only a few tones, the major becomes minor, and green transmutes into blue. The therapeutic effect of blues music (and other types of music) can be explained by recent scientific findings. Listening to music activates many parts of the brain, finds Levitin. First, the auditory cortex decodes and processes the sound. Eventually, the area of the brain involved in emotions and pleasure is activated, resulting in an increase in dopamine and serotonin.

In the early twentieth century, dance music and blues were often played at Saturday night parties. The next morning would bring spirituals from the church choir. Both the secularized blues and spiritual songs were cut from the same stone, that of affirmation. "Life may be a pile of shit, but at least you're looking at the stars," an aging jazz musician once told me. Blues music engenders "tragic optimism." The tragic nature of blues music is built on the "tragic triad" of pain, guilt, and death, themes that are central to many blues songs, including those of Blind Lemon Jefferson. The superstructure of Blind Lemon Jefferson can be removed to see the core infrastructural belief—that the tragic triad of life can be conquered with affirmation.[516] Instead of dying with suffering, seek release by singing what you feel.[517] Make do with what you have, from drummer Jo Jones tapping phonebooks to Hemingway's petite lexicon.[518] Hemingway skipped along the tips of each iceberg: from small word to smaller, only hinting at a hidden, deeper meaning.

At the dawn of a new chorus or legislative session, there are no scripts. The unknown canvass of what might become is terrifically optimistic: Things will get better. The *making* of democracy and jazz will lead to a solution. In Chapter 1, we addressed the open and invitational spirit of jazz and democracy, the resilient spirit to keep on and keep up. Shirley Horn gives this myth wings when she sang, "Here's to Life."

> *No complaints and no regrets*
> *I still believe in chasing dreams and placing bets*
> *but I have learned that all you give is all you get*
> *so give it all you got....*
> *So here's to life*
> *and every joy it brings*

so here's to life
to dreamers and their dreams

Psychotherapist Victor Frankl survived Auschwitz by subscribing to tragic optimism. Number 119,104 in the concentration camp, Frankl recognized his bareness: "While we were waiting for the shower, our nakedness was brought home to us: We really had nothing now except our bare bodies—even minus hair; all we possessed, literally, was our naked existence."[519] Prisoners turned inward. A simple sunrise would lift spirits like never before. In antebellum America, slaves often sang while they worked. The songs would lift spirits and the slaves seemed to work more diligently while they sang. Those with robust voices would sell for more at slave auctions.[520] Despite the unimaginable torture in the concentration camps, Frankl writes, "How content we were; happy in spite of everything."[521] He observed that the Nazis could take virtually every material thing away from the prisoners but couldn't always capture the internal attitude of optimism. That is, "the last inner freedom cannot be lost ... It is this spiritual freedom—which cannot be taken away—that makes life meaningful and purposeful."[522] To meet death with dignity is a noble act, for life means to suffer. We must stop questioning life, for life is questioning us, he says. Frankl's approach is known as "logotherapy," a will to finding meaning in life. There is always meaning, regardless of circumstance: "Is it not written in Psalms that God preserves all your tears?"[523] What is more, can man sacrifice his own suffering?[524] Suffering can become a crutch, an explanation for injustice. To suffer without seeking recourse or redemption is an abomination to the human will.

A friend related a story of his time at an inner city black neighborhood restaurant in Atlanta. Nearly all the workers were paid minimum wage; most worked two jobs to feed family members. Almost every day the kitchen would be ablaze with song, a smile on each face. The restaurant goers sang along and made music with the chef. Much like the jazz ambassadors who trumpeted democracy abroad while being rejected as first-class citizens at home, the restaurant workers were optimistic despite less-than-excellent circumstance. In the blues of life, the workers affirmed that joy was possible.

Norman Mailer says of boxer George Foreman in *The Fight*: "His mood was his property."[525] With jazz, you control your voice, temperament, and attitude. You and you alone control your view, outlook, and disposition—not the song's composer. "For the seed of triumph can be found in the *misery* of the disappointment."[526] Campbell recognizes that affirmation is grueling: "We always affirm with conditions. I affirm the world on condition that it gets to be the way Santa Claus told me it ought to be."[527] If everything was created by a divine power, then just as we accept joy, so take misery. Is joy the reward and pain the beneficial baptism? Poet Kahlil Gibran asked, "And is not the lute that soothes your spirit, the very wood that was hollowed with knives?"[528]

Jefferson's blindness pushed him to see with his heart. *The Myth of Blind Lemon Jefferson* reinterprets negative conditions into positive realities. The latter-day Jefferson, Ray Charles, sang "America the Beautiful." He couldn't see the "spacious skies" and "purple mountains," as the Reverend Al Sharpton observed.[529] He believed in America the beautiful, and the melody allowed him to escape the unfulfilled promise of democracy. *The Myth of Blind Lemon Jefferson* accentuates the positive: The American Dream isn't economic but emotional—sing like you're at the top! Despite the shortcomings of American democracy, the *Myth of Blind Lemon Jefferson* responds to Langston Hughes's call: "Let America Be America Again." Hughes felt the "rack and ruin of our gangster death" and the "rape and rot of graft" holding America down. Through suffering, he envisioned redemption. "We, the people, must redeem / The land, the mines, the plants, the rivers."[530] In line with the *Myth of Blind Lemon Jefferson*, in a Jazzocracy, music acts as a healer.

One way to enact blues music in our non-musical lives is to compare ourselves with those who have less. The first person with a

Rolex is rich and posh, whereas the tenth friend who buys one diminishes the perceived value for everyone. To compare via reference group results in unsatisfaction. Some Americans have avoided such comparisons. Known as "down shifters," they take pay decreases to spend more time with the real treasure of life—family and a more purposeful vocation. Like the "Millionaire Next Door," wealthy people can choose to drive used cars and shop at Wal-Mart. Is this not the first step of renunciation, to die to the world?[531] But these folks are few and far between. Millions of middle-class Americans compare their earnings with reference groups above them. While entertaining, watching *Cribs* will make some compare their consumer status to millionaires. An "untenable situation" is wrought by everyone coveting the same material things.[532] Author of *The Overspent American*, Juliet Schor gives the example of folks buying clothes and not removing the tags so that they can attend a glitzy party and return the items the next day. She found that twenty-seven percent of all households that make over $100,000 believe they can't afford everything they need: "Overall, half the population of the richest country in the world say they cannot afford everything they really need. And it's not just the poorer half."[533] Focusing on what we don't have makes us all poor, as Kipling reminded. But maybe, as *The Economist* notes, economic upward mobility is becoming too difficult: "If America is a ladder, the rungs have been moved further apart."[534] *The Myth of Blind Lemon Jefferson* flattens economic comparisons and helps us to escape the blues of life by transcending them with blues music.

Myths of Kinship

These myths deal with the organic evolvement of a people. These myths draw the boundaries of who is part of a family and who should be thrown out. In French colonies, for example, African school

children were taught of their French ancestors.[535] The African ancestors were not to be part of French national identity. In America, myths
of kinship include the Puritans, immigrants, colonialists, and Founding Fathers. All Americans can find a part of themselves in the shared
narratives of the earliest Americans. There is no prerequisite ethnic
group that qualifies one as American. The American kin is perpetually
in flux. As we search for myths, we find new frontiers of America.

The Myth of Jam Session

The first day of the American experiment was not July 4, 1776.
Nor was it when the *Niña, Pinta*, and *Santa Maria* set sail from Spain.
The pre-Columbian era of America, when Native Americans roamed
the land, reminds us that the New World was no *terra nullius*, an empty and bare land. America wasn't the "New World," as it was already
inhabited. When America's first immigrant Columbus discovered the
American continent, it was the dawn of the everybody world. It was
the dawn of the jam session era of America. Christopher Columbus
was himself a jam session: a Catholic sailor who Protestants lauded.
Father Michael McGivney founded the Knights of Columbus in 1882
to unionize Catholics when other unions wouldn't. McGivney recognized the jam session of Columbus, the minority sailor. The Japanese
live in Japan, the French in France, and the Italians in Italy. One *chooses*
to be an American. Early observers noted that on the tip of Manhattan
one could hear eighteen different languages.[536] America is a jam session where the rhythm section keeps the groove going, and every cat
speaks his or her own language.

One jazz musician remembered the jam sessions at the Victoria
Bar and Grill in New York City, where saxophonists Coleman Hawk-
ins, Lester Young, and Joe Thomas would play all day.[537] Running up
bar tabs, folks sat listening to these musicians jive and jam for hours.

Ellison wrote, "Dance hall jam sessions, along with recordings, are the true academy of jazz."[538] It's possible to learn more from the rapscallion than the dignitary. In the jam session, the individual blends into the greater group like the ingredients of cake batter: flour, butter, and sugar. Eventually these individual items blend into batter, yielding a lump character. It is not that jazz musicians lose their individuality, but contribute it to something grander, the plurality of a cultural and political democracy. The Jazzocracy honors the jam session motto of the antislavery newspaper *The Liberator*: "My country is the world. My countrymen are mankind."[539]

Peeled away, the superstructure of the jam session reflects the infrastructural belief that Americans understand the importance of "everybody." The jazz band has been a forerunner to integrated society since the earliest days: the mixed New Orleans bands and integrated bands touring through the Iron Curtain. Many white musicians played in the Miles Davis Nonet that recorded his acclaimed *Birth of Cool* album. Jazz aficionado Phil Schaap contends that jazz was the first American pastime to integrate before baseball.[540] In 1936, the Benny Goodman Trio was the first integrated band to play regularly in public. A manager told Goodman that he didn't want black musicians performing, to which Goodman responded, "This is my band. If you don't want them in the band, then screw yourself. We're walking out."[541]

The *Myth of Jam Session* extends to all parts of the ring. The audience is an integral part of the jazz performance. It claps, whistles, sighs, squeals, dances, calls, and *makes* with the musicians. Furthermore, the jazz audience is a reflection of the diversity on the bandstand. Whites and blacks come to shows. There are no rules as to what one should wear or look like. No need to look "hip" or dress a certain way to fit in. Come as you are. The audience is as integrated as the jazz jam session. In his 1981 introduction to *Invisible Man*, Ellison notes how literature and art can represent the democratic ideal:

So if the ideal of achieving a true political equality eludes
in reality…there is still available that fictional vision of
an ideal democracy in which the actual combines with
the ideal and gives us representations of a state of things
in which the highly placed and the lowly, the black and
the white….are combined to tell us of transcendent
truths and possibilities such as those discovered when
Mark Twain set Huck and Jim afloat on the raft…a
novel could be fashioned as a raft of hope.[542]

The raft of jazz teaches that borders, while important to self-
identity when perceived by foreigners, are almost inconsequential within a union. Borders, territories, and worlds melt away in the fizzy brew
of jazz. "When you see the earth from the moon, you don't see any
divisions, there, of nations or states. This might be the symbol, really,
for the new mythology to come," notes Campbell.[543] The update on
Campbell's quote is to look at the jazz jam session as if we were looking
at the world from afar. Many a gig has seen instrumentalists who can't
speak the same tongue *jazzing* in the one language of music. The jazz
band has always been an "everybody world" because it was borne out of
the mélange of African Americans, Creoles, and Europeans. *Your land
is my land.* The musical democracy of jazz brought folks together from
different backgrounds and did not monopolize the art as a "black only"
thing.[544] Ellington honored all big bands from 1925 to 1955—white
and black—in his 1962 tribute.

That's not to say that the jam session cannot lead to squabbles
and conflict. Perhaps one of the best ways to forget differences is to
laugh. Many bandleaders used humor to bring members together. In
Jazz Anecdotes, Bill Crow tells the tale of drummer Zutty Singleton
who was to play an exposed note on the xylophone at the culmina-
tion of the piece. He put a piece of paper on the xylophone to remind
him which note to strike. During intermission, another band mate

removed the paper. Singleton hit the wrong note and the band died laughing.[545] The fraternity of vagabond musicians urges a constant humor in which anyone can be poked. Bill Crow tells of bassist Junior Raglin who used to drink from bottles when others fell asleep on the bus. Clarinetist Barney Bigard was not amused when much of his alcohol went missing. Bigard turned the tables by filling a bottle with his urine and pretending to fall asleep. Raglin, playing his Dumb and Dumber part, took a sip. "Now, I hope you know what you just did," deadpanned Bigard.[546]

But is America still known for its jam session character? A survey of America in *The Economist* reported how a Vietnamese man saw an American car in Saigon during the Vietnam War that convinced him to move to America. The car "reinforced all those positive images of America. It ... stood for freedom."[547] The survey cites a worrisome Pew Poll: "Foreigners no longer saw America as a land of opportunity the way they once did."[548] The immigrants, the new everybodies, that supply America with an eager workforce pump perennial energy into America's economy, but "Has America become a centrifuge?"[549] Stepping away from politics, what does America export of its "art"? International MTV transmits semi-pornographic imagery, a dubious distinction. Our exported art evokes the rusted and saucy melting pot.

Sometimes a jam session includes "trading fours," where each member of the band takes four measures to solo. Often the soloist trades four measures with the drummer: tenor solo, drum solo, piano solo, drum solo, and on it goes until the end of the form whereupon one trades four again or returns to the melody. If someone forgets to play his four, there is a flagrant void of sound. If you play one measure extra, you're not respecting the form. In the jam session of a Jazzocracy, Americans trade fours with each other. Talk *and listen*. Escape the dueling thirty-second talking heads and actually listen; then offer new and compelling ideas. Instead of conceding a debate to traditional liberal and conservative talking points, look for the unusual perspective from the quiet voice in the musical mix. Even tenor saxophonist Sonny Rollins listened to the acoustic bass during his solos.[550] For instance: Why not negotiate retirement policies with Mexico so that US citizens can retire there, thus being removed from American social security rolls? The cost of living is cheaper in Mexico, and US citizens would help economic development with local spending. Then the border becomes a two-way street—workers come to the US and retirees move to Mexico. An unusual idea, to be sure, but not one to be readily dismissed. The difficulty of getting past the bifurcated political debate is immense; a plurality of ideas can be unearthed when the ear is put to the fertile ground of the American jam session.

Perhaps the most important aspect of trading fours is to remember oneself or self-remember. To behold an artwork, a Goya painting, or Rebirth Brass Band performance, one gives it full attention. When we discuss a political topic with our opponent, we push our attention onto him or her. Many times we forget to remember ourselves. When the drummer takes his four measures, not only is he playing, but *you are listening to him.* Your attention, then, is divided between the drummer and yourself. By remembering yourself, as Gurdjieff explains, we start to remember how we feel at particular moments.[551] Instead of becoming a mechanical listener or performer in jazz music, we are aware of ourselves, with heightened consciousness. Do you remember yourself while reading this text? "I am reading." It's not enough to go through the motions and trade fours. We lose ourselves in the *making*, adrift in a mechanical ocean of sleep – listening to the grid of the rhythm section groove but never realizing it's our turn to improvise and self-amend.

Self-remembering is certainly not an invitation to adopt an egotistical perspective. I have witnessed countless trading four sessions when a musician forgets it is his or her turn. After a measure of silence, the musician awkwardly enters. Remembering ourselves is consistent with the jazz-as-democracy trope because jazz is a performance-based music. We hold the eighty-eight piano keys to the interpretation, not the composer of the song. We must participate and not grow bored or tired of the exchange. Democracy is an arduous process and it can inflict the mortal wound of ambivalence into the electorate. By remembering ourselves, we are no longer just spectators but active participants in the *making* of democracy.

In recent times, some scholars contend that America's democracy suffers from an ambivalent and uninspired citizenry. Politics today has become a business. The 2004 election cost about $5 billion, enough to buy over 2,000 Super Bowl commercials.[552] Sociologist Robert Putnam finds that the professionalization of politics has made democracy less participatory. Political parties are becoming stronger financially, but the "brand loyalty" is becoming less meaningful.[553] Financial capital has supplanted social capital. Is voting turnout and lack of participation the declension of democracy? Technology (mainly the television and the broadcast culture) is often blamed for this trend, but it can help bring folks together, as with Meetup.com (a co-founder of the Web site was inspired by Putnam's findings).[554] When the unholy alliance of technology and voter segmentation occurs, the participatory nature of democracy takes on rust. Lincoln didn't describe our government as of the segmented people, by the media-focused issue, and for the political insiders.

In a Jazzocracy, perhaps the best way to enact trading fours in the domain of government is to open the legislative government to closer scrutiny. Evoke interest when the citizen feels his or her interests are at stake. Too often legislators drop bills into a black box where only insiders understand what happens. A simple solution is to put all considered legislation online. The black box of crafting legislation would disappear, ushering in transparent discussion and a fantasia of facts. Open-source government is a step in the direction of the "politics of liberty"—but it is also an attempt to show how the common man is affected by the machinations of Congress. In Australia, a political party has sprouted that allows anyone with an internet connection to vote on every bill brought to Parliament. With more knowledge, the citizen may self-remember his interests and his role as an instrument of democracy.

The Economist reports that legislative compromises have seen better days: "The conference stage—a last chance for a compromise—has occasionally been omitted altogether."[555] This leads to war-like Armageddon politics, where extremists battle instead of finding moderate solutions. Blame gerrymandering or polarizing cable television shows, America was once the land of reasoned compromise and negotiation. *The Showdown at Gucci Gulch* details how the 1986 tax reform act was an epic act of political compromise. America is "sorting" itself into like-minded groups, which in turn tend to absorb extremists, making common ground more difficult to find than Hillary's Step, the passage to the summit of Mount Everest.[556] Trading fours in the American jam session is about getting music and government back to balance. The healthy and unhealthy branches of the tree share interwoven roots: The good and bad must be accepted together. Instead of Jacobist retaliation against those who disagree, give the loyal opposition their four measures.[557] Americans might all be "mute inglorious Miltons," as poet Thomas Gray directs. But how do we know if we ain't listening?

The segregation of the electorate can be traced to the culture wars that are fought on the battlefield of ideology. Those who do not subscribe to a particular ideology or suffer from "institutionalized paranoia" are castigated as anti-American, jettisoned from the American kin.[558] The "culture war" is the intra-American fight between blue states and red states over social issues. It is the name given to America's apparent "deep division." America's deep division is hardly a culture war, according to Morris Fiorina, Senior Fellow at the Hoover Institution at Stanford. In *Culture War: The Myth of a Polarized America*, Fiorina sees America as closely divided but not deeply divided.[559] Taking a cue from Philip Converse's "The Nature of Belief Systems in Mass

Publics," Fiorina sees the large portion of the electorate as ambivalent and uncertain. Americans are moderates, centrists, and independents, just as Putnam found. It is the set of choices—the extreme Kennedys and Keyes—that polarize. In the 2004 election, 209 electoral votes went "barely" or "weakly" for a particular candidate. For example, Bush may have won in Texas by twenty percentage points, but one percent in New Mexico and almost three in Nevada. Kerry won by eleven points in California, but less than half a percent in Wisconsin. America is a *swing* nation. Massachusetts and Texas may be the extremes of liberal-conservative polarization, but most of America lives in the continuum of ambivalence. The primaries, dominated by extreme activists, determine the party nominees, making it more likely for extreme candidates to win the nomination and land on the ticket. Some pundits think that the primary process is an illiberal process of democracy, in which a small percent of the electorate acts as the sieve for millions of other Americans. Fiorina found that until recently, American presidents didn't even win fifty percent or more of the vote, an era of indecision like that of 1880 to 1892.[560] In a Pew Poll, he finds that even the social issues of religion and morality didn't polarize blue states and red states: There isn't a drastic difference in the number of churchgoers in blue and red states. Those living in blue and red states both think privatizing schools and prescription drug benefits ought to be explored. Furthermore, "the culture war" barely exists at a local level. Septic tank cleaning, trash collection, and animal control are hardly partisan issues.[561] Local politicians acquire more social capital because they live in the same community, humanizing their opponents. By and large, Americans are centrists. If the electorate is divided by the politicos, then music can be the bastion of unity. Whitman's cultural democracy is a canteen where all may eat, insofar as the mythology of art has not already caricatured a certain people.

To borrow the title of Murray's book, Americans are truly "Omni-Americans": We share cultural experiences. Our language is full of

Native American words; African Americans have given their musical sensibilities to popular idioms for centuries; Mexican culture is dominant in the southwest. Americans are part Native American, African, Chinese, Irish, Asian, Mexican, and to be determined—an irrefutable jam session. The mulatto culture of America can be seen in the arbitrary nature of our beginning. When was day one of America? A few possibilities include Columbus's maiden voyage; the 4th of July, 1776; the first settlers crossing the Bering Strait; or 1865 at the Appomattox Court House. Murray states, *"American culture, even in its most rigidly segregated precincts, is patently and irrevocably composite."*[562] America's kin is omni in nature. Indeed, Americans are closely divided along race, ethnicity, politics, religion, language, tattoos, and hair color. The mixing of American division has resulted in a broadmindedness that has led to ingenuity in the arts, literature, politics, and entrepreneurship. While Americans belong to a nation, we also belong to eternity, thought Tolstoy—how closed-minded to focus on the narrow.[563] To participate in the jazz jam session is to become American—to mix and create a lump character in which the pull and push of the composite is perpetually in flux.

There are those who feel the jazz jam session is not very inclusive. In *Blue: The Murder of Jazz*, Eric Nisenson asserts that some black jazz musicians today discriminate against white musicians. He blames the neoclassicalists—those who perform the canon of jazz (music from the early twentieth century to 1960). He attacks the philosophy of Crouch and Murray, who espouse a tradition of jazz that celebrates the African American inventor of the art. Nisenson labels the apparent discrimination of white musicians as "Crow Jim."[564] Others have attacked jazz for marginalizing women.

Such criticism stems from an inert assumption that Jazz at Lincoln Center, the neoclassicists, and documentary maker Ken Burns somehow create a canon for jazz. But how can so few distinguish a canon for such a pervasive music? In my time, conversing with so-called neoclassicists and those in the Lincoln Center big band, I've not observed any Crow Jim sentiment. The big band also has several white musicians and often collaborates with white celebrities. It is true that African Americans are the progenitors of jazz. But jazz is a language of re-definition because it depends on the sensibilities of the performers. Instead of bemoaning discrimination with the pen, fight with the horn. In the jam session of jazz, any Crow Jim sentiment fades as the ability and merit carries weight. Those who can play usually get the gigs. Miles Davis, for one, encountered criticism when he hired Bill Evans as his pianist. I imagine that when critics heard Evans play, any Crow Jim belief quickly ebbed. The tradition of jazz isn't Jim Crow or Crow Jim. It's omni-American.

The *Myth of Jam Session* establishes the Jazzocracy as a commons. Professor Lawrence Lessig writes on commons, "We permit neither the government to control how that resource is used nor the market to control how that resource is used."[565] Jazz is a commons in that everyone may participate in the making of music: Grab a horn and blow. Indeed, the more one practices, the better one gets. A distinction between resources should be made: Rivalrous resources are used at the expense of others. If three thousand cars jam a freeway, it prevents others from using the freeway. A nonrivalrous resource allows one to use something without preventing another to use the same resource. Jazz is a nonrivalrous resource because one person's participation does not preclude another from experiencing the music. It is an innovation commons, an omni-American commons. By adopting this myth, we understand the value of nonrivalrous commons: Americans share in the *making* of the political system, and judging by Fiorina's findings, are not deeply divided about the invitation.

Myths of Valor

These myths deal with the courage of a military in battle. But occasionally the hero, despite his noble deeds, grows wary and confused about his original intentions. He forgets his fellow knights and the damsel in distress. Similarly, in the jam session the soloist may remember only himself and forget the group. Rugged individualism and self-reliance are core American infrastructural beliefs. I reject the line of some populists who criticize America for its individualism.[566] Some of the greatest American heroes were exemplars of self-reliance: Benjamin Franklin was a self-made man.[567] President Theodore Roosevelt and pilot Charles Lindberg were strong individuals with perceptible purposes—to tame the trusts and fly trans-Atlantic. But sometimes the hero sees himself as the sole actor in his or her success. They even grow confused with their original intention. Rugged individualists like James Dean hanker to shape America in the image of the rebel without a cause.

How did the hero deviate from his cause? The good-bad man has taken on several transformations. Henry McCarty, also known as "Billy the Kid," didn't kill twenty-one people, as legend has it. He killed nine—five of which he murdered with the help of others. He wasn't always known as a noble bandit, an American Robin Hood. After Pat Garrett killed the Kid, media reports appeared portraying the death as an adventure story: Good triumphs over evil. The villain Kid represented the decaying devil and Garrett the destiny of light.

At the turn of the twentieth century, however, the Kid-Garrett story was transfigured and embellished: The Kid grew blonde hair, added a few inches, and by 1920, the Kid became the hero. The urban hair-slicked gangster became the bad-bad man, whereas the Kid was the *rebel with a cause*, fighting for the frontier against a corrupt government of New Mexico. The cultural context turned the Kid into a good bad man; in 1941, Life magazine tapped Kid as one of America's "best-loved bad men."[568] In the 1880s, civilization was destined to win, making the Kid bad, but in the 1920s, civilization had already won at the expense of liberty and individualism, possibly going too far with Prohibition. Alas, Kid became the shining hero to fight for liberty and freedom. Tatum points out that the Kid became a "tragic figure" after the 1920s, with Walter Noble Burns's *The Saga of Billy the Kid*. Kid possessed a "desperado complex," where he was internally conflicted with civilization and savagery and externally with lawfulness and lawlessness.[569] He was a balanced figure that preserved civilization because he promoted it. In other words, Kid felt that by killing the "bad men" in the Lincoln County War, civilization would continue. Even if he is a good bad man, community can't integrate him into society because of his vigilante violence—thus, the Kid *must* die as a purgative sacrifice for civilization. Burns's point is that we need *both* elements of the desperado complex—the Kid's rugged individualism during the Great Depression, and his defense of justice during periods of economic growth.[570] Audiences mythologized the transient Kid myths because of the "special temple" of the movie theater, the larger than life colorful character in that dark room.[571] Kid was a defender of community, taking justice into his own hands, not a rebel without a cause.

In the 1950s and '60s, in the wake of Vietnam, scholars questioned whether the Kid's sacrifice mattered. It was ironic that Garrett, the one-time hero, was killed by those who had him kill the Kid. You couldn't trust anyone. Society was too fractured. Thus, the hero became isolated and alienated. The Kid's sacrifice, his cause, didn't matter. Tatum writes that the new outlaw is "committed to no social values, founds no civilized world, and protects no oppressed peoples."[572] Because of the disaffection with broader society, the rebel without a cause was born. Life is meaningless.

American heroes have historically fought against a discernable cause: the colonialists against the crown, Homestead strikers against capitalists, Billy the Kid against the moneymen, even the Confederates against the Union. Once the cause is conquered, the hero is integrated into society. Author John G. Cawelti points out that even self-reliant Horatio Alger's boy rises to social respectability.[573] The hero was integrated into society. George Washington, the leader of the American rebellion, became commander-in-chief. When one rebels against something, one asserts a love of liberty. But one must also respect the desperado complex described by Burns: to assert our individuality and self-reliance during tough economic depression and hold respect for justice.

Crouch observes that Americans love the bad boy because he brings surprise.[574] But the element of surprise isn't unique to jazz music. In his Symphony No. 96 or Surprise Symphony, Haydn builds the melody with incremental steps, only to fool the listener when the orchestra blares with a larger interval, shaking stuck-in-the-mud expectations. In this case, Haydn is beguiling and innovative. When Haydn's works were canonized, however, his innovative spirit was knifed. Attending an opera performance didn't used to be a scripted and staid affair. Johnson reminds that the opera house was more like a club where casual listeners would come (and perhaps be surprised, or at least interface with music). It is true though, we enjoy the surprise-filled entertainment: Former basketball player Dennis Rodman surprised us with his off-the-court antics and on-the-court elbows. The comedic surprise is nothing new to America, e.g., vaudeville acts and frontier folklore featured raconteur-stars who provoked the audience. The modern day entertainer, however, apparently has little artistic cause. The entertainer is to amuse and profit from his act. In certain musical genres the entertainer screams anger—at everything. There is little veneration of myth, just an inflammation of stereotype à la 50 Cent or the twenty-first century minstrel show with Eminem. They are the rich and wealthy bad boys. But what is their cause?

Myth of Counterpoint

The *Myth of Counterpoint* resolves to understand the reconciliatory nature of jazz and the Constitution. While not only found in jazz music, counterpoint is the melodic material that is added to the melody, a supplement of sorts. It's a contrasting but parallel line that establishes a harmonic relationship while both lines remain independent. Counterpoint is not the shaping of identity in the individual's image but of the collective. We may respect Andrew Carnegie, the individualist, but also recognize that though he spent three-quarters of his life producing steel for battleships, he spent the remaining quarter promoting peace and building communities. The backwoodsman, in taming the wilderness, became part Indian because he learned from the *jam session* of pre-Columbian America. The Constitutional Convention was a meeting of reconciliation that drafted the governing documents for America. *We the people.* Those who subscribe to the *Myth of Counterpoint* "seek individuality through affirmation."[575] This myth accepts contradiction: America can be free and responsible, democratic and capitalistic, and red states with blue states. This view allows Americans to see contradictions as not opposed beliefs but complements to the greater system of democracy. To mythologize counterpoint is to understand that there are many lines at work between and within us. "Do I contradict myself? / Very well, then I contradict myself; / (I am large, I contain multitudes)," wrote Walt Whitman. Contradictions are. Many Americans don't trust government bureaucracy but believe democracy to be the great equalizer. Many believe in the free market, but the government must secure the market with regulation, fiscal policy, and monetary policy. Gurdjieff thought humans to be five-minute kingdoms: Isaac believes in promises, but breaks one when he's inebriated.[576] Are there many Isaacs within Isaac? Surely many Americas exist in America. Does the US need a Statue of Responsibility in the West to complement the Statue of Liberty in the East, as Frankl believed? Let us reclaim the image of Billy the Kid as the defender of justice and civilization. His "revolt" was purposeful. A Jazzocracy requires a recognition that self-reliance is part of the American experiment, but individualism that jettisons the band is anathema to the making of democracy.

Myths of Unjust Treatment

These myths portray a people oppressed by the dominant group in society. They focus on the tragic collective experience of a particular nation—like the Holocaust in Nazi Germany and slavery in the US.[577] While the Jim Crow days have vanished, modern music still places African Americans in the stranglehold of stereotype. In the late nineteenth century, whites smeared their faces with burnt cork to mimic black music that they overheard in the fields. Even today whites imitate black entertainment—at times reinforcing a wretched stereotype. The modern minstrel show of Eminem must be recognized for what it is.

Elvis Presley was not wholly innovative. He performed derivative black music. Elvis's first producer said, "[Elvis] tried not to show it, but he felt so *inferior*."[578] He was a white blues singer that made hip contortions and dancing lips appetizing to white America. While he certainly possessed a modicum of talent as a musician, he was still mimicking black musicians. Like Elvis, Eminem mimics blacks and is arguably the modern day minstrel entertainer. Eminem translates the bad of the black image, the human experience, into the worst. He raps of women, "So b*** me b****." Maybe it's generous to say that Eminem raps of the human plight, as blues music once did, but he offers hardly any words of sympathy and commiseration. And rap rhythm is largely repetitive, monotonous, and predictable. The repeated drum-and-bass of vulgar rap grinds the message home and provides little sonic or melodic release.

The blues are special because the low lyrics are canceled out by the harmonic progression of tension and release. A slow song sounded pensive, not gurgling with rage. The imprecision of the lyrics of the blues ballad are offset by the focused tonality of the song. Bessie Smith used incorrect words, saying "rural" instead of "ruler" in *Yellow Dog Blues*.[579] The effect of the blues ballad sings from the music, not the words.

Yeats questioned whether art could make its audience unhappy. John Coltrane explored and shared a range of emotions with audience members, often confusing and angering them. Pianist Bill Evans suggested to him: It is the artist's responsibility to select those emotions "most beneficial for his audience."[580] Coltrane once believed that jazz should bring joy to the listener, even if it talked about "the blues." Artists are the emotional sieves for the audience.

Mark Twain's humor was a thinly veiled jab at his societal surroundings.[581] What happens, however, when a certain wellspring of noise hurts more than it helps? Eminem's videos poke fun at societal happenings, but his style mocks himself. His minstrel act puts him back in the 1840s, except with more spinning rage and vitriol. Some mainstream rappers glorify themselves and scream of their sexual promiscuity all set to the beat of an IBM ThinkPad. But when you remove the musicians from the music, is it still music? They glorify bourgeoisie disaffection with the world. Why do people with so much wealth sound so angry? One can leap into the "bling bling," but one's temperance remains frozen. The rich rappers are leading the rage against (or for) the system that made them wealthy. Kanye West oddly decried the coverage of Hurricane Katrina's aftermath: "I hate the way they portray us in the media. You see a black family, it says, 'They're looting.'"[582] Such stereotyping may have existed in Katrina TV coverage. But such implicit and passive racism doesn't start on CNN or CNBC. It starts on Kanye's channels of choice: MTV and BET. Will Kanye awake to the real culprit in propagating the media stereotype ... himself? A sample from the Billboard Top 50:

> -"Lose Control" by Missy Elliott - "do ma thang m****f***** / ma rose royce lamborghini"

> -"Let Me Hold You" by Bow Wow - "N**** Look at me like now here you go / Really bout to blow some doe"

This perhaps stems from a greater problem—an overemphasis on freedom, capitalism, or "the politics of liberty." In rap there is little reconciliation and counterpoint with the group. One is free to act as one chooses and to say anything, offend everyone, and spew expletives. No consequences. There is no jam session (there are no musicians, just a computer beat). There is little balancing of tones (as such, rap is largely atonal). Rap is more like poetry; we should measure it by feet, *iambic pentameter*, rather than normal harmonic analysis. Rap largely dismisses the tenor of equality and focuses exclusively on personal freedom. Anything goes.

Rappers have been criticized by the likes of former US Senator Bob Dole and conservative commentator William Bennett.[583] Yet some folks ask the public to "understand" the anger of rappers. They reason that these entertainers have become scapegoats: Rappers simply parrot the angst in the ghetto, a rhyming mouthpiece. At its worst, the misunderstood anger can lead to black militancy and a complete breakdown of race relations. Sympathy is due for both parties, but critics of rap are right to find fault with it. Author Michael Eric Dyson writes that rap is often the expression of angst, sexual depravity, and cop killings. It turns the troubles of a people into crafted capital.[584] Male and female bodies are nothing more than commodities, giving voyeuristic titillation to white-paying audiences. Dyson observes that many whites think they're receiving a heapin' helpin' of ghetto life. Instead, rap provides a glamorization of such life. Rappers are often well-spoken individuals and articulate businessmen when the spicy video recorder isn't rolling. But as soon as the camera blinks green, they play the angry perverse part. They enact the stereotype.

"But Louis Armstrong enacted the black stereotype," one might say. Armstrong was accused of being an Uncle Tom—but he also possessed such extraordinary talent (and an upbeat outlook) that his horn overwhelmed the stereotype. "It's all fun and games; the lyrics don't matter," says the casual listener. Without rap, dear rap-buying listener, how else do you experience black culture? If we eat only the vulgarized stereotype, it undoubtedly affects our conception of black culture. The effects of rap on teenagers show deleterious trends. While causality is difficult to determine, a recent study finds teenagers who consume copious amounts of rap are more likely to hit a teacher, get arrested, have multiple sexual partners, try drugs, and consume alcohol.[585] Rap should not be the only synonym for "black culture," because it represents a distorted strain of it.

Possibly the most insightful analysis of rap in America comes from Professor Martha Bayles. She notes that the children of the punk generation crave obscene and vulgar lyrics. The Baby Boomers have seen an unprecedented rise in America's economic wealth via globalization and technology. But even the extraordinary wealth demonstrated by rappers is fantasy enough for Generations X and Y. Bayles notes that because rap feeds obscene lyrics to white America, the concept of "blackness" has been redefined.[586] Such "music" has become a mishmash of words, sans musicians, in order to provoke: "Obscenity is the preferred weapon of those willing to do anything to get a rise out of the public."[587] Bayles goes on to write about the rap strategy with her brilliant pen. "Seek out submerged, antisocial custom that is considered marginal even by its participants, drag it kicking and screaming to the surface, and celebrate it as 'art.'"[588]

In listening to materialism-cum-violent rap and singing its

praise, we cheer a marginal and antisocial creation. Once I was flipping through the channels and stopped on BET. The rappers surrounded a girl "dressed" with a skinny black thong, twirling herself around a strip pole. The beat was boring but the visual titillation convinced me to keep watching. Some scholars contend that the mainstream digestion of perpetual imagery leads to an "outlaw culture": Blacks aren't worth helping because they're angry and white America can't understand them.[589] The outlaw mentality has possibly conditioned many white Americans to lock the car door, tense up on Bourbon Street, and think unthinkable thoughts. There should not be such an automatic, perverse, and conditioned response towards blacks.

This increased vapidity of music is not limited to one musical genre. When jazz drummer Buddy Rich checked into a hospital, the nurse asked him if he had any allergies. He responded, "Country and Western music."[590] Next time a smash hit climbs the Billboard rankings, ask whether you like the song on its own merits. Or is it because you hear it, see the music video on MTV, and the song "grows" on you. Some record companies rely on independent promoters to pay radio stations to play their songs, according to New York Attorney General (now Governor) Elliot Spitzer. That is, a company pays to have you listen to the music, buying a chance to score a hit. Some songs have even been poll tested. Payola started in the 1950s as a way to promote music on the airwaves. Sony BMG paid a fine of $10 million for "bribing radio stations" to have tunes by Jennifer Lopez aired, among others.[591] Companies hire girls to call stations, to pose as listeners to dupe the singing-along audience. And the lyrics themselves may include moneymaking references to products. So much time is invested in marketing instead of the actual enterprise within the song. This isn't necessarily bad. Entertainment ought to be marketed. But the acceptance of the ugly and metal-mouth rapper as the African American image in mainstream America shows how entertainers have wrongly twisted the mythology of blacks in America. You can point to black rappers or white record companies that capitalize on perpetuating the stereotype, but because of the lack of pushback from the arts (and a ruptured mythology), the entertaining stereotype of black America prevails.

The Myth of the Modern Israelites

The Bible tells of Moses and the chosen people, and their odyssey to the Promised Land. God chooses Moses to lead the Israelites out from Egypt, where they were slaves under the Pharaoh. God comes to the rescue of the Israelites during their many battles. When the Israelites sparred with the Amalekites, Moses lifted the rod of God, which made the Israelites control the fight. However, Moses started to tire and the Israelites started to lose, so Aaron and Hur held up Moses' hand and the Israelites routed the Amalekites.

In his *Myths America Lives By*, Richard Hughes contends that early Americans believed they were the chosen people living in the chosen nation. He traces this sentiment to the reign of Henry VIII (1509–1547) and the English Reformation. When Edward VI became king, many saw him as the modern day Josiah who helped to establish the rule of law in the Bible. Catholicism was being suppressed in favor of Protestantism. However, when Mary Tudor assumed the throne, she tried to return England to Catholicism: Protestants fled England in fear of the Queen's heavy hand. Some of the exiles, known as radical Puritans, felt that Christianity had been besmirched and that the Pope was the anti-Christ.[592] The Puritans wanted to cleanse England of the Catholic traditions, still held over by the Anglican Church. When Elizabeth was crowned in 1558, she was pulled between the Puritans and the Anglican Church. She eventually chose to support the Church. The Puritans felt shunned and discouraged. Instead of trying to reform the Church, they chose to separate from the Church of England. In 1625, Charles I assumed the throne and openly perse-cuted the Puritans who fled to distant lands, including America.[593]

American Puritans felt deeply that they were God's chosen people, colonizing the empty New World. Puritans identified with the Israelites who had been oppressed. The trans-Atlantic journey was analogous to the passage to Canaan. Increasingly isolated from the Old Continent and spiritually alone, American Puritans felt they were chosen to abolish the corruption of the Catholic Church and start a Church in the true image of the New Testament. Decades later, Rabbi Isaac Mayer Wise, who had immigrated to the US in 1846, compared the wars between the Israelites and the Philistines with "God's chosen people" and the Native Americans.[594] He described the colonial period: "George Washington and his heroic compatriots were the chosen in-struments in the hands of Providence, to turn the wheel of events in favor of liberty forever."[595] Furthermore, when the Founding Fathers discussed the seal for the new nation, Benjamin Franklin suggested an image of Moses separating the waters of the Red Sea.[596]

Blacks also identified with the myth of the chosen people, for there was the direct parallel of slavery between Africans and the Israel-ites. Harriet Tubman was referred to as "Black Moses" in some quarters. African Americans often sang songs about liberty and freedom, often to the chagrin of white slave masters. The slaves learned to cloak their lyrics in tropes and conceits, referring to Biblical passages.[597]

The *Myth of the Modern Israelites* identifies current African Americans according to their history. Martin Luther King Jr. exclaimed "... we as a people will get to the Promised Land." Instead of stereotyp-ing black Americans as criminals and corrupt (and embodying them in stereotypic artistic images), Americans ought to understand the collective strength of character of African Americans. When White Americans were lynching and terrorizing blacks, they were ducking the promise of the Constitution. Frederick Douglass observed, "I am not the one that is being degraded on account of this treatment, but those who are inflicting it upon me."[598] Paradoxically, the tyrant is actually the victim. Albert Murray found that "slavery and oppression may well have made black people more human and more American while it has made white people less human and less American."[599] Murray notes that slave masters had a higher suicide rate than slaves.[600] Black Americans have been the most American members of the American experiment, as they did not violate the spirit of the Declaration of Independence for over three hundred years. Acceptance of slavery in political democracies stretches back to Athenian democracy, in which Aristotle and Plato advocated moral philosophies that opposed slavery, yet slaves were integral to the societal structure.[601] How many men or powers of government are required to change crime into virtue?[602] The *Myth of the Modern Israelites* urges Americans to find models of excellence in the black community. It can be a talented jazz musician, renowned social scientist, or the successful neighborhood doctor.

It is illuminating that those who were the most oppressed in America have created the most democratic of arts. Author Kurt Vonnegut recognizes the contribution of black Americans: "...but the priceless gift that African Americans gave the whole world...was a gift so great that it is now almost the only reason many foreigners still like us at least a little bit."[603] The black spirituals and cries for freedom were integrated into the music at the turn of the twentieth century "Jazz was a force for freedom, a visionary art form that offered hope even in the darkest of times ... [jazz] could illuminate the often dark American landscape."[604] American music has been perennially reinvented by African Americans. The American native self-expression, in fact, is rooted in the African American tradition. Why then, does the mainstream not venerate the Modern Israelite for his cultural contribution to the American collage?

Tocqueville observed that America was a nation run by the poor, however untrue that may be today.[605] Amercans have much to learn from those who often have the least. Blacks were the oppressed, like the Israelites, the chosen people. Santiago, the protagonist in Hemingway's *The Old Man and the Sea*, was dominated but never defeated while trying to reel in the marlin, the beaten fish. The human spirit cannot be defeated even in the most dire of circumstances. The *Myth of the Modern Israelites* means that Americans look at those suffering the most as those with the greatest character. Those who suffer and struggle for a better day become, in the words of Hemingway, "strong at the broken places." To adopt this myth is to set sail to distant shores of democracy across the Red Sea. It is to recognize the beauty of everyone, especially those who have been assailed and unjustly treated.

Myths of the Trickster

Almost all cultures feature trickster myths. Trickster is the maker of mischief, the force of joviality and improvisation, the bridge between heaven and hell. "Every group has its edge, its sense of in and out, and trickster is always there."[606] Always on the border, trickster is "the creative idiot" and "speaker of sacred profanities."[607] In Hindu mythology, Krishna is trickster when he steals butter despite his mother's warnings. In Greek mythology, Hermes is trickster when he steals Apollo's cattle, and Prometheus is trickster when he steals fire. The trickster is at work when abolitionist Frederick Douglass steals literacy from the white world. In his *Trickster Makes the World*, Lewis Hyde distinguishes between mischief and evil:

> … the Devil and the trickster are not the same thing
> … Those who confuse the two do so because they have
> failed to perceive trickster's great ambivalence. The Devil
> is an agent of evil, but trickster is amoral, not immoral.
> He embodies and enacts that large portion of our experi-
> ence where good and evil are hopelessly intertwined.[608]

Mischief is a playful annoyance or petty act to upset traditional order and illuminate truth on a higher plane of thought. It's as if trickster emerges to poke fun at man-made establishment. Trickster turns society on its side by allowing man to chuckle at himself without insisting upon broader revolt.

The thematic glue of the first trickster stories come from conquering appetite, contends Hyde. He offers an Apache story in which trickster Rabbit fools Coyote. Rabbit runs through a field of fruit and becomes ensnared by Farmer's trap. Coyote comes along and asks why Rabbit is stuck, to which Rabbit responds that Farmer trapped him because he wouldn't eat with Farmer. Soon Farmer will return with a chicken, but Rabbit won't eat with him. Coyote retorts, "You are foolish, I will take your place." Coyote frees Rabbit and takes his place in the trap. When the farmer returns, he sees Coyote and kills it.[609] In slaking his appetite, trickster's intelligence becomes apparent. His cunning and craft help him survive. His weapon is his language and elocution, improvising on the fly, a "plasticity of behavior," turning the blues of life into positive circumstance.[610]

Possibly the most distinct American incarnation of trickster is, as Hyde suggests, *The Confidence-Man* of Herman Melville. Confidence-Man wears many masks and never acts his true self. He is polytropic in face and pluralistic in intellect, riding life with an equipmental attitude, feigning the creative lie, a high priest of the advanced skill of semiotics. Confidence-Man, however, is not an agent of evil, rather "a savior who only seems dark because he must work in a fallen world."[611] In fact, in many cultures, trickster invents language or at least *jazzes* it with new thought, vitality, and form.

Modern entertainment has pushed trickster over the cliffs of evil. The veneration of the rough outlaw, rebel without a cause, the convicted protagonist, and hyperbolic rapper divorces playful mischief from American art. After all, trickster is not the convicted felon, pedestrian liar or middling thief. "Their disruptions are not subtle enough, or pitched at a high enough level ..."[612] The purpose of trickster's theft is to draw an image of cultural refraction so that society may reinvent and self-amend off the grid of reality.

An African trickster myth found in African American oral tradition is the "Signifying Monkey." The monkey sits in the tree and yells down to the lion that the elephant is talking about "yo' momma in a scandalous way!"[613] The lion runs to the elephant and attacks with bluster. The elephant slugs the lion and tramples it thoroughly. The monkey looks down at the lion and pokes fun. In his mockery and jubilation, the monkey slips and falls to the ground. The lion pounces, but the monkey talks his way out. They should have a fair fight; after all, the monkey fell. The lion frees the monkey, who quickly scampers up the tree to a safe distance. The Signifying Monkey employs the "psychic self-defense" of the African American.[614] In a white man's world, the African American must cope, but not protest with violence. Instead, the African American signifies "a way of saying one thing and meaning another ... it is tropological thought ... all to achieve reverse power, to improve situations."[615] The joke is ultimately on the lion, for it gets caught in the invented language or "cultural code" of the monkey.[616]

Taken to music, signifyin(g) can be found in musical imitation and the call and response *making* of jazz. A jazz musician copes with his blues by invention and adopting an equipmental attitude of pragmatism: An open revolt is unnecessary when quiet and coded subversion can bring about change. The jazz musician pokes fun and mimics fellow band members. To enter the jazz ring is to step nose-first into the cultural code of the musicians. That black music was able to enmesh (and enlighten) white Americans is perhaps the grandest example of cultural signifyin(g). Mainstream white audiences and music companies continually borrow from black music. Perhaps "borrow" is too kind a word. In *Jazz Consciousness*, Paul Austerlitz contends that whites appropriate black culture, only to spur black musicians to re-appropriate (or invent and signify) another musical form. In the nineteenth century, black minstrels were popular among white audiences. African Americans eventually performed black minstrel roles, mocking themselves, but also gaining the status of entertainers. African Americans invented blues music and jazz. Whites appropriated the music as white swing bands out-earned black bands. African Americans answered with bebop, and whites appropriated the blues with rock music. African Americans spawned funk, hip hop, and rap. White audiences have already appropriated these recent black creations as mainstream entertainment. Austerlitz calls this practice *"stereotype and reappropriation."* The cultural code of black music duped the white lion and invented American music. And the modern trickster who signified on the mainstream was the most famous musician of his time.

The Myth of the Modern Trickster

Some scholars say Louis Armstrong was born on July 4, 1900; others say August 1, 1901. Whatever his birth date, the founding father Armstrong was the quintessential American. Born into poverty, he grew up in the violent neighborhood of Jane Alley in New Orleans. With no conservatory or classroom training, he changed the stylization of America as we know it, elevating the solo to a synonym of jazz. After playing in New Orleans, he rode his horn to Chicago and then New York. Like the roving reporter Charles Kuralt, Armstrong roamed across America. He played over three hundred gigs per year, appeared in over thirty films, and recorded endlessly. He was a superstar like no other. The Italians enlarged his picture to the same size as Mussolini's. He broke formality while performing when he said to George V: "This one's for you, Rex."[619] He took part in the perennial jam session, collaborating with pianist Earl Hines—who had a strong classical influence—even with Hawaiian musicians. Armstrong was an unparalleled jazz-pop singer. Crooner Bing Crosby thought there would never be a better pop singer than Armstrong: "It's so simple. When he sings a sad song you feel like crying, and when he sings a happy song you feel like laughing. What the hell else is there with pop singing?"[620]

Despite the success and genius of Armstrong, intellectuals have criticized him for his Uncle Tom stage persona. Even Marsalis once thought Armstrong was the Uncle Tom minstrel caricature that pleased white audiences. His music was the ultimate form of social commentary. As Giddins's biography explains it, "[Armstrong's] ability to balance the emotional gravity of the artist with the communal good cheer of the entertainer helped enable him to demolish the Jim Crow/ Zip Coon/ Ol' Dan Tucker stereotypes."[621] Armstrong recognized his role as an entertainer: to amuse. Though much like the monkey trickster, Armstrong "was as much himself rolling his eyes and mugging as he was playing the trumpet."[622] Thomas Jefferson felt that every generation needed a revolution. Marrying gradual revolutionary changes with tradition makes the oncoming change easier to swallow. Armstrong's talent overwhelmed the humorous setting and lyrics. Louis Armstrong's Uncle Tom persona disguised the oncoming changes in American civil society just as "proletarian music" camouflaged jazz (and its looming lessons) in the Soviet Union. Some thought Armstrong had doctored his horn, using chewing gum to make the mouthpiece smaller. How could he possibly play so high? In Columbus, Ohio, he allowed a group of orchestral players to try his horn, which only proved the singularity of Armstrong's talent.[623] His stage persona was deeper than he let on. He signified and communicated in a manner "characterized by irony, indirection, needling, and trickery."[624] He was saying more than his white audiences could hear: He was subtle enough to criticize the position of blacks in broader American society. He was economical in his words and brought added depth to his melodic phrases, stressing an unstressed note or singing a lyric one beat before it is normally due. He demonstrated liberty through his trumpet, flinging off the nets that tried to catch his soul, but acquiesced to the puerile entertainer's role of his era. His music was sophistically creative and replete with message. Traditional values would remain static, but terrific change was on the heavenly horizon.[625] His rhythm may not have saved the world. It certainly changed it.

The modern trickster of Armstrong is Hermes reincarnate. The audience to which he performs evokes the Apolline part of society. The Apolline audience members come to the Armstrong-Hermes performance in order to escape the order and rules of society, and the audience very much "follows the rules of the game," or the *logos* of life.[626] When modern trickster Armstrong performs, he enchants Apollo. It is the modern trickster who signifies on the Apolline audience, camouflaging, suggesting, and hinting at change. Hyde gives the example of Lévi-Strauss's bifurcated view: "life and death, agriculture and warfare, herbivore and carnivore."[627] The trickster lives in the middle and at the boundaries. The trickster is often the bridge, taking on the image of "carrion eater" (resolving herbivore and carnivore), for example.[628] Louis Armstrong was America's modern trickster straddling the Jim Crow era and oncoming Civil Rights movement. Armstrong was the trickster bridge for cultural liberalism to instruct political democracy.

The *Myth of Modern Trickster* pushes the Apolline citizen to recognize the subtly of signifying, abstracting, and encoding. The newness of an idea can be cloaked in the cover of the past. The inherent complexity of this myth can be simplified when we step away from the reason of Apollo and see the intentions of the artist. Indeed, to determine the intentions of an artist is largely an interpretive task, but such questioning is the very decoding of trickster. The delicacy and intricacy of purpose is often lost on the audience. To the few who understand the signifying, the laugh isn't at them.

Composing a Jazzocracy

To create a Jazzocracy is a game of "what if?" The infusion of a new strain of myth, even one borrowed from the usable history of a nation, takes decades, perhaps even centuries to implement. And it remains to be seen if a cultural mythology can be subverted from an unconcealed attempt. A fully conscious march beyond price and towards art may not be possible, as the friction of debate would surely slow any radical movement. Perhaps a modern trickster is needed to lure America's oral tradition onto the grid of myth.

Although a Jazzocracy thrives in the world of make believe, it also dwells in the hearts of those Americans who desire a more perfect union. Thought, of course, is antecedent to action. And for any change to occur, to infuse mythical art into twenty-first century cultural liberalism, it must begin with the individual mind.

An individual can revolt in the mind. To recognize the absurdity at work in America's oral tradition is difficult but necessary. "Even the strongest current of water cannot add a drop to a cup which is already full," penned Tolstoy.[629] To awaken the mind to question cultural currents pushes one towards the "in-between" and invisible. In II Corinthians, Paul recognizes that while the visible world may be in constant decay, the touch of spirit dwells within. The invisible steers the soul and renews the spirit.

Tolstoy scolded those for accepting Jesus Christ, yet not changing their lives.[630] "Faith without deeds is dead," it is written in the Bible.[631] To question America's oral tradition is not enough. A constant effort to seek beauty and radiance must be put forth. With sustained effort, a collective movement may sprout and fashion wings, and bring, in the words of Attali, "public opinion in harmony with the new truth."[632]

Campbell recognized artists as the mythmakers of our era. The *Myth of the Modern Israelites* can shape a new conception of African

Americans in mainstream expressions. The power of oral tradition is immense. Music is more than an object or property. Just as Dizzy Gillespie conceived in rhythm, so too can we think in counterpoint and harmony. In this way, life becomes art—tension and release, call and response, and steady antiphony.

Some Eastern philosophies consider the universe as the divine's dance, dream, and reflection; *our* universe is our reflection upon it. Imagine the universe as the trumpet solo of Gabriel, and we the humble staccato notes. To conceive in such a manner, art will begin to reflect the jam session of American thought. To think in terms of art helps to translate the tenor of the times into an emergent American style, one that speaks to the potentiality of America's cultural and political democracy. "In music, man is revealed and not in a noise," writes Tagore.[633]

To think in terms of art is to return to *making* music. It pushes us past the fleeting tastes of music-as-entertainment. We need not think *about* music. Just as we don't think *about* physics; we think *in* physics, contends Johnson. We ought to think *in* music. Instead of conceiving of music as a performance or an act of entertainment, consider life-as-music as the twenty-first century American trope. Music, in this way, "becomes superfluous, the unfinished, the relational. It even ceases to be a product separable from its author."[634] Such a "connectedness principle," writes Ted Gioia, suggests that "all music creates linkages with our daily lived experiences."[635] Art can always be reinterpreted and recast; thus, the connectedness of music to our daily lives serves as a timeless mirror that presents us with a challenging vision. Over time the mirror will depict what it once showed the world. East of the sun and west of the moon, America the Beautiful rises again.

Epilogue
Swan Song

*I*n Goethe's *Faust*, the beginning is the "act." What are the appropriate steps to take in constructing a Jazzocracy? What is our act? Admittedly, arguing for an infusion of jazz-based myth into the broader American mythology is an academic task. I am quite sure that some may think I did not go far enough in forecasting how to enact the five proposed myths. This text, however, is not meant to be an instructional guide in incorporating myth into society. Nor can it be seen as a comprehensive guide to the intricate and labyrinthine domain of aesthetic theory. This work merely suggests an appropriate metaphor with which to view cultural liberalism and how it refracts an image of America and Americans. This section, however, is a departure from the rest of the text because it escapes the domain of myth and suggests a few tangible ideas for honoring the jazz tradition and enacting its lessons.

Another Way to Listen

My grandfather, Piara Singh Gill, was an accomplished cosmic ray physicist. When I was a child, he would sit me down at the wooden kitchen table and explain the nuts and bolts of science. He started to explain about the periodic table and protons, neutrons, and electrons. After a few moments, he was onto quarks, helium nuclei, and solar cosmic rays. My attention would flag, my ears secretly listening to the TBS telecast of the Atlanta Braves in the adjacent room. I had trouble understanding his lectures because I was unfamiliar with the vocabulary of physics. Because it took effort to understand, I quickly grew bored.

Many of my friends profess a similar reason for not listening to jazz: "I just don't understand it," or "It doesn't make sense." If one is not familiar with a type of music, then one probably won't listen to it. Levitin suggests that if a song is too simple, like nursery rhymes, they are not challenging enough. And if the song is too multifaceted or unpredictable (presumably like a jazz song), it is too challenging. The casual listener selects mainstream music because it is a balance of simplicity and complexity. The only way to gain familiarity with jazz music is to listen to it. And the initial attempts may be uncomfortable and challenging. It is no doubt a difficulty to find jazz music. Jazz records make up only five percent of the market if that. But then again, Apple computers make up roughly five percent of the personal computer market, and very few think Apple is "uncool." Maybe jazz just needs to find its iPod. Historically, jazz has emphasized the virtuosity of instrumentals over vocals. That is not to say that there aren't excellent examples of jazz singers. Nowadays, popular music is just the opposite—stressing lyrics over the quality of the vocals and musical accompaniment. Both approaches have their merits. The emphasis on instrumental virtuosity, I believe, helps to abstract expression, recasting the music as an interpretive art. In other words, the jazz solo invites the listener to bring his or her interpretation to the work. If jazz is difficult to understand, it may be because of the unfamiliarity with instrumental music. It's one thing not to enjoy jazz after listening intently to a few albums or attending a jazz club. It's quite another to dismiss it without listening to it. Ignorance should not lead to contempt. Knowledge should help form opinions.

In listening to jazz, it helps to get past the notes or at least understand them as veneer. Each note, every silence, is merely the surface package for a depth of meaning and expression. One of my bass teachers suggested that I think in images while listening to jazz. Taken to the jazz-as democracy metaphor, it can help to think of images suggested in the text while listening to jazz: the shout section of a big band ensemble as the final days of a political campaign, or the call and response of a trading four session as a reasoned debate within the electorate. In John Coltrane's rendition of *Syeeda's Song Flute*, think of the beginning riff as a hammer nailing the grid of rhythm. The successive chorus in which Coltrane runs up the scale builds the three-dimensional grid of the skyscraper. To think in images is a helpful first step to decode the abstraction of jazz.

Thinking in images or decoding the message of the music convinces the critic that jazz is an inaccessible and elitist music. The fact that one can write a text on jazz-as-democracy arguably convinces the critic that jazz is museum music, something to be visited and analyzed, with little role in the entertainment sphere. Celebrated jazz musicians don suits and tuxedos, provoking more cries of elitism. Trumpeter Bernie Privin once subbed for Marty Napoleon's trumpet player. He showed up in a tuxedo because nobody informed him of the sports coat attire. "Don't worry about it. You can be the leader tonight," said Napoleon. "Nothing doing. If I was the leader, do you think I would have hired you guys?" replied Privin.[636]

I can understand why critics may think of jazz as an inaccessible art, but I reject such a view. If there is such a distinction as "highbrow" and "lowbrow," jazz successfully navigates both. For the majority of the twentieth century, jazz was the popular music of the day. In some quarters it represented American vice, part of the lowbrow circle of entertainment. Only from the 1970s until now has jazz qualified as "high brow" art. Indeed, one can receive a doctorate in jazz studies. The ivory tower may have accepted jazz, but I hardly think the scat singing of Ella Fitzgerald on *Lemon Drop* can be imprisoned in a museum. Such emotional tunes refuse to qualify as elitist, especially when the lyrics are deeply personal expressions of the performer. To consider jazz elitist is to consider the solo of human expression snobby. When I put on the Count Basie Orchestra's rendition of "Do Nothin' Till You Hear From Me," even my jazz-avoiding friends start to tap their foots. Maybe Duke Ellington was right when he said there are only two types of music: good and bad (not high and low).

Nourishing the Ear

American school children read Twain, Whitman, and Poe. American literature teaches us about America's history, ideals, values, and aspirations. The adventurous escapades of Huckleberry Finn inspire children, Ichabod Crane mesmerizes lore lovers, and *The Catcher in the Rye* questions the loss of innocence of America's youth. The narratives of American literature are part of the literary mythology and create a unified narrative. The stories many learned in school have become the conscience of our nation, uniting Americans behind a usable literature to inspire and enthuse.

Music is audible and aural literature. And just as American schools teach the works of America's greatest writers, so too should schools educate about America's classical art, the music of Armstrong, Ellington, and Gillespie. Mike Huckabee, former Republican Governor of Arkansas, refers to the arts as "weapons of mass instruction."[637] In Arkansas, it is law for every elementary school to teach forty minutes of music or art each week. A *Boston Globe* editorial agrees with him, calling the right brain "a terrible thing to waste."[638] A 2002 National Governors Association report states:

> School districts are finding that the arts develop many
> skills applicable to the 'real world' environment. In a study
> of 91 school districts across the nation, evaluators found
> that the arts contribute significantly to the creation of the
> flexible and adaptable workers that businesses demand to
> compete in today's economy.[639]

Whether art makes one smarter is debatable.[640] Professors Ellen Winner and Lois Hetland stress that art teaches different types of skills, like persistence and innovation, not found in other classes.[641] While many classes stress rote learning, art teaches the student to invent, innovate, and imagine—skills for life. I think American schools should teach American arts. There will no doubt be debate over what type of music or genre to teach. Children need not listen to John Coltrane's "sheets of sound" in the second grade. That's like reading Joyce's *Finnegans Wake* without the mental preparedness. But just as the high school student graduates with a more advanced knowledge of literature, so too should he possess a more critical ear. In this way, jazz and other music will stand as audible literature. Just as Hemingway's *Farewell to Arms* and Hawthorne's *The Scarlet Letter* contribute to the American literary narrative, the works of Armstrong and Ellington will help create a unified oral tradition of music.

Hearing is perhaps our most undernourished sense. When was the last time you listened to an instrumental song with complete attention? That is, the song wasn't put on to establish the mood of a party or accompany you on a drive home. To read a book requires real concentration. To discover the invisibility of music also takes effort. Because listening to music is a plug-and-play experience, we often don't think critically of our musical oral tradition. Music can be entertainment. But some music is more than just amusing and droll sounds. An active and sustained attempt at understanding American music will instruct school children that art doesn't have to start with MTV and end with BET.

The upbeat news is that certain universities feature jazz history courses, Jazz at Lincoln Center has devised online curricula, and the National Endowment for the Arts (NEA) has invested millions to preserve jazz since the days of the Nixon administration. But the jazz education initiative is hardly a nationwide effort. Even the once jazz broadcasting Voice of America faces budget cuts, making it more difficult to spread the music abroad. George Washington once addressed Congress by saying that "There is nothing that can better deserve your patronage than the promotion of science and literature."[642] He even proposed a national university that made good on his beliefs. America's Second President, John Adams, observed that he studied politics and war so that his grandchildren could have the freedom to study literature and arts. After a country is secure, the freedom to create must be wrought by poets, painters, and musicians.

Looking at our rich history we see an evolution of a jam session country. Our ancestors bequeathed a rich cultural tradition which helps to reconcile the interests of the individual with that of the group. But when we turn on the radio, we listen to a parade of nothing: trashy rhyming lyrics that are increasingly vapid and self-stereotyping of their propagators. We might enjoy the novels of Mark Twain but why not also the music of Louis Armstrong? Jazz *is* worth the effort. In our musical quest, America's communion with the world will surface— ordering noise and touching (not torching) the soul. Let's put something more beautiful in our iPods and in our minds.

The Need for Buffers

"Whatever survives should become art," one might think. Jazz is dead. Rap survives because it's commercially viable, so it follows that rap will become the cultural legacy of the times. Do we want our cultural legacy to be that of vapid materialism? What will the next generation think of those who lived at the dawn of the twenty-first century? If we are judged by our popular music, then it's not hard to think of America today as a land that promotes vulgarity and materialism. Then again, later observers might not even notice, since the vapidity and meaningless of American art might increase (if it's possible to increase the absence of meaning).

Arthur Schlesinger Jr. believes, "If the arts are worth pursuing at all, they are worth pursuing for their own sake."[643] That is, art is a universal good of society. Everyone should have access to emotive and accessible art. As Schlesinger points out, many institutions like schools, hospitals, and libraries serve the good of community through public support. The Smithsonian museums offer a priceless look at America's history, for instance. These entities wouldn't survive without help. American art needs help, too. Its inherited cultural legacy ought to be preserved because it's part of America's history, a part of us. The universal good of art should be available to everyone, rich and poor. Everyone's soul deserves to be touched. It's important not to institutionalize ingenuity in art, but it's necessary to provide the right conditions for creativity.

The incongruence of art and entertainment is similar to that of democracy and capitalism. One is built on equality, the other on inequality. Philosopher Karl Polanyi recognized that American society is based on "gain."[644] The interplay of capitalism and democracy invites leaders of all political stripes to comment. In his farewell address, President Eisenhower warned of the marriage of the private defense sector with the government. Hitler felt capitalism and democracy incongruent: "Private enterprise cannot be maintained in a democracy."[645] Jazz was once the commercial art-cum-entertainment, but must be thought of now as the democratic art.[646] Art has often been tied to a supporting entity, whether it was the Renaissance courts, the Middle Age temples, or the American dollar. Jazz deserves to be preserved, encouraged, and promoted because it retains certain fundamental American qualities that speak to a shared history for all omni-Americans. The cultural democracy imbued within the jam session of jazz instructed political democracy to integrate and melt with its era. Now that jazz is no longer the popular music, political democracy ought to return the noble gesture to jazz by creating buffers to preserve an American tradition. Running a hospital is often a money-losing affair, but government needs to support such institutions for the good of society. Jazz buffers like Jazz at Lincoln Center (JALC) should exist as an artistic buffer. JALC has its critics within and without the jazz world, but it should be recognized for what it is. In a time of cultural decay, it is a fortress for art.

The Creative Economy

Although I think there is a need for jazz buffers, I am not willing to concede the coin of capitalism in helping jazz to survive. For instance, the Internet has helped casual listeners to discover classical music. They can read reviews and learn for themselves, instead of feeling threatened by the classical cognoscenti.[647] Jazz record labels and musicians should consider how the Internet can sell music. The record store may not stock copious jazz records, but the Internet has a virtually infinite warehouse of options. Jazz musicians must discover the long tail of e-commerce—it can be profitable to sell less of more. I understand the criticisms to fund the arts, but when there is a strong economic return, one should be in favor of it. In his *The Rise of the Creative*

Class, Richard Florida writes extensively about the burgeoning of the "creative class." He uses fairly broad parameters, suggesting 38 million Americans belong to the creative class, roughly 30 percent of the total workforce. He includes those who works in publishing, design, music, film, advertising, and other fields. As manufacturing and service sector jobs are increasingly outsourced and sent offshore, Americans are turning to creative jobs (arts, design, advertising, etc.) to seek profit.

I believe there is a kernel of truth in Florida's findings. After Hurricane Katrina, I helped prepare a report that studied the economic impact of the arts in New Orleans. In brief, the creative economy of the birthplace of jazz is significant. The text that follows is an adaptation from my research for the "Bring New Orleans Back" Commission Report, and an essay I penned for *Issues & Concerns* magazine.

After Hurricane Katrina wrecked New Orleans, then-Speaker of the House Dennis Hastert opined that it made no sense to rebuild a city some seven feet below sea level. Hurricane Katrina killed more than 1,300 people, led to rampant looting, displaced inhabitants, and spotlighted America's dirty little secret of poverty. But ever since the hurricane, city planners have beavered away beneath the radar trying to rebuild a broken city. To rebuild a city is to restore hope, optimism, and spirit to citizens. Building levees, power grids, and roads are obviously important and necessary. After rebuilding the infrastructure, it is also important to rebuild and reinvest in that which makes New Orleans unique: its culture and arts.

[Promoting America's "identity" and "character" may win support in some quarters but won't loosen the purse strings of government funding. An economic case must be made for the arts.] The creative sector is a chief contributor of New Orleans's greater economy. The creative industries generate around $300 million for the city with $259 million coming from arts audiences and $43 million from arts organization spending. The economic impact is even wider, with almost 10,000 jobs being created. This translates into $187 million in household earnings. The patrons of the arts aren't just tourists, as 70 percent of nonprofit art audiences are citizens of New Orleans. Over 10 million tourists visited New Orleans pre-Katrina, spending $5 billion.

Creative industries make for large economic engines. London's creative industry is the second largest industry in the city, and that's without including tourism. Dun & Bradstreet finds that America's creative industry grew at 5.5 percent from 2004 to 2005, whereas the national average for all industries was 3.8 percent.[648] And total non-profit arts generate a whopping $134 billion in revenue and $24.4 billion in tax receipts. Tourism only boosts the economic impact of the cultural economy. The Americans for the Arts Congressional Report shows that as of January 2005, some 600,000 arts businesses were open for commerce in the US. These businesses employ almost 3 million workers. Artists also create intellectual property right value through copyrights, and add to a city's reputation.

The US government, however, allocates meager funds for the arts. This is despite a return on investment of $8 for every $1 that the government invests.[649] Only 2 percent of funding for the arts comes from the federal government. The US federal budget allocates 0.02 percent to the arts. The arts excel, despite a lack of government funding. Some might say that the US government's laissez-faire approach to creative industries somehow helps the arts. But after crunching the numbers from other cities and countries around the world, the US government could be doing more to support the arts.

Austria allocates 1.58 percent of its federal budget for the arts, the Netherlands 0.83 percent, and Russia 0.50 percent. Austria leverages its cultural history by promoting Austrian composers Haydn and Mozart. The 250th birth year of Mozart occurred in 2006, and a grand, yearlong festival of 2,500 performances attracted tourists and boosted the performance of the greater economy. How will America celebrate Dizzy Gillespie's 100th birthday in 2017? In Amsterdam, Netherlands, there is a continual campaign waged by political action groups to allocate 1 percent of the federal budget for culture. St. Petersburg, Russia, is fresh from investing $1.3 billion on rebuilding infrastructure and cultural sites for its tri-centennial celebration. Even Japan goes to lengths to promote and fund its cultural industry. The Japanese Constitution ensures that citizens have access to a level of culture. Some 120 acclaimed artists receive a stipend from the Japanese government for life. The Japanese have rewritten their tax policy to make it easier for individuals to donate artwork to museums and galleries. The commonality among most art policies is that they focus on the preservation of heritage. The Japanese fund the *Japanese* arts and the French preserve *French* art. So, too, should America preserve its artistic heritage.

While the potential for New Orleans to become a vibrant creative economy exists, it still continues to lag. Pre-Katrina, the city received $2 million in investment per year, which led to $45.5 million in cultural spending—a return on investment of 22 to 1. San Francisco sees a return on investment of 13 to 1, and Montreal—10 to 1. Vienna, for instance, generates cultural spending of $500 million, and San Francisco: $706 million.[650] New Orleans's lag is because politicians have not recognized the economic importance of the arts.

Now more than ever, the arts in New Orleans need help. Hurricane Katrina wrecked the cultural industry: 75 percent of New Orleans's nonprofit creative institutions were closed. The uninsured damage of creative facilities is over $80 million. After Katrina, some 90 percent of musicians had left. More musicians have returned, but the numbers are still grim. The images of death and destruction wrought by Katrina should not lead Americans to give up on the Gulf Coast. Instead, we should recognize that those who were afflicted are Omni-Americans, the modern Israelites.

It is debatable whether New Orleans will ever be rebuilt to what it once was. And let us be clear that New Orleans had turned into a caricature of itself long before Katrina. The population was dwindling.

Hurricane Katrina could have catalyzed investment and growth for an entire region, much like the Tennessee Valley Authority during the presidency of Franklin Delano Roosevelt. It is not too late for the public and private sectors to show initiative in growing the region. New Orleans has the creative ingredients needed to thrive: a unique music, delectable cuisine, and strong-willed citizens yearning to create. Any plan to rebuild New Orleans into a first-rate city should consider the creative economy as the lifeblood of the city. That is, of course, if there is a significant commitment to rebuild New Orleans at all.

The rise of the creative economy, I hope, will lead jazz writers, economists, politicians, and urban planners to propose solutions on how to embed and sell jazz music in capitalist society. There's a gem waiting to be discovered in promoting America's native art of jazz through creative economy proposals.

Acknowledgements

I opened this book by calling it my solo. By now, however, we've come to understand that every solo is not an individual journey, but a collective experiment. My jazz heroes—Charlie Parker, Miles Davis, and Bill Evans—had supportive rhythm sections, and I've been fortunate to find mine at BetterWorld Books. My sincerest thanks to Xavier Helgesen, David Murphy, Geoff Schwarten, and others at Better-World. Before it was hip to "go green" or be mindful of the broader community, they built an enterprise that advances the "triple bottom line." It is because of BetterWorld that this book is not just a collection of words but an instrument to help literacy in New Orleans and displaced musicians. My deep gratitude goes surely to the leader of the rhythm section, my editor John Probst, a rare individual who is professional and imaginative, durable and cool. Thank you for not working me too hard and helping me navigate the dizzying labyrinth of manuscript and minutiae. Also a note of thanks to Ellis Marsalis III and Kelly Powers at Obie Joe for believing in (and promoting) this work, and Katie Clark at Ideo who is a creative dynamo. While I'm at it, how can I not thank the folks at USPS, UPS, and DHL for shuttling manuscripts around the world?

Jazz music has been a tireless passion for me. I have many people to thank for turning me on to America's finest art. Until now, my life has been one long music rehearsal. First and foremost - my music teachers, Mr. Stutz Wimmer and Georgia Ekonomou at the Lovett School in Atlanta. Adam Nitti, Lyn DeRamus and my many professors at Dartmouth, which also includes Donald Glasgo, William Summers, Hafiz Shabazz, Jim Moor, Donald Pease, William Cook, and Don Baldini. Thank you, Dean Carolynne Krusi and Dean Stuart Lord and Professor Ian Angell at the London School of Economics. Also thanks to the staff at Tulane University, the Hogan Archive, and Mr. Walter Isaacson. My thanks to those who have inspired my ideas and prose over the years: Ken Prichard (the finest English teacher), John Allman, Dr. Jeff Rosensweig at Emory University, Dr. C. Everett Koop at Dartmouth, Peter Israel, and literary agent Ron Konecky.

Next time you're in New Orleans, I encourage you to visit Hotel Jeff. The accommodation is Spartan (a futon, eggs and A1 sauce) but the company and conversation is moving and magnificent. It's run by one of my best friends, Jeff DellaVolpe, M.D., who scooted me back and forth in his yellow Jeep and stayed up late talking music. Brent Reidy is yet another who I am forever grateful, helping me edit the manuscript, develop arguments, and sympathize with brief episodes of frustration. Adam Starr, my friend from graduate school, is nothing short of a star with the pen. His bombastic flare (think the 1999 movie Office Space) was influential in the development of the text. One day I expect to see many titles to his name and credits to his intelligent actor brother Chris, the champion of the Nevada spelling bee (eventually "f-l-o-c-c-u-l-e-n-t" tripped him in the nationals). My thanks to my friend from graduate school, Ariana Pieper, for her critiques and insight.

My thanks to my friends who have helped and challenged me: Derek Hansen, Grady Hannah, Alexa and Arthur Pulitzer, Nancy Falco, Ron Markham, Andrew Schutzbank, Tivon Pennicott, Colin Fagan, Lindsey Davis, Dan Regenstein, Billy Mathis, Andrew Travers, Ben Phillips, Aruturo O'Farrell, Christian Littejohn, David Gardner, Joanne Kim, Shahara Ahmad-Llewellyn, Ling Yan, Xiang Yan, Steven Frank, Taylor Thompson, James Stuart Castiglione Baehr, Emma Juniper, Mark Romig, Anantha Krishnan, Josh Bower, Dhruv Parekh, Dustin Reidy, Irvin Mayfield. Thanks to my capitalist comrades at JP-Morgan: Dominic Myers, Kevin Sun, and Lee Kirbach for looking the other way while I (ahem) worked. Thank you to Senator Max Cleland, Senator John Kerry, and Jonathan Powell who gave me opportunities of a lifetime.

There are two who deserve my strongest and deepest gratitude, Wynton Marsalis and Doug Brinkley. I met Mr. Marsalis while in high school in New York and am a proud student turned disciple. To set foot in his shadow is to encounter genius. Besides my father, you have been the strongest influence on these words and my life. I hope one day to make you proud. Professor Brinkley and his gracious wife Anne are two of the finest examples of how to live. They welcomed me into their home and mentored me through this process. Professor Doug Brinkley is spectacular with the pen, but even more so with his heart.

My father Raghbir, mother Surishtha, and sister Kashi (and late grandfather Nanaji) encouraged me – and those who lost their homes and jobs during Hurricane Katrina inspired me. I admire the musicians of New Orleans who have come back home, and encourage more to return. You may leave the music, but it will never leave you.

Notes

[1] "The Top 100, the most influential figures in American history," <http://www.theatlantic.com/doc/200612/influentials/>

[2] Gary Giddins, *Satchmo*, Da Capo Press, 1988. pg. 62

[3] André Malraux, *Picasso's Mask*. Holt, Rinehart and Wilson, 1974. pg. 35.

[4] Albert Murray, *The Hero and the Blues*. Vintage Books, 1973. pg. 65

[5] Cited in Samuel A. Floyd, *The Power of Black Music*, Oxford University Press. pg. 106

[6] Zachary Roth, "The Establishmentarian," *Washington Monthly*. Nov. 2006. <http://www.washingtonmonthly.com/features/2006/0611.roth.html>

[7] "A Trumpeter Unmuted," *Newsweek*. October 2004 <http://www.msnbc.msn.com/id/6212850/site>

[8] Rick Lewis, "Art and Soul" *Philosophy Now*. September/October 2006. <http://www.philosophynow.org/issue57/57lewis.htm>

[9] Gary Giddins, *Satchmo*, Da Capo Press, 1988. pg. 123

[10] Nat Hentoff, *Jazz is*. New York: Limelight Editions, 1984, c1976. pg. 21.

[11] Thelonious Monk Institute of Jazz, "Jazz in America," <http://www.jazzinamerica.org/lp.asp?LPOrder=3&Grade=8&PageID=205>

[12] Ibid.

[13] Interview with Ken Burns. <http://www.pbs.org/jazz/about/about_behind_the_scenes2.htm>

[14] William Maxwell, "Ralph Ellison and the Constitution of Jazzocracy," *Journal of Popular Music Studies*, Volume 16, Page 40. April 2004: 40.

[15] Jacques Attali, *Noise: The Political Economy of Music*, University of Minnesota Press, 1985. pg. 10.

[16] Marshall McLuhan, *Understanding Media*. Routledge, 2001. pg. 71.

[17] David Mark, *Going Dirty: The Art of Negative Campaigning*, Rowman & Littlefiled Publishers, 2006. pg. 20-22.

[18] Dana Gioia, "Trade easy pleasures for more complex ones," 17 June 2007. <http://news-service.stanford.edu/news/2007/june20/gradtrans-062007.html>

[19] Ibid.

[20] Ibid.

[21] John Baines, "Egyptian Myth and Discourse: Myths, Gods, and the Early Written and Iconographic Record" in *Journal of Near Eastern Studies*, 1999. pg. 91

[22] Samuel A. Floyd, Jr. *The Power of Black Music*, Oxford University Press, pg. 26-27.

[23] Erik von Kuehnelt-Leddihn, Introduction to *Democracy in America Volume 1*. New Rochelle, New York, 1966

[24] Stephen Tatum, *Inventing Billy the Kid* . University of New Mexico: 1982, pg. 135 James Madison, *Federalist* No. 51, Penguin Books, 1987. pg. 259-265.

[25] Albert Murray, *The Hero and the Blues*. Vintage Books, 1973. pg. 62

[26] James Madison, *Federalist* No. 51, Penguin Books, 1987. pg. 259-265. .

[27] Albert Murray, *The Hero and the Blues* . Vintage Books, 1973. pg. 6

[28] Miles Davis, "*The Autobiography*," Simon & Schuster, 1989. pg. 136.

[29] Miles Davis, "*The Autobiography*," Simon & Schuster, 1989. pg. 101.

[30] Ibid.

[31] Ibid, pg. 226.

[32] Vijay Iyer, "Exploding the Narrative in Jazz Improvisation," in (eds) Robert G. O'Meally, Brent Hayes Edwards, & Farah Jamine Griffin, *Uptown Conversation: The New Jazz Studies*, Columbia University Press, 2004. pg. 393-395

[33] Ibid.

[34] Ibid.

[35] Cited in Jorge Daniel Veneciano, "Louis Armstrong, Bricolage, and the Aesthetics of Swing," in (eds) Robert G. O'Meally, Brent Hayes Edwards, & Farah Jamine Griffin, *Uptown Conversation: The New Jazz Studies*, Columbia University Press, 2004. pg. 256

[36] Cited in David P. Brown, *Noise Orders: Jazz Improvisation, and Architecture*. University of Minnesota Press, 2006. pg. 25

[37] Samuel A. Floyd, Jr. *The Power of Black Music*, Oxford University Press, pg. 97.

[38] Thomas Paine, *Rights of Man*. Penguin Classics, 1984. pg.42.

[39] Ibid, pg. 91

[40] Kramnick, Isaac, *The Federalist Papers*, Editor's Introduction. Penguin, 1987. pg. 22.

[41] Thomas Paine, *Rights of Man*. Penguin Classics, 1984. pg.79.

[42] "Jazz An American Story," Jazz at Lincoln Center / NEA <http://media.jalc.org/nea/lesson5/essay4.php?uv=s>

[43] George Lakoff and Mark Turner. *More than Cool Reason*, University of Chicago Press. pg. Xi.

[44] Ibid, pg. 3

[45] Albert Murray, *The Hero and the Blues*. Vintage Books, 1973. pg. 32. 2004: 185.

[46] Michael Mandelbaum, *Democracy's Good Name: The Rise and Risks of the World's Most Popular Form of Government*, Public Affairs, 2007. pg. 45.

[47] Bill Crow, *Jazz anecdotes*. New York: Oxford University Press, 1990 pg. 21.

[48] Chris Goddard, *Jazz away from home*. New York: Paddington Press, 1979. pg. 192.

[49] Alan P. Merriam and Fradley H. Garner, "Jazz—The Word" in Robert G. O'Meally, *The Jazz Cadence of American Culture*. Columbia University Press, 1998: pg. 8.

[50] Ibid, pg. 16.

[51] Bill Crow, *Jazz anecdotes*. New York: Oxford University Press, 1990. pg. 21.

[52] John A. Kouwenhoven, *The Beer Can By the Highway*. John Hopkins University Press: 1961.

[53] Ibid, pg. 40.

[54] Cornell West, *Democracy Matters*. Penguin, 2004. pg. 23.

[55] Alexis de Tocqueville, *Democracy in America Volume 1*. New Rochelle, New York: 1966

[56] Thomas Mann, *The Coming Victory of Democracy*. Alfred A. Knopf, 1938, pg. 28.

[57] Alexis de Tocqueville, *Democracy in America Volume 1*. New Rochelle, New York: 1966, pg. 24.

[58] Roy N. Lokken, "The Concept of Democracy in Colonial Political Thought," in *The William and Mary Quarterly*. 1959. 3rd Ser., Vol. 16, No. 4, pg. 568.

[59] Ibid, pg. 571

[60] Ibid, pg. 572.

[61] John A. Kouwenhoven, *The Beer Can By the Highway*. John Hopkins University Press: 1961.

[62] Interview with Ken Burns. <http://www.pbs.org/jazz/about/about_behind_the_scenes2.htm

[63] Thomas Paine, *Rights of Man*. Penguin Classics, 1984. pg. 71.

[64] Alexis de Tocqueville, *Democracy in America Volume 1*. New Rochelle, New York: 1966, pg. 98

[65] Alexander Hamilton, *Federalist* No. 120, Penguin Books, 1987. pg. 120-121

[66] Kramnick, Isaac, *The Federalist Papers*, Editor's Introduction. Penguin, 1987. pg. 31.

[67] Alexis de Tocqueville, *Democracy in America Volume 1*. New Rochelle, New York: 1966. pg. 98.

[68] Ibid. pg. 101

[69] Charles Beard, "The Constitution: A Minority Document," in *Conflict and Consensus in Early American History*. D.C. Heath and Company: 1980, pg. 125.

[70] Alexis de Tocqueville, *Democracy in America Volume 1*. New Rochelle, New York: 1966, pg. 105

[71] Michael Mandelbaum, *Democracy's Good Name: The Rise and Risks of the World's Most Popular Form of Government*, Public Affairs, 2007. pg. 40.

[72] Lucy M. Salmon, "Democracy in the Household," in *The American Journal of Sociology*, Vol. 17, No. 4. Jan. 1912, pg. 439.

[73] Thomas Paine, *Rights of Man*. Penguin Classics, 1984. pg. 180.

[74] "Constitutional Topic: The Constitutional Convention" *The U.S. Constitution Online*. 3 July 2005. <http://www.usconstitution.net/consttop_ccon.htm>

[75] Max Farrand, "Compromises of the Constitution" in *The American Historical Review*. Vol. 9, No. 3. April. 1904, pg. 489.

[76] Alexis de Tocqueville, *Democracy in America Volume 1*. New Rochelle, New York: 1966, pg. 143.

[77] Henry Steele Commager, "A Constitution for All the People," in *Conflict and Consensus in Early American History*. D.C. Heath and Company: 1980, pg. 136.

[78] John A. Kouwenhoven, *The Beer Can By the Highway*. John Hopkins University Press: 1961. pg. 54.

[79] Michael P. Fitzsimmons, *The Remaking of France*. Cambridge University Press: 1994.

[80] Donald S. Lutz, "Toward a Theory of Constitutional Amendment," in *American Political Science Review*. Vol. 88, No. 2. June 1994, pg. 355.

[81] Ibid, pg. 356.

[82] Cited in Donald S. Lutz, "Toward a Theory of Constitutional Amendment," in *American Political Science Review*. Vol. 88, No. 2. June 1994, pg. 356.

[83] Ibid, pg. 359.

[84] Ibid, pg. 362.

[85] Stanley Crouch, "Blues to be Constitutional: A Long Look at the Wild Wherefores of Our Democratic Lives as Symbolized in the Making of Rhythm and Tune" Robert G. O'Meally, *The Jazz Cadence of American Culture*. Columbia University Press, 1998, pg. 42.

[86] Walt Whitman, *Democratic Vistas*. Walter Scott Publishing: 1970. pg. 14.

[87] John A. Kouwenhoven, *The Beer Can By the Highway*. John Hopkins University Press: 1961. pg. 41.

[88] John A. Kouwenhoven, *The Beer Can By the Highway*. John Hopkins University Press: 1961. pg. 50.

[89] Phil Hirschkorn, "Freedom Tower to rise 1,776 feet from ashes," *CNN.com*. 20 December 2003. http://www.cnn.com/2003/US/Northeast/12/19/wtc.plan/>

[90] John A. Kouwenhoven, *The Beer Can By the Highway*. John Hopkins University Press: 1961. pg. 45.

[91] Alan Trachtenberg, "The Rainbow and the Grid," in *American Quarterly*. Vol. 16, No. 1, Spring, 1964. pg. 8

[92] Ibid.

[93] Ibid, pg. 9.

[94] Ibid.

[95] John A. Kouwenhoven, *The Arts in Modern American Civilization*. W.W. Norton & Company, 1948. pg. 48.

[96] John A. Kouwenhoven, *The Arts in Modern American Civilization*. W.W. Norton & Company, 1948. pg. 50.

[97] Cited in Alex Krieger, "The American City: Ideal and Mythic Aspects of a Reinvented Urbanism" In *Assemblage*. No. 3, July 1987. pg. 41-42.

[98] John Carlos Williams, *Paterson*, New Directions Publishing Corporation, 1995.

[99] David P. Brown, *Noise Orders: Jazz Improvisation, and Architecture*. University of Minnesota Press, 2006. pg. 4-5.

[100] Valerie Wilmer, *Jazz People*. Da Capo Press, 1970. pg. 44.

188

Kabir Sehgal

Notes to pages 21 to 26

[101] Salim Washington, " 'All the Things You Could Be by Now': *Charles Mingus Presents Charles Mingus* and the Limits of Avant-Garde Jazz," in (eds) Robert G. O'Meally, Brent Hayes Edwards, & Farah Jamine Griffin, *Uptown Conversation: The New Jazz Studies*, Columbia University Press, 2004. pg. 33.

[102] Gary Giddins, *Satchmo*, Da Capo Press, 1988. pg. 26.

[103] Ibid, pg. 27.

[104] Cited in Samuel A. Floyd, Jr. *The Power of Black Music*, Oxford University Press, pg. 15.

[105] Ibid, pg. 15.

[106] Ibid, pg. 21

[107] J. H. Kwabena Nketia, "The Interrelations of African Music and Dance," in *Studia Musicologica Academiae Scientiarum Hungaricae*, T. 7, Fasc. 1/4, The Present Volume Contains the Papers Read at the International Folk Music Council (IFMC) Conference Held in Budapest in August 1964 (1965), pp. 91-101.

[108] Samuel A. Floyd, Jr. *The Power of Black Music*, Oxford University Press, pg. 32.

[109] Ted Gioia, *Work Songs*. Duke University Press, 2006. pg. 9-10.

[110] Samuel A. Floyd, Jr. *The Power of Black Music*, Oxford University Press. pg. 38

[111] Interview with Ken Burns. <http://www.pbs.org/jazz/about/about_behind_the_scenes2.htm>

[112] Samuel A. Floyd, Jr. *The Power of Black Music*, Oxford University Press pg. 52

[113] Ibid, pg. 56-57.

[114] Ibid, pg. 74

[115] Carol S. Gould and Kenneth Keaton, "The Essential Role of Improvisation in Musical Performance," in *The Journal of Aesthetics and Art Criticism*. Vol. 58, No. 2, Improvisation in the Arts, Spring 2000, pg. 143.

[116] Ibid.

[117] Ibid.

[118] Ibid, pg. 144.

[119] David P. Brown, *Noise Orders: Jazz Improvisation, and Architecture*. University of Minnesota Press, 2006. pg. xiv.

[120] Lee Brown, "The Theory of Jazz Music 'It Don't Mean a Thing…'" in *The Journal of Aesthetics and Art Criticism*. Vol 49, No. 2, Spring 1991, pg. 119.

[121] LeRoi Jones, *Blues People: Negro Music in White America*. Perennial: 2002. pg. 66.

[122] Ibid.

[123] Louis Harap, "The Case for Hot Jazz," *The Music Quarterly*, Vol. 27, No. 1, Jan. 1941. pg. 35.

[124] Walt Whitman, *Democratic Vistas*. Walter Scott Publishing: 1970. pg. 16.

[125] Bill Russell, *New Orleans style*. eds Barry Martyn and Mike Hazeldine, Jazzology Press, 1994. pg. 8.

[126] Ibid. pg. 52.

[127] Lee Brown, "The Theory of Jazz Music 'It Don't Mean a Thing...'" in *The Journal of Aesthetics and Art Criticism*. Vol 49, No. 2, Spring 1991, pg. 116.

[128] Ibid, pg. 118.

[129] David P. Brown, *Noise Orders: Jazz Improvisation, and Architecture*. University of Minnesota Press, 2006. pg. 10.

[130] Cited in David P. Brown, *Noise Orders: Jazz Improvisation, and Architecture*. University of Minnesota Press, 2006. pg. 67.

[131] Lee Brown, "The Theory of Jazz Music 'It Don't Mean a Thing...'" in *The Journal of Aesthetics and Art Criticism*. Vol 49, No. 2, Spring 1991, pg. 120.

[132] Ibid.

[133] Ibid, pg. 121.

[134] Scott DeVeaux, "Constructing the Jazz Tradition: Jazz Historiography" in *Black American Literature Forum*. Indiana State University, 1991. pg. 538.

[135] Eric Nisenson, *Ascension: John Coltrane And His Quest*. St. Martin's Press, 1993. pg. 116.

[136] Bill Crow, *Jazz anecdotes*. New York: Oxford University Press, 1990. pg. 185.

[137] Ibid, pg. 186.

[138] Ibid, pg. 117.

[139] Cited in Chris Goddard, *Jazz away from home*. New York: Paddington Press, 1979. pg. 18.

[140] LeRoi Jones, *Blues People: Negro Music in White America*. Perennial: 2002. pg. 25.

[141] Ibid.

[142] Ibid, pg. 27.

[143] Valerie Wilmer, *Jazz People*. Da Capo Press, 1970. pg. 75.

[144] Louis Harap, "The Case for Hot Jazz," *The Music Quarterly*, Vol. 27, No. 1, Jan. 1941, pg. 55.

[145] George Lewis, "Experimental Music in Black and White: The AACM in New York, 1970-1985"," in (eds) Robert G. O'Meally, Brent Hayes Edwards, & Farah Jamine Griffin, *Uptown Conversation: The New Jazz Studies*, Columbia University Press, 2004.

[146] Ibid, pg. 51.

[147] Bill Russell, *New Orleans style*. eds Barry Martyn and Mike Hazeldine, Jazzology Press, 1994. pg. 12.

[148] Ibid, pg. 29.

[149] Ibid, pg. 84.

[150] Ibid., pg. 30.

[151] Stanley Crouch, "Blues to be Constitutional: A Long Look at the Wild Wherefores of Our Democratic Lives as Symbolized in the Making of Rhythm and Tune" Robert G. O'Meally, *The Jazz Cadence of American Culture*. Columbia University Press, 1998. pg. 199.

[152] Bill Russell, *New Orleans style*. eds Barry Martyn and Mike Hazeldine, Jazzology Press, 1994. pg. 164.

[153] Michael Wines, "Republicans' Boomerang," *New York Times*. 6 January 1996. pg. 1

[154] Bill Russell, *New Orleans style*. (eds) Barry Martyn and Mike Hazeldine, Jazzology Press, 1994. pg. 138.

[155] Cited in Robert Walser, "Out of Notes: Signification, Interpretation, and the Problem of Miles Davis," in *The Music Quarterly*. Oxford University Press: 1993, pg. 348.

[156] Bill Russell, *New Orleans style*. eds Barry Martyn and Mike Hazeldine, Jazzology Press, 1994. pg. 55.

[157] Albert Murray, *The Hero and the Blues*. Vintage Books, 1973. pg. 107

[158] Martha Bayles, *Hole in our Soul: The Loss of Beauty & Meaning in American Popular Music*, University of Chicago, 1994, pg. 3.

[159] Ralph Ellison, *Living With Music: Ralph Ellison's Jazz Writings*. Modern Library, 2001. pg. 35.

[160] Bill Crow, *Jazz anecdotes*. New York: Oxford University Press, 1990. pg. 99.

[161] Dale A. Somers, "Black and White in New Orleans: A Study in Urban Race Relations, 1865-1900," *The Journal of Southern History*, Southern Historical Association, 1974. pg. 1-24.

[162] Ibid.

[163] Albert Murray, *The Hero and the Blues*. Vintage Books, 1973. pg. 25.

[164] Douglas Malcom, "'Jazz America': Jazz and African American Culture in Jack Kerouac's 'On the Road'" in *Contemporary Literature*. University of Wisconsin Press, 1999. pg. 85.

[165] Ibid, pg. 90.

[166] Ibid, pg. 91.

[167] Sidney H. Bremer, "Home in Harlem, New York: Lessons from the Harlem Renaissance Writers," *PMLA*, 1990. pg. 52.

[168] Ibid.

[169] "Wild ones," *The Guardian*. 11 December 2004. <http://www.guardian.co.uk/arts/features/story/0,11710,1370298,00.html>

[170] Ibid.

[171] Alfred Appel Jr. *Jazz Modernism*. Alfred A. Knopf, 2002. pg. 65.

[172] Vijay Iyer, "Exploding the Narrative in Jazz Improvisation," in (eds) Robert G. O'Meally, Brent Hayes Edwards, & Farah Jamine Griffin, *Uptown Conversation: The New Jazz Studies*, Columbia University Press, 2004. pg. 394

[173] Eric Nisenson, *Ascension: John Coltrane And His Quest*. St. Martin's Press, 1993. pg. 122.

[174] LeRoi Jones, *Blues People: Negro Music in White America*. Perennial: 200, pg. 153.

[175] Rafi Zabor, *The Bear Comes Home*. W. W. Norton & Company, 1998. pg. 453.

[176] "Literary Paws." PBS Online NewsHour. 13 April 1998. < http://www.pbs.org/newshour/bb/entertainment/jan-june98/bear_4-13.html >

[177] Joseph Campbell, *The Power of Myth*. Anchor, 1988. pg. 19.

[178] Walt Whitman, *Democratic Vistas*. Walter Scott Publishing: 1970. pg. 42.

[179] Ibid, pg. 62.

[180] Walt Whitman, *Democratic Vistas*. Walter Scott Publishing: 1970. pg. 63.

[181] John A. Kouwenhoven, *The Arts in Modern American Civilization*. W.W. Norton & Company, pg. 1.

[182] Rabindranath Tagore, *The Religion of Man*. Rupa & Co. 2005.

[183] Kahlil Gibran, *The Prophet*. Knopf, 1923. pg. 55.

[184] Ibid, pg. 56.

[185] Leo Tolstoy, *The Kingdom of God is Within You*. University of Nebraska Press, 1985. pg. 88.

[186] Erik von Kuehnelt-Leddihn, Introduction to *Democracy in America Volume 1*. New Rochelle, New York, 1966, pg. x.

[187] Horace A. Porter, *Jazz Country: Ralph Ellison in America*. Iowa City University Press, 2001. pg. 39.

[188] Cited in David Ake, "Negotiating National Identity Among American Jazz Musicians in Paris," *Journal of Musicological Research* 23, 2004.: 185.

[189] David Ake, *Jazz Cultures*. University of California Press, pg. 20.

[190] Michael Mandelbaum, *Democracy's Good Name: The Rise and Risks of the World's Most Popular Form of Government*, Public Affairs, 2007. pg. 17.

192

 Kabir Sehgal

[191] Dave Brubeck, "The Beat heart 'Round the World," *The New York Times*. 15, June 1958. pg. S M2. pg. 119.

[192] Ibid.

[193] Robert McG Thomas Jr., "Willis Conover Is Dead at 75; Aimed Jazz at the Soviet Bloc." In *The New York Times*. May 19, 1996. pg. 1.35

[194] Rajiv Chandrasekaran, "Imperial Life in the Emerald City: Inside Iraq's Green Zone," Knopf, 2006.

[195] Albert Murray, *The Hero and the Blues*. Vintage Books, 1973. pg. 29-30.

[196] "Marsalis, Clinton and Others Dissect Jazz at Symposium" *The New York Times*. 11 December 2003

[197] Thomas A. Bailey, "The Mythmakers of American History," in Nicolas Cords and Patrick Gerster, *Myth and the American Experience*. New York, Glencoe Press, 1973. pg. 11.

[198] Leo Tolstoy, *The Kingdom of God is Within You*. University of Nebraska Press, 1985. pg. 131. 7, pg. C17.

[199] Peter J. Spiro, "The Paradox of American Power: Why the World's Only Superpower Can't Go It Alone by Joseph S. Nye, Jr." in *The American Journal of International Law*. Vol. 97, No. 3. July 2003, pg. 732.

[200] Cited in Peter J. Spiro, "The Paradox of American Power: Why the World's Only Superpower Can't Go It Alone by Joseph S. Nye, Jr." in *The American Journal of International Law*. Vol. 97, No. 3. July 2003, pg. 732.

[201] Kenneth A. Osgood, "Hearts and Minds: The Unconvential Cold War," *Journal of Cold War Studies* 4.2 (2002): pg. 85.

[202] William Manchester, *The Last Lion: Winston Spencer Churchill: Alone, 1932-1940*. Delta, 1989. pg. 581.

[203] Anthony Leviero, "U.S. To Take Offensive in Psychological War," *The New York Times*. 1 February 1953, pg. E6.

[204] Kenneth A. Osgood, "Hearts and Minds: The Unconvential Cold War," *Journal of Cold War Studies* 4.2 (2002) pg. 88.

[205] Albert Murray, *The Hero and the Blues*. Vintage Books, 1973. pg. 12.

[206] Joseph Campbell, *The Power of Myth*. Anchor, 1988. pg. 277.

[207] Ibid.

[208] Ibid, pg. 99.

[209] Ibid, pg. 99.

[210] Bill Crow, *Jazz anecdotes*. New York: Oxford University Press, 1990. pg. 189.

[211] James Critchlow, "Public Diplomacy during the Cold War: The Record and Its Implications," *Journal of Cold War Studies* 6.1 (2004): pg. 77.

[212] Arthur Kavaler, "State Department Opens New Service Next Week," *The New York Times*. 9 February 1947, pg. X11.

[213] Drew Middleton, "Russians Discuss U.S. Broadcasts In Stores, Shops, and Other Places," *The New York Times*. 28 March 1947, pg. 6.

[214] James Critchlow, "Public Diplomacy during the Cold War: The Record and Its Implications," *Journal of Cold War Studies* 6.1 (2004): pg. 81.

[215] James Critchlow, "Public Diplomacy during the Cold War: The Record and Its Implications," *Journal of Cold War Studies* 6.1 (2004): pg. 79.

[216] Robert McG Thomas Jr., "Willis Conover Is Dead at 75; Aimed Jazz at the Soviet Bloc." In *The New York Times*. May 19, 1996. pg. 135.

[217] Felix Belair Jr., "United States Has Secret Sonic Weapon—Jazz," *The New York Times*. 6 November 1950 pg. 3.

[218] Welles Hangen, "Soviet Finds Jazz Is A Acceptable Art," *The New York Times*. 8 January 1955, pg. 1.

[219] Ibid.

[220] Ibid.

[221] C. L. Sulzberger, "Restrictions on U.S. Press Growing in Soviet Sphere," *The New York Times*. 3 November 1947, pg. 8.

[222] "'Voice' Is Reported Upsetting Kremlin," *The New York Times*. 28 May 16, pg. 109.

[223] Penny M Von Eschen, *Satchmo Blows Up the World: Jazz Ambassadors Play the Cold War*. Harvard University Press, 2004, pg. 6

[224] Cited in Ibid, pg. 12.

[225] "Gillespie Starts Tour Today," *The New York Times*. 23 March 1956. pg. 26.

[226] Cited in Penny M. Von Eschen, *Satchmo Blows Up the World: Jazz Ambassadors Play the Cold War*. Harvard University Press, 2004, pg. 28.

[227] Ibid, pg. 34.

[228] Cited in Penny M. Von Eschen, *Satchmo Blows Up the World: Jazz Ambassadors Play the Cold War*. Harvard University Press, 2004, pg. 251.

[229] John Forham, "Dizzy for president!" *The Guardian*. 20 October 2004. <http://www.guardian.co.uk/arts/features/story/0,11710,1331548,00.html>

[230] Cited in Penny M. Von Eschen, *Satchmo Blows Up the World: Jazz Ambassadors Play the Cold War*. Harvard University Press, 2004, pg. 131.

[231] Nan Robertson, "Duke Ellington, 70, Honored at White house," *The New York Times*. 30

April 1969, pg. 1.

[232] Bill Crow, *Jazz anecdotes*. New York: Oxford University Press, 1990. pg. 149.

[233] Alan Rich, "Benny Goodman To Tour In Soviet," *The New York Times*. 9 March 1962, Pg. 2.

[234] Ibid.

[235] Penny M. Von Eschen, *Satchmo Blows Up the World: Jazz Ambassadors Play the Cold War*. Harvard University Press, 2004, pg. 106.

[236] "Soviet Blessing Goes to Goodman," *The New York Times*. 3 June 1962, pg. 13.

[237] Theodore Shabad, "Russians Greet Benny Goodman," *The New York Times*. 29 May 1962, pg. 20.

[238] "UNT presents honorary degree to King of Thailand in March ceremony," 4 July 2004. <http://www.unt.edu/inhouse/april22004/thailandannounce.htm>

[239] Linda Martin and Kerry Segrave, *Anti-Rock: The Opposition to Rock 'n' Roll*. Da Capo Press, 1993.

[240] Martha Bayles, *Hole in our Soul: The Loss of Beauty & Meaning in American Popular Music*, University of Chicago, 1994. pg. 197.

[241] Michael Mandelbaum, *Democracy's Good Name: The Rise and Risks of the World's Most Popular Form of Government*, Public Affairs, 2007. pg. 69-70.

[242] Ibid, pg. 71.

[243] S. Frederick Starr, *Red & Hot: The Fate of Jazz in the Soviet Union*. Limelight Editions, pg. 20.

[244] Cited in Michael Mandelbaum, *Democracy's Good Name: The Rise and Risks of the World's Most Popular Form of Government*, Public Affairs, 2007. pg. 109.

[245] Michael Mandelbaum, *Democracy's Good Name: The Rise and Risks of the World's Most Popular Form of Government*, Public Affairs, 2007. pg. 33.

[246] "Sam Wooding and His Orchestra," 2 May 2005. <http://www.redhotjazz.com/woodingo.html>

[247] "Thomas 'Tommy' Ladnier (1900-1939)," 2 May 2005 <http://www.redhotjazz.com/Ladnier.html>

[248] S. Frederick Starr, *Red & Hot: The Fate of Jazz in the Soviet Union*. Limelight Editions, 2004. pg. 6

[249] Ibid, pg 70.

[250] Ibid, pg 72.

[251] "Joseph Schillinger (1895-1943)" 2 May 2005 <http://archivesofamericanart.si.edu/exhibits/piano/schillinger.htm>

252 Nicolas Slominsky, *A Think or Two About Music.* 2 May 2005 <http://www.anecdotage.com/index.php?aid=1014>

253 "Maxim Gorky," 2 May 2005. <http://www.imagi-nation.com/moonstruck/clsc73.html>

254 "Maxim Gorky," 2 May 2005 <http://www.spartacus.schoolnet.co.uk/RUSgorky.htm>

255 S. Frederick Starr, *Red & Hot: The Fate of Jazz in the Soviet Union.* Limelight Editions, 2004. pg. 93

256 Bruce Wilson, "Ukrainians refuse to accept Kremlin's man after rigged election Flashback to the Cold War" in *The Advertiser.* 27 Novem ber 2004.

257 "Soviet Now Bans Phonograph Jazz Records; Calls Our Music 'Bourgeois Music'" *The New York Times.* 9 January 1927, pg. 6.

258 "Jazz Gains in Popularity as Soviet Lifts Ban; Modern Dances Frowned On as Bourgeois," in *The New York Times.* 17 May 1933. pg. 15.

259 Ibid.

260 S. Frederick Starr, *Red & Hot: The Fate of Jazz in the Soviet Union.* Limelight Editions, 2004. pg. 109

261 "Killing in Soviet Held Aid to Stalin" *The New York Times.* 11 July 1937. pg. 15.

262 "Abroad." *The New York Times.* 25 August 1946. pg. 75.

263 "Emigré's Memories: Leo Feigin on Soviet jazz, freedom and Willis Conover" 2 May 20005 <http://www.jazzhouse.org/library/index.php3?read= ripmaster1>

264 "Americans Abroad Celebrate Fourth." *The New York Times.* 5 July 1950, pg. 15.

265 "Jazz Bootlegged All Over Russia." *The New York Times.* 23 October 1953. pg. 10.

266 "Soviet Sweetens Tone on Some Types of Jazz." *The New York Times.* 19 March 1955. pg. 17.

267 "Jazz Bootlegged All Over Russia." *The New York Times.* 23 October 1955, pg. 17

268 Ibid.

269 Leon Steinmetz. "The Four Soviet Cultures." In *National Review;* 23 October 1987, Vol. 39 Issue 20, p32, 4p.

270 S. Frederick Starr, *Red & Hot: The Fate of Jazz in the Soviet Union.* Limelight Editions, 2004, pg. 300.

271 Alex Kan, "Golden Years of Soviet Jazz: A Brief History of New Improvised Music in Russia." 2 May 2005 <http://www.jazz.ru/eng/history/default.htm>

272 Ibid.

273 "Soviets Arts Trace Political Pattern." *The New York Times.* 10 February 1948. pg. 12.

274 Aleksandr Solzhenitsyn, "Misconceptions about Russia are a threat to America." In *Foreign Affairs*; Spring 80, Vol.

275 "Shakespeare As Kultur." *The New York Times*. 15 May 1921. pg. 26

276 Ibid.

277 "Dadaism" *Florida Holocaust Museum*. 15 August 2007. <http://www.flholocaustmuseum. org/history_wing/thirdreich/weimar_dadaism.cfm>

278 Carole Kew, "From Weimar Movement Choir to Nazi Community Dance: The Rise and Fall of Rudolf Laban's Festkultur." Dance Research, 0264-2875, December 1, 1999, Vol.17, Issue 2

279 Ibid.

280 Ibid.

281 Ibid.

282 Friedrich Nietzche, *The Birth of Tragedy* (originally published 1872; this ed. tr. Shaun Whiteside; ed. Michael Tanner) London: Penguin Books. Pg. 18.

283 Art Napoleon, "A Pioneer Looks Back: Sam Wooding 1967," *Storyville*. 10 (Apr. – May 1967): 37.

284 Susan Cook, "Jazz as Deliverance: The Reception and Institution of American Jazz during the Weimar Republic." In *American Music*. Volume 7, No. 1, Special Jazz Issue. Spring, 1989. pg. 31.

285 Michael Kater, *Different Drummers: Jazz in the Culture of Nazi Germany*. Oxford University Press, 1992. pg. 82.

286 "Swing is the thing in Germany," *The New York Times*. 14 November 1937, pg. 95.

287 Michael Kater, *Different Drummers: Jazz in the Culture of Nazi Germany*. Oxford University Press, 1992, pg. 14.

288 Peter Jelavick, "If Only the Kaiser Had Danced Jazz…Parting the Curtains of Berlin's Legendary Stages." *German Life*. July 31, 1994. Volume 1, Issue 1, pg. 26.

289 Susan Cook, "Jazz as Deliverance: The Reception and Institution of American Jazz during the Weimar Republic." In *American Music*. Volume 7, No. 1, Special Jazz Issue. Spring, 1989. pg. 36.

290 Ibid, pg. 40.

291 Ibid, pg. 41.

292 Michael Kater, *Different Drummers: Jazz in the Culture of Nazi Germany*. Oxford University Press, 1992, pg, 17.

293 Peter Jelavick, "If Only the Kaiser Had Danced Jazz…Parting the Curtains of Berlin's Legendary Stages." *German Life*. July 31, 1994. Volume 1, Issue 1, pg. 26.

[294] Ibid.

[295] Michael Kater, *Different Drummers: Jazz in the Culture of Nazi Germany*. Oxford University Press, 1992. pg. 5.

[296] William Manchester, *The Last Lion: Winston Spencer Churchill: Alone, 1932-1940*. Delta, 1989. pg. 55.

[297] Jennifer Fay, "That's Jazz Made in Germany!": Hallo, Fraulein! and the Limits of Democratic Pedagogy." In *Cinema Journal* - 44, Number 1, Fall 2004, pg. 6.

[298] "Eugenics Bureau to Advise Berlin Couples on Marriage." *The New York Times*. May 29, 1926. pg. 17.

[299] Walter Laqueur, "Weimar – The left wing intellectuals," in *Weimar, a Cultural History, 1918-1933*, London: Weidenfeld and Nicolson, 1974.

[300] Carole Kew, "From Weimar Movement Choir to Nazi Community Dance: The Rise and Fall of Rudolf Laban's Festkultur." Dance Research, 0264-2875, December 1, 1999, Vol. 17, Issue 2

[301] Jacques Attali, *Noise: The Political Economy of Music*, University of Minnesota Press, 1985. pg. 87.

[302] Michael Kater, *Different Drummers: Jazz in the Culture of Nazi Germany*. Oxford University Press, 1992. pg. 25.

[303] Michael Kater, "Forbidden Fruit? Jazz in the Third Reich" in *The American Historical Review*, Volume 94, No. 1 (Feb., 1989).

[304] Edward Rosthstein, "Is Music Ever Mute On Politics?" *The New York Times*. June 13, 1993. pg. 74.

[305] Phil Daoust, "Out & about: Jazz: Swingtime for Hitler." *The Guardian*. October 27, 2004, pg. G2.

[306] Ibid.

[307] Michael Kater, *Different Drummers: Jazz in the Culture of Nazi Germany*. Oxford University Press, 1992. pg. 31.

[308] "Reich Admits Saxophone" *The New York Times*. 4 August 1935. pg 22.

[309] Michael Kimmelman, "The Lure of Fordism, Jazz and 'Americanismus'" *The New York Times*. 11 February 1990. pg. H37.

[310] Michael Kater, "Forbidden Fruit? Jazz in the Third Reich" in *The American Historical Review*, Volume 94, No. 1 (Feb., 1989), pg. 13.

[311] Charles A Beard, "Education Under the Nazis." In *Foreign Affairs*. New York: April 1936, Volume 15, Iss. 0000003, pg. 440.

[312] Michael Kater, *Different Drummers: Jazz in the Culture of Nazi Germany*. Oxford University Press, 1992. pg. 41.

[313] Michael Kater, "Forbidden Fruit? Jazz in the Third Reich" in *The American Historical Review*, Volume 94, No. 1 (Feb., 1989), pg. 16.

[314] Michael Kater, *Different Drummers: Jazz in the Culture of Nazi Germany*. Oxford University Press, 1992. pg. 49.

[315] "Swing is the thing in Germany," *The New York Times*. 14 November 1937. pg. 95.

[316] Ibid.

[317] Michael Kater, "Forbidden Fruit? Jazz in the Third Reich" in *The American Historical Review*, Volume 94, No. 1 (Feb., 1989), pg. 30.

[318] Michael Kater, *Different Drummers: Jazz in the Culture of Nazi Germany*. Oxford University Press, 1992. pg. 120.

[319] Ibid, pg. 126.

[320] Jack Fleisher, "Nazi Propaganda Put On Defensive." *The New York Times*. 19 May 1942. pg. 5.

[321] Ibid.

[322] William L Shirer, "The Propaganda Front." *The Washington Post*. 12 July 1942. pg. B7.

[323] Herbert Mitgang, "In This Air War, the Nazis Fired Words and Music." *The New York Times*. 8 September 1997, pg. C17.

[324] "You're The Top" 2 May 2005. <http://www.assumption.edu/dept/history/HI14Net/Porterlyrics.html>

[325] Herbert Mitgang, "In This Air War, the Nazis Fired Words and Music." *The New York Times*. 8 September 1997, pg. C17.

[326] "Swing Sessions with Bill Gottlieb." *The Washington Post*. August 1940. pg. A7.

[327] "President's Call to Youth to Meet Problems of the War and the Future." *The New York Times*. 4 September 1942. pg. 4.

[328] Ibid, pg. 4.

[329] Anton Tantner, "Jazz Youth Subcultures in Nazi Europe." In: ISHA Journal. Publication Series of the International Students of History Association. February 1994. [=ABELS, Bodien/RHIJN, Carine van (ed.): History of Daily Life. Papers of the fifth Isha Conference Utrecht, TheNetherlands, April 4–8, 1994. Atalanta: Houten, 1994.] S. 22-23.

[330] Ibid, pg. 24.

[331] Ibid, pg. 26.

[332] Ibid, pg. 26.

[333] Ibid, pg. 27.

334 Michael Kater, "Forbidden Fruit? Jazz in the Third Reich" in *The American Historical Review*, Volume 94, No. 1 (Feb., 1989), pg. 32.

335 "Glen Miller" 2 May 2005 <http://www.icebergradio.com/artist/491/glenn_miller.html>

336 Herbert Mitgang. "In This Air War, the Nazis Fired Words and Music." *The New York Times.* 8 September 1997, pg. C17.

337 Michael J. Budds, *Jazz and the Germans: Essays on the Influence of "Hot" American Idioms on 20th-Century German Music*, Michael J. Budds (Hillsdale, NY: Pendragon Press, 2002). pg. 2.

338 Jennifer Fay, "That's Jazz Made in Germany!": Hallo, Fraulein! and the Limits of Democratic Pedagogy." In *Cinema Journal* - 44, Number 1, Fall 2004, pg. 4.

339 Ibid, pg. 5.

340 Ibid, pg. 8

341 William A. Shack, *Harlem in Montmartre: A Paris Jazz Story between the Great Wars.* University of California Press, 2001. pg. 68.

342 Miles Davis, "*The Autobiography*," Simon & Schuster, 1989. pg. 128.

343 Cited in Michael Mandelbaum, *Democracy's Good Name: The Rise and Risks of the World's Most Popular Form of Government*, Public Affairs, 2007. pg. 11.

344 Thomas Paine, *Rights of Man*. Penguin Classics, 1984. pg.118.

345 Cornell West, *Democracy Matters*. Penguin, 2004. pg. 203.

346 Cynthia Verba. *Music and the French Enlightenment: Reconstruction of a Dialogue 1750-1764.* Oxford University Press, 1993. pg. 1.

347 Ibid, pg. 16.

348 Ibid, pg. 14.

349 James A. Fulcher, *French Cultural Politics & Music: From the Dreyfus Affair to the First World War*. Oxford University Press, 1999. pg. 4.

350 Norman Mailer, "The White Negro: Spiritual Reflections on the Hipster" City Light Books, 1957.

351 Jeffrey H. Jackson, *Making Jazz French: Music and Modern Life in Interwar Paris*. Duke University Press, 2003. pg. 26.

352 Thomas Morgan, *James Reese Europe*, 1992. 4 April 2005, <http://www.jass.com/Others/europe.html>.

353 William A. Shack, *Harlem in Montmartre: A Paris Jazz Story between the Great Wars.* University of California Press, 2001. pg. 17.

354 "Colored Troops In Today: Part of Old 15th Infantry Should Reach Pier This Morning," *The New York Times.* 9 February 1919. pg. 9.

355 "Clef Club In Lively Music," *The New York Times*. 16 February 1919. pg. 18.

356 Ibid, pg. 19.

357 Anatol Rapoport, "Introduction by Anatol Rapoport," in *On War*, (Penguin, 1982), pg. 20.

358 Cited in Jeffrey H. Jackson, *Making Jazz French: Music and Modern Life in Interwar Paris*. Duke University Press, 2003. pg. 16.

359 "Clef Club In Lively Music," *The New York Times*. 16 February 1919. pg. 19.

360 Thomas Morgan, *James Reese Europe*, 1992. 4 April 2005, <http://www.jass.com/Others/europe.html>.

361 Floyd Levin, "Jim Europe's 369th Infantry 'Hellfighters' Band." 15 April 2005 < http://www.redhotjazz.com/hellfighters.html>

362 Thomas Morgan, *James Reese Europe*, 1992. 4 April 2005, <http://www.jass.com/Others/europe.html>.

363 William A. Shack, *Harlem in Montmartre: A Paris Jazz Story between the Great Wars*. University of California Press, 2001. pg. 20.

364 Timothy R. Mangin, "Notes on Jazz in Senegal," in (eds) Robert G. O'Meally, Brent Hayes Edwards, & Farah Jamine Griffin, *Uptown Conversation: The New Jazz Studies*, Columbia University Press, 2004. pg. 228.

365 Jeffrey H. Jackson, *Making Jazz French: Music and Modern Life in Interwar Paris*. Duke University Press, 2003. pg. 29.

366 "Origin of the Saxophone," *The New York Times*. 16 December 1928. pg. X11.

367 Jeffrey H. Jackson, *Making Jazz French: Music and Modern Life in Interwar Paris*. Duke University Press, 2003. pg. 31.

368 "Says Jazz Originated in Old French Music," *The New York Times*. March 25, 1928. pg. 28.

369 Cited in Jeffrey H. Jackson, *Making Jazz French: Music and Modern Life in Interwar Paris*. Duke University Press, 20090. pg. H37

370 Michael Nowlin, "Making Sense of the American 1920s." *Studies in the Novel*: Spring 2002, Vol. 34 Issue 1, p. 81

371 Jeffrey H. Jackson, *Making Jazz French: Music and Modern Life in Interwar Paris*. Duke University Press, 2003. pg. 45.

372 Michael Mandelbaum, *Democracy's Good Name: The Rise and Risks of the World's Most Popular Form of Government*, Public Affairs, 2007. pg. 99.

373 James M. Harding, "Adorno, Ellison, and the Critique of Jazz," in *Cultural Critique*, No. 31. The Politics of Systems and Environments, Part II (Autumn, 1995) pg. 129.

374 Charles Egert. "Love and Homicide in the Jazz Age novel" in *Journal of Narrative Theory*. *Journal of Narrative Theory* 34.1 (2004), pg. 54-87.

[375] Ibid.

[376] Ryan Jerving, "Jazz Language and Ethic Novelty." In *Modernism/modernity*. 10.2 (2003) pg. 243.

[377] Ibid, pg. 251.

[378] Bill Crow, *Jazz anecdotes*. New York: Oxford University Press, 1990. pg. 5.

[379] Ryan Jerving, "Jazz Language and Ethic Novelty." In *Modernism/modernity*. 10.2 (2003), pg. 252.

[380] William A. Shack, *Harlem in Montmartre: A Paris Jazz Story between the Great Wars*. University of California Press, 2001. pg. 27.

[381] Ibid, 29.

[382] Bill Moody, *The Jazz Exiles: American Musicians Abroad*. University of Nevada Press: 1993, pg. 21.

[383] William A. Shack, *Harlem in Montmartre: A Paris Jazz Story between the Great Wars*. University of California Press, 2001. pg. 33.

[384] "American Nights In Paris." *The New York Times*. 6 May 1928. pg. 83.

[385] Ibid.

[386] Elaine Brody, *Paris The Musical Kaleidoscope 1870-1925*. New York: George Braziller, 1987. pg. 243.

[387] William A. Shack, *Harlem in Montmartre: A Paris Jazz Story between the Great Wars*. University of California Press, 2001. pg. 36.

[388] Ibid, 38.

[389] Cited in Elaine Brody, *Paris The Musical Kaleidoscope 1870-1925*. New York: George Braziller, 1987. Pg. 243.

[390] "Montparnasse" Lockergnome Encyclopedia. 28 April 2005 <http://www.uga.edu/profile/pride.html>

[391] William A. Shack, *Harlem in Montmartre: A Paris Jazz Story between the Great Wars*. University of California Press, 2001. pg. 39.

[392] Cited in Jeffrey H. Jackson, *Making Jazz French: Music and Modern Life in Interwar Paris*. Duke University Press, 2003. pg. 62.

[393] "Montparnasse Jazz Is Stilled by Police," *The New York Times*. 20 November 13. pg. 32.

[394] Cited in Ibid, pg. 37.

[395] Cited in Ibid., pg. 39.

[396] "Montmartre Clubs Close." *The New York Times*. 11 January1927. pg. 11.

[397] Cited in William A. Shack, *Harlem in Montmartre: A Paris Jazz Story between the Great Wars.* University of California Press, 2001. pg. 77.

[398] Ibid, pg. 78

[399] William Manchester, *The Last Lion: Winston Spencer Churchill: Alone, 1932-1940.* Delta, 1989. pg. 52.

[400] William A. Shack, *Harlem in Montmartre: A Paris Jazz Story between the Great Wars.* University of California Press, 2001. pg. 80.

[401] John D. Pelzer, "Django, Jazz and the Nazis in Paris." *History Today.* Oct2001, Vol. 51 Issue 10, p33, 7 p, 2c, 10bw

[402] "Quintette of the Hot Club of France." 28 April 2005 <http://www.redhotjazz.com/hotclubfrance.html>

[403] John D. Pelzer, "Django, Jazz and the Nazis in Paris." *History Today.* Oct2001, Vol. 51 Issue 10, p33, 7 p, 2c, 10bw

[404] Joseph Dinkins, "Django Reinhardt," <http://www.redhotjazz.com/django.html>

[405] Jeffrey H. Jackson, "Music-Halls and the Assimilation of Jazz in the 1920s Paris." *Journal of Popular Culture.* Fall 2000, Vol. 34 Issue 2, p69,

[406] Ibid.

[407] Gerald C. Hynes, *A Biographical Sketch of W.E.B. DuBois.* 18 April 2005. <http://www.duboislc.org/html/DuBoisBio.html>

[408] Fredrick Cunliffe-Owen. C. B. E., "Black Labor New Problem in France." *The New York Times.* 14 September 1924. pg. E7.

[409] Cited in Andy Fry, "Beyond Le Boeuf: Interdisciplinary Rereadings of Jazz in France," *Journal of the Royal Music Association* 128: 139.

[410] William A. Shack, *Harlem in Montmartre: A Paris Jazz Story between the Great Wars.* University of California Press, 2001. pg. 24. pg. E7.

[411] Jeffrey H. Jackson, *Making Jazz French: Music and Modern Life in Interwar Paris.* Duke University Press, 2001, pg. 75.

[412] Ibid.

[413] Jeffrey H. Jackson, *Making Jazz French: Music and Modern Life in Interwar Paris.* Duke University Press, 2003. pg. 96.

[414] "Musical Life in France." *The New York Times,* 5 January 1941. pg. X6.

[415] William A. Shack, *Harlem in Montmartre: A Paris Jazz Story between the Great Wars.* University of California Press, 2001. pg. 103.

[416] Cited in Andy Fry, "Beyond Le Boeuf: Interdisciplinary Rereadings of Jazz in France," *Journal of the Royal Music Association* 128: 140.

417 G. H. Archambault, "France To Mourn." *The New York Times*, 25 June 1940. pg. 1.

418 "Nazis Order Blackout in Paris," *The New York Times*, 13 July 1941. pg. 9.

419 William A. Shack, *Harlem in Montmartre: A Paris Jazz Story between the Great Wars*. University of California Press, 2001 . pg. 106.

420 John D. Pelzer, "Django, Jazz and the Nazis in Paris." *History Today*. Oct 2001, Vol. 51 Issue 10, p33, 7 p, 2c, 10bw

421 Ibid.

422 Cited in Ibid.

423 Ibid.

424 Ibid.

425 William A. Shack, *Harlem in Montmartre: A Paris Jazz Story between the Great Wars*. University of California Press, 2001. pg. 117.

426 John D. Pelzer, "Django, Jazz and the Nazis in Paris." *History Today*. Oct 2001, Vol. 51 Issue 10, p33, 7 p, 2c, 10bw

427 William A. Shack, *Harlem in Montmartre: A Paris Jazz Story between the Great Wars*. University of California Press, 2001. pg. 117.

428 Bill Crow, *Jazz anecdotes*. New York: Oxford University Press, 1990. pg. 183.

429 Bill Moody, *The Jazz Exiles: American Musicians Abroad*. University of Nevada Press: 19

430 Cited in David Strauss, *American Quarterly*. John Hopkins University Press, 1965 Vol. 3, No. 3, pg. 585.

431 Miles Davis, "*The Autobiography*," Simon & Schuster, 1989. pg. 129.

432 David Ake, "Negotiating National Identity Among American Jazz Musicians in Paris," *Journal of Musicological Research* 23, 2004: 168.

433 Ibid, pg. 170.

434 "Singer Brings a Modern Sound to Chinese Jazz," *NPR*. 16 August 2007. <http://www.npr.org/templates/story/story.php?storyId=12808843>

435 Penny M. Von Eschen, "The Real Ambassadors," in (eds) Robert G. O'Meally, Brent Hayes Edwards, & Farah Jamine Griffin, *Uptown Conversation: The New Jazz Studies*, Columbia University Press, 2004. pg. 393-395

436 Susannah Lockwood Smith, "From Peasants to Professionals: The Socialist-Realist Transformation of a Russian Folk Choir." *Kritika: Explorations in Russian and Eurasian History-* Volume 3, Number 3, Summer 2002, pg. 408.

437 Lee Harris, "The Future of Tradition" in *Policy Review*. June/July 2005. Number 131. <http://www.policyreview.org/jun05/harris.html>

[438] Ibid.

[439] Penny M. Von Eschen, "The Real Ambassadors," in (eds) Robert G. O'Meally, Brent Hayes Edwards, & Farah Jamine Griffin, *Uptown Conversation: The New Jazz Studies*, Columbia University Press, 2004. pg. 192.

[440] Marilyn Berlin Snell, "Charlie Parker Didn't Give a Damn." in *NPQ: New Perspectives Quarterly*. Summer 1991, Vol. 848. pg. 2.

[441] Ralph Ellison, *Living With Music: Ralph Ellison's Jazz Writings*. Modern Library, 2009. pg. 201.

[442] Joanna Overing, "The Role of Myth: An Anthropological Perspective, or: 'The Reality of the Really Made-Up'" in *Myths & Nationhood* eds Geoffrey Hosking and George Schöpflin. Routledge, 11. pg. 107.

[443] Cited in W. B. Yeats, *Autobiographies* eds William H. O'Donnell and Douglas N. Archibald. Scribner, 1999, pg. 281.

[444] Stephen Hawking, *A Brief History of Time: From the Big Bang to Black Holes*. Bantam, 1988. pg. 55. 997. pg. 2.

[445] S. H. Hooke, "Myth, Ritual and History" in *Folklore*, Folklore Entreprises, 1939. pg. 138.

[446] Percy S. Cohen, "Theories of Myth," in *Man*. Royal Anthropological Institute of Great Britain and Ireland. pg. 337.

[447] Joanna Overing, "The Role of Myth: An Anthropological Perspective, or: 'The Reality of the Really Made-Up'" in *Myths & Nationhood* eds Geoffrey Hosking and George Schöpflin. Routledge, 1997. pg. 5.

[448] Joanna Overing, "The Role of Myth: An Anthropological Perspective, or: 'The Reality of the Really Made-Up'" in *Myths & Nationhood* eds Geoffrey Hosking and George Schöpflin. Routledge, 1997. pg. 4.

[449] Joseph Campbell, *The Power of Myth*. Anchor, 1988. pg. 2.

[450] Ibid.

[451] "Centrifugal forces," *The Economist*. 16 July 2005. pg. 4.

[452] James Oliver Robertson, *American Myth, American Reality*. Hill & Wang: New York, 1980. pg. xv.

[453] Ibid, pg. xvii.

[454] Deepak Chopra, *The Spontaneous Fulfillment of Desire*. Three Rivers Press, 2004. pg. 149.

[455] Lee Harris, "The Future of Tradition" in *Policy Review*. June/July 2005. Number 131. <http://www.policyreview.org/jun05/harris.html>

[456] Lee Harris, "The Future of Tradition" in *Policy Review*. June/July 2005. Number 131. <http://www.policyreview.org/jun05/harris.html>

[457] Joseph Campbell, *The Power of Myth*. Anchor, 1988. pg. xiii.

[458] "Centrifugal forces," *The Economist*. 16 July 2005. pg. 4.

[459] George Schöpflin, "The Functions of Myth and a Taxonomy of Myths," in *Myths & Nationhood* eds Geoffrey Hosking and George Schöpflin. Routledge, 1997, pg. 29.

[460] Mark A. Gabriel, *Jesus and Muhammad: Profound Differences and Surprising Similarities*. Charisma House, 2004. pg. 46.

[461] Ibid, pg. 49.

[462] Joseph Campbell, *The Power of Myth*. Anchor, 1988. pg. 31.

[463] James Oliver Robertson, *American Myth, American Reality*. Hill & Wang: New York, 1980. pg. 33.

[464] Joseph Campbell, *The Power of Myth*. Anchor, 1988. pg. 32.

[465] Thomas J. Schlereth, "Columbia, Columbus, and Columbianism," in *The Journal of American History*. Organization of American Historians, 1992. pg. 939.

[466] Ibid, pg. 941.

[467] Ibid, pg. 952.

[468] "Mister Christopher Columbus" 25 July 2005. <http://www.niehs.nih.gov/kids/lyrics/columbus.htm >

[469] James Oliver Robertson, *American Myth, American Reality*. Hill & Wang: New York, 1980. pg. 14.

[470] Ibid, pg. 16.

[471] Ibid, pg. 57.

[472] Eric Nisenson, *Ascension: John Coltrane And His Quest*. St. Martin's Press, 1993. pg.186

[473] Neil Leonard, *Jazz: myth and religion*. New York: Oxford University Press, 1987. pg. 128.

[474] "Wild ones," *The Guardian*. 11 December 2004. <http://www.guardian.co.uk/arts/features/story/0,11710,1370298,00.html>

[475] Joanna Overing, "The Role of Myth: An Anthropological Perspective, or: 'The Reality of the Really Made-Up'" in *Myths & Nationhood* eds Geoffrey Hosking and George Schöpflin. Routledge, 1997. pg. 7.

[476] Ibid, pg. 9.

[477] George Schöpflin, "The Functions of Myth and a Taxonomy of Myths," in *Myths & Nationhood* eds Geoffrey Hosking and George Schöpflin. Routledge, 1997, pg. 28-34.

[478] Jacob Slichter, "The Price of Fame," *The New York Times*. 29 July 2005. pg. A21.

[479] Kay S. Hymowitz, "The Trash Princess," in *City-Journal*. <http://www.city-journal.org/html/16_4_urbanities-paris_hilton.html>

[480] Brooks Boliek, "Senators fight hidden sex in 'Grand Theft Auto'"*Reuters*. 15 July 2005. <http://today.reuters.com/News/newsArticle.aspx?type=entertainmentNews&storyID= 2005-07-15T073501Z_01_N15610958_RTRIDST_0_ENTERTAINMENT-MEDIA-SEX-DC.XML>

[481] Wynton Marsalis, *To a Young Jazz Musician: Letters from the Road*. Random House, 2004. pg. 84.

[482] Ibid.

[483] Joseph Campbell, *The Power of Myth*. Anchor, 1988. pg. 9.

[484] Ibid.

[485] Joseph Campbell, *The Power of Myth*. Anchor, 1988. pg. 10.

[486] Eric Nisenson, *Ascension: John Coltrane And His Quest*. St. Martin's Press, 1993. pg. 207.

[487] Miles Davis, "*The Autobiography*," Simon & Schuster, 1989. pg. 212.

[488] Jacques Attali, *Noise: The Political Economy of Music*, University of Minnesota Press, 1985. pg. 43.

[489] Martha Bayles, *Hole in our Soul: The Loss of Beauty & Meaning in American Popular Music*, University of Chicago, 1994. pg. 336.

[490] Wynton Marsalis, *To a Young Jazz Musician: Letters from the Road*. Random House, 2004. pg. 90.

[491] Ted Gioia, *Work Songs*. Duke University Press, 2006. pg. 6.

[492] André Malraux, *Picasso's Mask*. Holt, Rinehart and Wilson, 1974. pg. 58.

[493] Ibid.

[494] André Malraux, *Picasso's Mask*. Holt, Rinehart and Wilson, 1974. pg. 69.

[495] Joseph Campbell, *The Power of Myth*. Anchor, 1988. pg. 25.

[496] Olly Wilson, "Black Music as an Art Form" in Robert G. O'Meally, *The Jazz Cadence of American Culture*. Columbia University Press, 1998: pg. 87

[497] James Joyce, *A Portrait of the Artist as a Young Man*, Viking: New York. pg. 213

[498] Kahlil Gibran, *The Prophet*. Knopf, 1923. pg. 76.

[499] Olly Wilson, "Black Music as an Art Form" in Robert G. O'Meally, *The Jazz Cadence of American Culture*. Columbia University Press, 1998: pg. 84.

[500] David P. Brown, *Noise Orders: Jazz Improvisation, and Architecture*. University of Minnesota Press, 2006. pg. 1-2.

[501] Jorge Daniel Veneciano, "Louis Armstrong, Bricolage, and the Aesthetics of Swing," in (eds) Robert G. O'Meally, Brent Hayes Edwards, & Farah Jamine Griffin, *Uptown Conversation: The New Jazz Studies*, Columbia University Press, 2004. pg. 256-277.

[502] André Malraux, *Picasso's Mask*. Holt, Rinehart and Wilson, 1974. pg. 28.

[503] Richard Layard, *Happiness: Lessons from a New Science*. Penguin, 2005. pg. 67.

[504] Chris Goddard, *Jazz away from home*. New York: Paddington Press, 1979. pg. 21.

[505] "Jay-Z Lyrics" 29 July 2005. <http://www.azlyrics.com/lyrics/jayz/pussy.html>

[506] Ibid.

[507] Lee Harris, "The Future of Tradition" in *Policy Review*. June/July 2005. Number 131. <http://www.policyreview.org/jun05/harris.html>

[508] Thomas A. Bailey, "The Mythmakers of American History," in Nicolas Cords and Patrick Gerster, *Myth and the American Experience*. New York, Glencoe Press, 1973. pg. 2.

[509] John Gennari, "Jazz Criticism: Its Development and Ideologies," *Black American Literature Forum*, Vol. 25. No. 3. (Autumn, 1991), 449.523.

[510] Albert Murray, *The Omni-Americans: Black Experience and American Culture*. Da Capo, 1970. pg. 7.

[511] Alan Govenar, "Blind Lemon Jefferson: The Myth and the Man." In *Black Music Research Journal*, 2000. pg. 8.

[512] Ibid, pg. 9.

[513] Ibid, pg. 12.

[514] Ibid, pg. 18.

[515] Albert Murray, *Stomping the Blues*. Da Capo, 1976. pg. 45.

[516] Victor Frankl, *Man's Search For Meaning*. Touchstone, 1984. pg. 139.

[517] Nat Hentoff, *Jazz is*. New York: Limelight Editions, 1984, c1976. pg. 18.

[518] Alfred Appel Jr. *Jazz Modernism*. Alfred A. Knopf, 2002. pg. 17.

[519] Victor Frankl, *Man's Search For Meaning*. Touchstone, 1984. pg. 28.

[520] Samuel A. Floyd, *The Power of Black Music*, Oxford University Press. pg. 50.

[521] Victor Frankl, *Man's Search For Meaning*. Touchstone, 1984. pg.59.

[522] Ibid, pg. 75.

[523] Ibid, pg. 123.

[524] P. D. Ouspensky, *In Search of the Miraculous: Fragments of an Unknown Teaching*. Harvest,

2001. pg. 274.

525 Norman Mailer, *The Fight*. Little, Brown & Company, 1975. pg. 54.

526 Ibid, pg. 26.

527 Joseph Campbell, *The Power of Myth*. Anchor, 1988. pg. 81.

528 Kahlil Gibran, *The Prophet*. Knopf, 1923. pg. 29.

529 Al Sharpton, "2004 Democratic National Convention Address" 17 July 2005. <http://www.americanrhetoric.com/speeches/convention2004/alsharpton2004dnc.htm>

530 Langston Hughes, "Let America Be America Again." 17 July 2005. <http://www.poetryconnection.net/poets/Langston_Hughes/2385>

531 P. D. Ouspensky, *In Search of the Miraculous: Fragments of an Unknown Teaching*. Harvest, 2001. pg. 44.

532 Juliet B. Schor, "The Overspent American: Upscaling, Downshifting, And The New Consumer" in CNN.com. 25 June 1998. <http://www.cnn.com/books/beginnings/9806/overspent.americans.cnn/>

533 Ibid.

534 "Middle of the class," *The Economist*. 16 July 2005. pg. 12.

535 George Schöpflin, "The Functions of Myth and a Taxonomy of Myths," in *Myths & Nationhood* eds Geoffrey Hosking and George Schöpflin. Routledge, 1997, pg. 34.

536 Nathan Glazer and Daniel P. Moynihan, "The Myth of the Melting Pot," in Nicolas Cords and Patrick Gerster, *Myth and the American Experience*. New York, Glencoe Press, 1973. pg. 132.

537 Bill Crow, *Jazz anecdotes*. New York: Oxford University Press, 1990. pg. 95.

538 Ralph Ellison, *Living With Music: Ralph Ellison's Jazz Writings*. Modern Library, 2001. pg. 23.

539 Howard Zinn, "The Power and the Glory: Myths of American exceptionalism." in *Boston Review*. < http://bostonreview.net/BR30.3/zinn.html>

540 Wynton Marsalis, *To a Young Jazz Musician: Letters from the Road*. Random House, 2004. pg. 64-65.

541 Bill Crow, *Jazz anecdotes*. New York: Oxford University Press, 1990. pg. 136.

542 Ralph Ellison, *Invisible Man*, Vintage. 1980. pg. xx.

543 Joseph Campbell, *The Power of Myth*. Anchor, 1988. pg. 41.

544 Ibid, pg. 208.

545 Ibid, pg. 159.

546 Bill Crow, *Jazz anecdotes*. New York: Oxford University Press, 1990. pg. 161.

547 "Degrees of separation," *The Economist*. 16 July 2005. pg. 3

548 Ibid.

549 Ibid, pg. 4.

550 Valerie Wilmer, *Jazz People*. Da Capo Press, 1970. pg. 57

551 P. D. Ouspensky, *In Search of the Miraculous: Fragments of an Unknown Teaching*. Harvest, 2001. pg. 117.

552 "Cost of 2004 elections: $4 billion and counting" USA Today. 2 November 2004. <http://www.usatoday.com/news/politicselections/nation/2004-11-02-election-costs_x. htm?POE=NEWISVA>

553 Robert D. Putnam, *Bowling Alone: The Collapse and Revival of American Community*. Simon & Schuster, 2001. pg. 38.

554 "The glue of society," *The Economist*. 16 July 2005. pg. 16.

555 "Motion dismissed," *The Economist*. 16 July 2005. pg. 18.

556 "Motion sustained," *The Economist*. 16 July 2005. pg. 20.

557 Leo Tolstoy, *The Kingdom of God is Within You*. University of Nebraska Press, 1985. pg. 6.

558 Albert Murray, *The Omni-Americans: Black Experience and American Culture*. Da Capo, 1970. pg. 79.

559 Morris P. Fiorina, *Culture War? The Myth of a Polarized America*. Longman, 2004. pg. ix.

560 Ibid, pg. 12.

561 Cindy Simon Rosenthal, "Local Politics: A Different Front in the Culture War?" in *The Forum*: Vol. 3: No. 2, Article 5. 2005. <http://www.bepress.com/forum/vol3/iss2/art5>

562 Albert Murray, *The Omni-Americans: Black Experience and American Culture*. Da Capo, 1970. pg. 22.

563 Leo Tolstoy, *The Kingdom of God is Within You*. University of Nebraska Press, 1985. pg. 365.

564 Eric Nisenson, Blue: The Murder of Jazz, Da Capo Press, 1997. pg. 42.

565 Lawrence Lessig, *The Future of Ideas*. Vintage, 2002. pg. 92.

566 Steven Lukes, "The Meanings of 'Individualism'" in *The Journal of History of Ideas*, 1971. pg. 60.

567 John Harmon McElroy, *American Beliefs: What Keeps a Big Country And a Diverse People United*. Ivan R. Dee, 1999. pg. 102.

568 Stephen Tatum, *Inventing Billy the Kid*. University of New Mexico: 1982. pg. 87.

[569] Ibid, pg. 104.

[570] Ibid, pg. 106.

[571] Joseph Campbell, *The Power of Myth*. Anchor, 1988. pg. 21.

[572] Stephen Tatum, *Inventing Billy the Kid*. University of New Mexico: 1982. pg. 133.

[573] John G. Cawelti, "From Rags to Respectability: Horatio Alger," in Nicolas Cords and Patrick Gerster, *Myth and the American Experience*. New York, Glencoe Press, 1973. pg. 111.

[574] Stanley Crouch, "Blues to be Constitutional: A Long Look at the Wild Wherefores of Our Democratic Lives as Symbolized in the Making of Rhythm and Tune" Robert G. O'Meally, *The Jazz Cadence of American Culture*. Columbia University Press, 1998: pg. 156.

[575] Ibid, pg. 159.

[576] P. D. Ouspensky, *In Search of the Miraculous: Fragments of an Unknown Teaching*. Harvest, 2001. pg. 14.

[577] George Schöpflin, "The Functions of Myth and a Taxonomy of Myths," in *Myths & Nationhood* eds Geoffrey Hosking and George Schöpflin. Routledge, 1997, pg. 31.

[578] Cited in Martha Bayles, *Hole in our Soul: The Loss of Beauty & Meaning in American Popular Music*, University of Chicago, 1994. pg. 122.

[579] Albert Murray, *Stomping the Blues*. Da Capo, 1976. pg. 82.

[580] Eric Nisenson, *Ascension: John Coltrane And His Quest*. St. Martin's Press, 1993. pg. 184.

[581] Constance Rourke, *American Humor: A Study of National Character*. Harcourt, Brace and Company: New York, 1931. pg. 211.

[582] Lisa de Moraes, "Kanye West's Torrent of Criticism, Live on NBC," in *The Washington Post*. 3 September 2005. pg. C01.

[583] Michael Eric Dyson, *Between God and gangsta rap: bearing witness to Black culture*. New York: Oxford Unviersity Press, 1996. pg. 176.

[584] Ibid, pg. 177.

[585] Sid Kirchheimer, "Does Rap Put Teens at Risk?" 2003, WebMD. 13 Sept. 2005, <http://my.webmd.com/content/article/61/68559.htm>

[586] Martha Bayles, *Hole in our Soul: The Loss of Beauty & Meaning in American Popular Music*, University of Chicago, 1994. pg. 342.

[587] Ibid, pg. 352.

[588] Ibid.

[589] Ibid, pg. 353.

[590] Bill Crow, *Jazz anecdotes*. New York: Oxford University Press, 1990. pg. 192.

591 "Sing a song of Spitzer." *The Economist*. 30 July 2005. pg. 54.

592 Richard Thomas Hughes, *Myths to Live By*. University of Illinois Press, 2004. pg. 25-45.

593 Ibid.

594 Richard Thomas Hughes, *Myths to Live By*. University of Illinois Press, 2004. pg. 33.

595 Cited in Richard Thomas Hughes, *Myths to Live By*. University of Illinois Press, 2004. pg. 33.

596 Richard Thomas Hughes, *Myths to Live By*. University of Illinois Press, 2004. pg. 25-45.

597 Ibid.

598 James Oliver Robertson, *American Myth, American Reality*. Hill & Wang: New York, 1980. pg. 105.

599 Albert Murray, *The Omni-Americans: Black Experience and American Culture*. Da Capo, 1970. pg. 36.

600 Kurt Vonnegut, *Man Without a Country*, Seven Stories Press, 2004. pg. 68.

601 Leo Tolstoy, *The Kingdom of God is Within You*. University of Nebraska Press, 1985. pg. 134.

602 Ibid, pg. 10.

603 Kurt Vonnegut, *Man Without a Country*, Seven Stories Press, 2004. pg. 67.

604 Eric Nisenson, *Blue: The Murder of Jazz*, Da Capo Press, 1997. pg. 43.

605 Alexis de Tocqueville, *Democracy in America Volume 1*. New Rochelle, New York: 1966, pg. 238.

606 Lewis Hyde, *Trickster Makes This World*. North Point Press, 1998. pg. 7.

607 Ibid, pg. 7

608 Ibid, pg. 10.

609 Ibid, 19-20.

610 Ibid, pg. 43.

611 Ibid, pg. 54.

612 Ibid, pg. 13.

613 Cited in Cited in Samuel A. Floyd, *The Power of Black Music*, Oxford University Press. pg. 93.

614 Cited in Samuel A. Floyd, *The Power of Black Music*, Oxford University Press. pg. 92.

615 Cited in Samuel A. Floyd, *The Power of Black Music*, Oxford University Press. pg. 95.

616 Lewis Hyde, *Trickster Makes This World*. North Point Press, 1998. pg. 277.

617 "Louis Armstrong Statue Unveiling - July 4, 2000" 19 July 2005. <http://www.satchmo.com/louisarmstrong/statue.html>

618 Jeffrey Taylor, "Louis Armstrong, Earl Hines, and 'Weather Bird'" in *The Music Quarterly*, 1988. pg. 3.

619 "Louis the First," *Time Magazine*. 21 February 1949. <http://www.time.com/time/time100/artists/profile/satchmo_related.html>

620 Gary Giddins, *Satchmo*, Da Capo Press, 1988. pg. xii-xiii.

621 Cited in "Explaining Armstrong" 19 July 2005. <http://xroads.virginia.edu/~ug99/graham/conclusion.html>

622 Gary Giddins, *Satchmo*, Da Capo Press, 1988. pg. 8.

623 Bill Crow, *Jazz anecdotes*. New York: Oxford University Press, 1990. pg. 209.

624 Gary Tomlinson, "Cultural Dialogues and Jazz: A White Historian Signifies," *Black Music Journal*, Vol. 11, No. 2, 1991.pp. 229-264.

625 "Explaining Armstrong" 19 July 2005. <http://xroads.virginia.edu/~ug99/graham/conclusion.html>

626 Lewis Hyde, *Trickster Makes This World*. North Point Press, 1998. pg. 266.

627 Ibid, pg. 267.

628 Ibid.

629 Ibid, pg. 49.

630 Leo Tolstoy, *The Kingdom of God is Within You*. University of Nebraska Press, 1985. pg. 45.

631 Cited in Mark A. Gabriel, *Jesus and Muhammad: Profound Differences and Surprising Similarities*. Charisma House, 2004. pg. 93.

632 Ibid, pg. 252.

633 Rabindranath Tagore, *The Religion of Man*. Rupa & Co. pg. 114.

634 Jacques Attali, *Noise: The Political Economy of Music*, University of Minnesota Press, 1985. pg. 141.

635 Ted Gioia, *Work Songs*. Duke University Press, 2006. pg. 7.

636 Jacques Attali, *Noise: The Political Economy of Music*, University of Minnesota Press, 1985. pg. 187.

637 "The Sound of Music," *Boston Globe*. 23 August 2007. <http://www.boston.com/news/globe/editorial_opinion/editorials/articles/2007/08/23/the_sound_of_music_and_arts/>

[638] Ibid.

[639] Creative Industries 2005: Congressional Report," Americans for the Arts, March 2005. 1.

[640] Ellen Winner and Lois Hetland, "Art for our sake," *The Boston Globe*. 2 September 2007.

[641] Ibid.

[642] Arthur Schlesinger, Jr. "America, the Arts, and the Future: The First Nancy Hanks Lecture on the Arts and Public Policy," in David B. Pankratz and Valerie B. Morris, *The Future of Arts: Public Policy and Arts Research*. Praeger, 1990. pg. 4.

[643] Ibid, pg. 5.

[644] Ibid, pg. 96.

[645] William Manchester, *The Last Lion: Winston Spencer Churchill: Alone, 1932-1940*. Delta, 1989. pg. 64.

[646] W. McNeil Lowry, *The Arts: Public policy in the United States*. Prentice-Hall, 1984. pg. 95.

[647] Alex Ross, "The Well-Tempered Web," *The New Yorker*, 22 October 2007. < http://www.newyorker.com/reporting/2007/10/22/071022fa_fact_ross?currentPage=all?>

[648] "Creative Industries 2005: Congressional Report," Americans for the Arts, March 2005. 1.

[649] "Arts & Economic Prosperity: The Economic Impact of Nonprofit Arts Organizations And Their Audiences," Americans for the Arts, National Report, 2003. 3.

[650] "Report of the Cultural Committee of the Mayor's Bring New Orleans Back Commission," 10 January 2006. <http://www.aeaconsulting.com/site/bnob/BNOB%20EXECUTIVE%20 SUMMARY%2020060202.pdf>

Bibliography

Ake, David. *Jazz Cultures*. University of California Press.

Ake, David. "Negotiating National Identity Among American Jazz Musicians in Paris." *Journal of Musicological Research* 23 (2004). Pg. 159-186

"American Nights in Paris." *The New York Times*, 6 May 1928, 83.

"Americans Abroad Celebrate Fourth." *The New York Times*, 5 July 1950, 15.

Appel, Jr., Alfred. *Jazz Modernism*. New York: Alfred A. Knopf, 2002.

Archambault, G. H. "France To Mourn." *The New York Times*, 25 June 1940, 1.

Arendt, Hannah. *The Origins of Totalitarianism*. New York: Meridian Books, 1958.

Attali, Jacques. Noise: *The Political Economy of Music*. Minneapolis: University of Minnesota Press, 1985.

Austerlitz, Paul. *Jazz Consciousness*. Middletown, CT: Wesleyan University Press, 2005.

Bailey, Thomas A. "The Mythmakers of American History." In *Myth and the American Experience*. Edited by Nicolas Cords and Patrick Gerster. New York: Glencoe Press, 1973.

Bailey, Thomas A. "The Mythmakers of American History." *The Journal of American History*, Vol. 55, No. 1 (Jun. 1968) 5-21.

Baines, John. "Egyptian Myth and Discourse: Myths, Gods, and the Early Written and Iconographic Record." *Journal of Near Eastern Studies* (1991): 81–105. Volume 50, No. 2.

Barrett, Frank J. "Coda: Creativity and Improvisation in Jazz and Organizations: Implications for Organizational Learning." *Organization Science*, (1998): 605–622.

Bayles, Martha. *Hole in Our Soul: The Loss of Beauty & Meaning in American Popular Music.* Chicago: University of Chicago, 1994.

Beard, Charles. "The Constitution: A Minority Document." *In Conflict and Consensus in Early American History*, 109–127. Boston: D. C. Heath and Company, 1980.

Beard, Charles A. "Education Under the Nazis." *Foreign Affairs* 15 (April 1936): 440.

Belair, Jr., Felix. "United States Has Secret Sonic Weapon—Jazz." *The New York Times*, 6 November 1955, 1.

Bidney, David. "Myth, Symbolism, and Truth." *The Journal of American Folklore* (1955): 379–392. Volume 68, No. 270

Boliek, Brooks. "Senators Fight Hidden Sex in 'Grand Theft Auto.'" *Reuters*, 15 July 2005. http://today.reuters.com/News/newsArticle.aspx?type=entertainmentNews &storyID=2005-07-15T073501Z_01_N15610958_RTRIDST_0_ ENTERTAINMENT-MEDIA-SEX-DC.XML. 15 July 2005

Bremer, Sidney H. "Home in Harlem, New York: Lessons from the Harlem Renaissance Writers." *PMLA* (1990): 47–56. Volume 105, No. 1.

Brody, Elaine. *Paris: The Musical Kaleidoscope*, 1870–1925. New York: George Braziller, 1987.

Brown, David P. *Noise Orders: Jazz, Improvisation, and Architecture.* University of Minnesota Press, 2006.

Brown, Lee. "The Theory of Jazz Music: 'It Don't Mean a Thing…'" *The Journal of Aesthetics and Art Criticism* 49 (Spring 1991): 115–127.

Brubeck, Dave. "The Beat Heard 'Round the World." *The New York Times*, 15 June 1958, SM14.

Budds, Michael J. *Jazz and the Germans: Essays on the Influence of "Hot" American Idioms on 20th-Century German Music.* Hillsdale, N.Y.: Pendragon Press, 2002.

Campbell, Joseph. *The Power of Myth.* New York: Anchor, 1991.

Cawelti, John G. "From Rags to Respectability: Horatio Alger." In *Myth and the American Experience.* Edited by Nicholas Cords and Patrick Gerster. New York: Glencoe Press, 1973.

"Centrifugal Forces." T*he Economist*, 16 July 2005, 4.

Chopra, Deepak. *The Spontaneous Fulfillment of Desire: Harnessing the Infinite Power of Coincidence.* New York: Three Rivers Press, 2004.

"Clef Club in Lively Music." *The New York Times*, 16 February 1919, 18.

Cockburn, Alexander. *The Golden Age Is in Us: Journeys & Encounters*, 1987–1994. New York: Verso, 1995.

Cohen, Percy S. "Theories of Myth." In *Man*, 337–353. Royal Anthropological Institute of Great Britain and Ireland. Man, Volume 4, No. 3 (1969).

Collier, Paul. "Rebellion as a Quasi-Criminal Activity." *The Journal of Conflict Resolution* (2000): 839–853. Volume 44, No. 6

"Colored Troops in Today: Part of Old 15th Infantry Should Reach Pier This Morning." *The New York Times*, 9 February 1919, 9.

Commager, Henry Steele. "A Constitution for All the People." *In Conflict and Consensus in Early American History*, 128–139. Boston: D. C. Heath and Company, 1980.

"Constitutional Topic: The Constitutional Convention." *The U.S. Constitution Online*, 3 July 2005. http://www.usconstitution.net/consttop_ccon.html#sherman.

Cook, Susan. "Jazz as Deliverance: The Reception and Institution of American Jazz During the Weimar Republic." *American Music* 7 (Spring 1989), 31.

"Cost of 2004 Elections: $4 Billion and Counting. *USA Today*, 2 November 2004. http://www.usatoday.com/news/politicselections/nation/2004-11-02-election-costs_x.htm?POE=NEWISVA.

Critchlow, James. "Public Diplomacy During the Cold War: The Record and Its Implications." *Journal of Cold War Studies* 6.1 (2004): 77.

Crouch, Stanley. "Blues To Be Constitutional: A Long Look at the Wild Wherefores of Our Democratic Lives as Symbolized in the Making of Rhythm and Tune." In *The Jazz Cadence of American Culture.* Edited by Robert G. O'Meally, 154–165. New York: Columbia University Press, 1998.

Crow, Bill. *Jazz Anecdotes.* New York: Oxford University Press, 1990.

Cunliffe-Owen. C. B. E., Fredrick. "Black Labor New Problem in France." *The New York Times,* 14 September 1924, E7. Frederick Cunliffe-Owen. C.B.E.

Davis, Miles. *Autobiography.* Simon & Schuster, 1990.

Daoust, Phil. "Out & About: Jazz: Swingtime for Hitler." *The Guardian,* 27 October 2004, G2.

de Moraes, Lisa. "Kanye West's Torrent of Criticism, Live on NBC." *The Washington Post,* 3 September 2005, C1.

de Tocqueville, Alexis. *Democracy in America.* New York: Arlington House: 1966. Delbanco, Andrew. *The Real American Dream: A Meditation on Hope.* Cambridge, Mass.: Harvard University Press, 1999.

"Degrees of Separation." *The Economist,* 16 July 2005, 3.

DeVeaux, Scott. "Constructing the Jazz Tradition: Jazz Historiography." *Black American Literature Forum* 25 (1991): 525–560.

DiMaggio, Paul J. "The Nonprofit Instrument and the Influence of the Marketplace on Policies in the Arts." In *The Arts: Public policy in the United States.* Edited by W. McNeil Lowry. Upper Saddle River, N.J.: Prentice Hall, 1984.

Dyson, Michael Eric. *Between God and Gangsta Rap: Bearing Witness to Black Culture.* New York: Oxford University Press, 1996.

Egert, Charles. "Love and Homicide in the Jazz Age Novel." *Journal of Narrative Theory* 34.1 (2004): 54–87.

Ellison, Ralph. *Invisible Man.* Vintage, 1995.

Ellison, Ralph. *Living with Music: Ralph Ellison's Jazz Writings.* New York: Modern Library, 2001.

"Emigré's Memories: Leo Feigin on Soviet Jazz, Freedom, and Willis Conover." 2 May 2005. http://www.jazzhouse.org/library/index.php3?read=ripmaster1.

"Eugenics Bureau to Advise Berlin Couples on Marriage." *The New York Times,* 29 May 1926, 17.

"Explaining Armstrong." 19 July 2005. http://xroads.virginia.edu/~ug99/graham/conclusion.html.

Fantasia, Rick. "Fast Food in France." *Theory and Society* 24, no. 2 (1995): 2.

Farrand, Max. "Compromises of the Constitution." *The American Historical Review* 9, no. 3 (1904): 479–489.

Fay, Jennifer. "That's Jazz Made in Germany!": Hallo, Fraulein! and the Limits of Democratic Pedagogy." *Cinema Journal* 44, no. 1 (2004): 6.

Fiorina, Morris P. *Culture War? The Myth of a Polarized America.* Longman, 2004.

Fitzsimmons, Michael P. *The Remaking of France.* Cambridge University Press, 1994.

Fleisher, Jack. "Nazi Propaganda Put on Defensive." *The New York Times,* 19 May 1942, 5.

Floyd Jr., Samuel A. *Power of Black Music.* USA: Oxford University Press, 1996.

Forham, John. "Dizzy for president!" *The Guardian,* 20 October 2004. http://www.guardian.co.uk/arts/features/story/0,11710,1331548,00.html?gusrc=rss.

Frankl, Victor. *Man's Search For Meaning.* Touchstone, 1984. New York

"French Critics and American Jazz." *American Quarterly* 3, no. 3 (1965): 585.

Fry, Andy. "Beyond Le Boeuf: Interdisciplinary Rereadings of Jazz in France." *Journal of the Royal Music Association* 128. Volume 128, Number 1. (2003) pg. 137-153

Fulcher, James A. *French Cultural Politics & Music: From the Dreyfus Affair to the First World War.* New York: Oxford University Press, 1999.

Gabriel, Mark A. *Jesus and Muhammad: Profound Differences and Surprising Similarities*. Lake Mary, Fla.: Charisma House, 2004.

"General William Westmoreland." *The Economist*, 30 July 2005, 79.

"Georgia's 2003 SAT Scores Show Improvement, but Lag Behind National Pace." Georgia Department of Education. http://www.doe.k12.ga.us/_documents/curriculum/testing/scores_sat_03.pdf.

Glazer, Nathan, and Daniel P. Moynihan. "The Myth of the Melting Pot." In *Myth and the American Experience*, Nicholas Cords and Patrick Gerster. New York: Glencoe Press, 1973.

Gibran, Kahlil. *The Prophet*. New York: Alfred A. Knopf, 1923.

Giddins, Gary. *Satchmo: The Genius of Louis Armstrong*. Da Capo Press, 2001.

"Gillespie Starts Tour Today." *The New York Times*, 23 March 1956, 26.

Gioia, Ted. *Work Songs*. Duke University Press, 2006.

Goddard, Chris. *Jazz Away from Home*. New York: Paddington Press, 1979.

Gould, Carol S., and Kenneth Keaton. "The Essential Role of Improvisation in Musical Performance." The Journal of Aesthetics and Art Criticism 58, no. 2 (2000): 143–148.

Govenar, Alan. "Blind Lemon Jefferson: The Myth and the Man." *Black Music Research Journal* (2000): 7–21. Volume 20, No. 1.

Hahn, Gerald J., William H. Hill, Roger W. Hoerl, and Stephen A. Zinkgraf. "The Impact of Six Sigma Improvement—A Glimpse Into the Future of Statistics." *The American Statistician* (1999): 208–215. Volume 53, No. 3.

Hamilton, Alexander. *Federalist*. No. 120, Penguin Books, 1987.

Hangen, Welles. "Soviet Finds Jazz Is a Acceptable Art." *The New York Times*, 8 January 1956, 109.

Harap, Louis. "The Case for Hot Jazz." *The Music Quarterly* 27, no. 1 (1941): 47–61.

Harris, Lee. "The Future of Tradition." *Policy Review* no. 131 (2005). http://www.policyreview.org/jun05/harris.html. Number 131, June & July 2005.

Hawking, Stephen. *A Brief History of Time: From the Big Bang to Black Holes*. New York: Bantam, 1988.

Hentoff, Nat. *Jazz Is*. New York: Limelight Editions, 1984.

Higgins, Charlotte. "Beethoven (1.4m) beats Bono (20,000) in Battle of the Internet Downloads." *The Guardian*, 21 July 2005. http://www.guardian.co.uk/online/news/0,12597,1532890,00.html.

Hill, Erica. "Rural Internet Use on the rise." *CNN.com*, 18 February 2004. http://www.cnn.com/2004/TECH/02/18/hln.wired.rural.internet/.

Hill, Karl A. "The Amos Tuck School of Business Administration: Its Origin and Present Program." *The Journal of Higher Education* 32, no. 9 (1961): 475.

Hirschkorn, Phil. "Freedom Tower to Rise 1,776 Feet from Ashes." *CNN*.com, 20 December 2003. http://www.cnn.com/2003/US/Northeast/12/19/wtc.plan/.

Hooke, S. H. "Myth, Ritual, and History." *Folklore* (1939): 137–147. Volume 50, No. 2.

Hughes, Langston. "Let America Be America Again." 17 July 2005. http://www.poetryconnection.net/poets/Langston_Hughes/2385.

Hughes, Richard Thomas. *Myths to Live By*. University of Illinois Press, 2004.

Hyde, Lewis. *Trickster Makes This World: Mischief, Myth, and Art*. North Point Press, 1999.

Hynes, Gerald C. *A Biographical Sketch of W. E .B. DuBois*. 18 April 2005. http://www.duboislc.org/html/DuBoisBio.html.

Isenberg, M. W. "Plato's Sophist and the Five Stages of Knowing." In *Classical Philology*, 201–211. Chicago: University of Chicago, 1951.

Jackson, Jeffrey H. *Making Jazz French: Music and Modern Life in Interwar Paris*. Durham, N.C.: Duke University Press, 2003.

Jackson, Jeffrey H. "Music Halls and the Assimilation of Jazz in the 1920s Paris." *Journal of Popular Culture* 34, no. 2 (2000): 69.

Jacobson, Robert, and Robert Cropp. "Dairy Cooperatives and Their Roles in the United States." *Dairy Markets and Policy* (August 1995). http://www.cpdmp.cornell.edu/CPDMP/Pages/Publications/Pubs/M9.pdf.

"Jay-Z Lyrics." 29 July 2005. http://www.azlyrics.com/lyrics/jayz/pussy.html.

"Jazz Bootlegged All Over Russia." *The New York Times*, 23 October 1953, 10.

"Jazz Gains in Popularity as Soviet Lifts Ban; Modern Dances Frowned On as Bourgeois." *The New York Times*, 17 May 1933, 15.

Jelavick, Peter. "If Only the Kaiser Had Danced Jazz…Parting the Curtains of Berlin's Legendary Stages." *German Life* 1, no. 1 (1994): 26.

Jerving, Ryan. "Jazz Language and Ethic Novelty." *Modernism/Modernity* 10.2 (2003): 243.

Jones, LeRoi. *Blues People: Negro Music in White America*. New York: Perennial, 2002.

"Joseph Schillinger (1895–1963)." http://archivesofamericanart.si.edu/exhibits/piano/schillinger.htm.

Joyce, James. *A Portrait of the Artist as a Young Man*. New York: Viking. 1966.

Kahn, Ashley. "After 70 Years, the Village Vanguard Is Still in the Jazz Swing." *Wall Street Journal Online*, 8 February 2005. http://www.villagevanguard.net/html/history.htm.

Kan, Alex. "Golden Years of Soviet Jazz: A Brief History of New Improvised Music in Russia." 2 May 2005. http://www.jazz.ru/eng/history/default.htm.

Kater, Michael. *Different Drummers: Jazz in the Culture of Nazi Germany*. New York: Oxford University Press, 1992.

Kater, Michael. "Forbidden Fruit? Jazz in the Third Reich." *The American Historical Review* 94, no. 1 (1989): 13.

Katz, Stanley N. "Influences on Public Policies in the United States." In *The Arts: Public Policy in the United States*. Edited by W. McNeil Lowry. Upper Saddle River, N.J.: Prentice Hall, 1984.

Kavaler, Arthur. "State Department Opens New Service Next Week." *The New York Times*, 9 February 1947, X11.

Kemp-Welch, Tony. "Khrushchev's 'Secret Speech' and Polish Politics: The Spring of 1956." *Europe-Asia Studies* 48, no. 2 (1996): 181.

Kew, Carole. "From Weimar Movement Choir to Nazi Community Dance: The Rise and Fall of Rudolf Laban's Festkultur." *Dance Research* 17, no. 2 (1999). Pg. 73-96.

"Killing in Soviet Held Aid to Stalin." *The New York Times*, 11 July 1937, 15.

Kimmelman, Michael. "The Lure of Fordism, Jazz, and 'Americanismus.'" *The New York Times*, 11 February 1990, H37.

Kirchheimer, Sid. "Does Rap Put Teens at Risk?" *WebMD*, 13 Sept. 2005. http://my.webmd.com/content/article/61/68559.htm.

Kouwenhoven, John A. *The Arts in Modern American Civilization*. New York: W. W. Norton & Company, 1948.

Kouwenhoven, John A. *The Beer Can by the Highway*. Baltimore, Md.: Johns Hopkins University Press, 1961.

Kramnick, Isaac. *The Federalist Papers*. Editor's Introduction. Penguin, 1987.

Krieger, Alex. "The American City: Ideal and Mythic Aspects of a Reinvented Urbanism." *Assemblage* no. 3 (1987): 38–59.

Lakoff, George and Turner, Mark. *More than Cool Reason*. University Of Chicago Press, 1989.

Landon, Charles. "The Chewing Gum Industry." *Economic Geography* 11, no. 2 (1935): 183–190.

Layard, Richard. *Happiness: Lessons from a New Science*. New York: Penguin, 2005.

"Louis Armstrong Statue Unveiling—July 4, 2000." 19 July 2005. http://www.satchmo.com/louisarmstrong/statue.html.

"Louis the First." *Time Magazine*, 21 February 1949. http://www.time.com/time/time100/
artists/profile/satchmo_related.html.

Leonard, Neil. *Jazz: Myth and Religion.* New York: Oxford University Press, 1987.

Lessig, Lawrence. *The Future of Ideas: The Fate of the Commons in the Connected World.* New York:
Vintage, 2002.

Leviero, Anthony. "U.S. To Take Offensive in Psychological War." *The New York Times*, 1
February 1953, E6.

Levin, Floyd. "Jim Europe's 369th Infantry 'Hellfighters' Band." 15 April 2005. http://www.
redhotjazz.com/hellfighters.html.

Lewis, Rick. "Art and Soul." *Philosophy Now* (September/October 2006). http://www.
philosophynow.org/issue57/57lewis.htm.

"Literary Paws." *PBS Online NewsHour*, 13 April 1998. http://www.pbs.org/newshour/bb/
entertainment/jan-june98/bear_4-13.html.

Littler, Craig R. "Understanding Taylorism." *The British Journal of Sociology* 29, no. 2 (1978):
185–202.

Lokken, Roy N. "The Concept of Democracy in Colonial Political Thought." *The William and
Mary Quarterly* 16 (1959): 568–580.

Lowry, W. McNeil. *The Arts: Public Policy in the United States.* Prentice-Hall, 1984.

Lukes, Steven. "The Meanings of 'Individualism.'" *The Journal of History of Ideas* (1971): 45–66.
Volume 32, No. 1.

Lutz, Donald S. "Toward a Theory of Constitutional Amendment." *American Political Science
Review* 88 (1994): 355–370.

Madison, James. *Federalist.* No. 51. Penguin Books, 1987.

Mailer, Norman. *The Fight.* Boston: Little, Brown & Company, 1975.

Mailer, Norman. *The White Negro: Spiritual Reflections on the Hipster.* San Francisco: City
Lights, 1957.

Malcolm, Douglas. "'Jazz America': Jazz and African American Culture in Jack Kerouac's 'On
the Road.'" *Contemporary Literature* 40, no. 1 (1999): 85–110.

Malraux, André. *Picasso's Mask.* New York: Holt, Rinehart and Winston, 1974.

Manchester, William. *The Last Lion: Winston Spencer Churchill: Alone, 1932–1940.* Delta, 1989.

Mandelbaum, Michael. *Democracy's Good Name: The Rise and Risks of the World's Most
Popular Form of Government.* Public Affairs, 2007.

Mann, Thomas. *The Coming Victory of Democracy.* New York: Alfred A. Knopf, 1938.

"Marsalis, Clinton, and Others Dissect Jazz at Symposium." *The New York Times*, 11
December 2003. http://query.nytimes.com/gst/fullpage.html?res=9502E1DC173C
F932A25751C1A9659C8B63

Mark, David. *Going Dirty: The Art of Negative Campaigning.* Rowman & Littlefield
Publishers, 2006.

Marsalis, Wynton. *To a Young Jazz Musician: Letters from the Road.* New York: Random
House, 2004.

Martin, Linda and Segrave, Kerry. *Anti-Rock: The Opposition to Rock 'n' Roll.* Da Capo
Press, 1993.

"Maxim Gorky." 2 May 2005. http://www.imagi-nation.com/moonstruck/clsc73.html.

Maxwell, William. "Ralph Ellison and the Constitution of Jazzocracy." *Journal of Popular Music
Studies* 16 (April 2004): 40.

McElroy, John Harmon. *American Beliefs: What Keeps a Big Country and a Diverse People United.*
Chicago: Ivan R. Dee, 1999.

McLuhan, Marshall. *Understanding Media.* Routledge, 2005.

Merriam, Alan P., and Fradley H. Garner. "Jazz—The Word." In *The Jazz Cadence of American Culture*. Edited by Robert G. O'Meally, 7–31. New York: Columbia University Press, 1998.

Merriam Webster Online Dictionary. http://www.merriam-webster.com/

"Middle of the Class." *The Economist*. 16 July 2005, 12.

Middleton, Drew. "Russians Discuss U.S. Broadcasts In Stores, Shops, and Other Places." *The New York Times*, 28 March 1947, 6.

Miller, Jr., Laurence H. "On the 'Chicago School of Economics.'" *The Journal of Political Economy*. (1962): 64–69. Volume 70, No. 1.

"Mister Christopher Columbus." 25 July 2005. http://www.niehs.nih.gov/kids/lyrics/columbus.htm.

Mitgang, Herbert. "In This Air War, the Nazis Fired Words and Music." *The New York Times*, 8 September 1997, C17.

"Montmartre Clubs Close." *The New York Times*, 11 January 1927, 11.

"Montparnasse." *Lockergnome Encyclopedia*, 28 April 2005. http://www.uga.edu/profile/pride.html.

"Montparnasse Jazz Is Stilled by Police." *The New York Times*, 20 November 1927, 2.

Moody, Bill. *The Jazz Exiles: American Musicians Abroad*. Reno: University of Nevada Press, 1993.

Morgan, Thomas. *James Reese Europe*, 1992. 4 April 2005. http://www.jass.com/Others/europe.html.

"Motion Dismissed." *The Economist*, 16 July 2005, 18.

"Motion Sustained." *The Economist*, 16 July 2005, 20.

Murray, Albert. *The Omni-Americans: Black Experience and American Culture*. Da Capo, 1970. New York.

Murray, Albert. *Stomping the Blues*. Da Capo, 1976. New York.

Murray, Albert. *The Blue Devils of Nada*. New York: Vintage, 1996.

Murray, Albert. *The Hero and the Blues*. Vintage, 1996.

"Musical Life in France." *The New York Times*, 5 January 1941. X6.

Napoleon, Art. "A Pioneer Looks Back: Sam Wooding 1967." *Storyville* 10 (April–May 1967). pg. 37.

"Nazis Order Blackout in Paris." *The New York Times*, 13 July 1941, 9.

Nietzsche, Friedrich. *The Birth of Tragedy*. Translated by Shaun Whiteside and edited by Michael Tanner. London: Penguin. 1993.

Nisenson, Eric. *Ascension: John Coltrane and His Quest*. New York: St. Martin's Press, 1993.

Nisenson, Eric. Blue: The Murder of Jazz. Da Capo Press, 1997.

Nowlin, Michael. "Making Sense of the American 1920s." *Studies in the Novel* 34, no. 1 (2002): 81.

O'Meally, Robert (Editor), Edwards, Brent Hayes (Editor), and Griffin, Farah Jasmine (Editor). *Uptown Conversation: The New Jazz Studies*. Columbia University Press, 2004.

"Origin of the Saxophone." *The New York Times*, 16 December 1928, X11.

Osgood, Kenneth A. "Hearts and Minds: The Unconventional Cold War." *Journal of Cold War Studies* 4.2 (2002): 85.

Ouspensky, P. D. *In Search of the Miraculous: Fragments of an Unknown Teaching*. Fort Washington, Pa.: Harvest Books, 2001.

Overing, Joanna. "The Role of Myth: An Anthropological Perspective, or: 'The Reality of the Really Made-Up.'" In *Myths & Nationhood*. Edited by Geoffrey Hosking and George Schöpflin, 1–18. Routledge, New York. 1997.

Paine, Thomas. *Common Sense, The Rights of Man and Other Essential Writings of Thomas Paine*. Signet Classics, 2003.

Pelzer, John D. "Django, Jazz and the Nazis in Paris." *History Today* 51, no. 10 (2001): 33.

Porter, Horace A. *Jazz Country: Ralph Ellison in America.* Iowa City: Iowa University Press, 2001.

"President's Call to Youth to Meet Problems of the War and the Future." *The New York Times,* 4 September 1942, 4.

Putnam, Robert D. *Bowling Alone: The Collapse and Revival of American Community.* New York: Simon & Schuster, 2001.

"Quintette of the Hot Club of France." 28 April 2005. http://www.redhotjazz.com/hotclubfrance.html.

Rapoport, Anatol. "Introduction by Anatol Rapoport." In *On War.* Penguin, 1982. Pg. 11-83. England.

Rathbone, Perry T. "Influences of Private Patrons: The Art Museum as an Example." *In The Arts: Public Policy in the United States.* Edited by W. McNeil Lowry. Upper Saddle River, N.J.: Prentice Hall, 1984.

"Reich Admits Saxophone." *The New York Times,* 4 August 1935, 22.

Rich, Alan. "Benny Goodman To Tour in Soviet." *The New York Times,* 9 March 1962, 2.

Robertson, James Oliver. *American Myth, American Reality.* New York: Hill & Wang; 1980.

Robertson, Nan. "Duke Ellington, 70, Honored at White House." *The New York Times,* 30 April 1969, 1.

Rosenthal, Cindy Simon. "Local Politics: A Different Front in the Culture War?" *The Forum* 3, no. 2 (2005). http://www.bepress.com/forum/vol3/iss2/art5. Pgs. 1-8.

Ross, Alex. "The Well-Tempered Web". *The New Yorker,* 22 February, 2008.

Rossiter, Clinton, (Editor). *Federalist Papers.* Signet Classics, 2003.

Rothstein, Edward. "Is Music Ever Mute on Politics?" *The New York Times,* 13 June 1993, 74.

Rourke, Constance. *American Humor: A Study of National Character.* New York: Harcourt, Brace and Company, 1931.

Russell, Bill. *New Orleans Style.* Edited by Barry Martyn and Mike Hazeldine. New Orleans, La.: Jazzology Press, 1994.

Salmon, Lucy M. "Democracy in the Household." *The American Journal of Sociology* 17, no. 4, (1912): 437–457.

"Sam Wooding and His Orchestra." 2 May 2005. http://www.redhotjazz.com/woodingo.html.

"Says Jazz Originated in Old French Music." *The New York Times,* 25 March 1928, 28.

Schlereth, Thomas J. "Columbia, Columbus, and Columbianism." *The Journal of American History* (1992): 937–968. Volume 79, No. 3.

Schlesinger, Jr., Arthur. "America, the Arts, and the Future: The First Nancy Hanks Lecture on the Arts and Public Policy." In *The Future of Arts: Public Policy and Arts Research.* Edited by David B. Pankratz and Valerie B. Morris. Westport, Conn.: Praeger, 1990.

Schöpflin, George. "The Functions of Myth and a Taxonomy of Myths." In *Myths & Nationhood.* Edited by Geoffrey Hosking and George Schöpflin, 19–35. Routledge, New York. 1997.

Schor, Juliet B. "The Overspent American: Upscaling, Downshifting, and the New Consumer." *CNN.com,* 25 June 1998. http://www.cnn.com/books/beginnings/9806/overspent.americans.cnn/.

Seidman, Joel. "Democracy and Trade Unionism: Some Requirements for Union Democracy." *The American Economic Review* (1958): 35–43. Volume 48, No. 2.

"Senators Compromise on Filibusters." *CNN.com,* 24 May 2005. http://www.cnn.com/2005/POLITICS/05/23/filibuster.fight/.

Shabad, Theodore. "Russians Greet Benny Goodman." *The New York Times.* 29 May 1962, 20.

Shack, William A. *Harlem in Montmartre: A Paris Jazz Story between the Great Wars.* Berkeley: University of California Press, 2001.

"Shakespeare as Kultur." *The New York Times,* 15 May 1921, 26.

Sharpton, Al. "2004 Democratic National Convention Address." 17 July 2005. http://www.americanrhetoric.com/speeches/convention2004/alsharpton2004dnc.htm.

Shirer, William L. "The Propaganda Front." *The Washington Post*, 12 July 1942, B7.

"Sing a Song of Spitzer." *The Economist*, 30 July 2005, 54.

Slichter, Jacob. "The Price of Fame." *The New York Times*, 29 July 2005, A21.

Slominsky, Nicolas. A Think or Two About Music. 2 May 2005. http://www.anecdotage.com/index.php?aid=1014.

Smith, Anthony. "The 'Golden Age' and National Renewal." In *Myths & Nationhood*. Edited by Geoffrey Hosking and George Schöpflin, 36–59. Routledge, New York. 1997.

Smith, Susannah Lockwood. "From Peasants to Professionals: The Socialist-Realist Transformation of a Russian Folk Choir." *Kritika: Explorations in Russian and Eurasian History* 3, no. 3 (2002): 408.

Snell, Marilyn Berlin. "Charlie Parker Didn't Give a Damn." *NPQ: New Perspectives Quarterly* 8, no. 3 (1991): 60–63.

Somers, Dale A. "Black and White in New Orleans: A Study in Urban Race Relations, 1865–1900." *The Journal of Southern History* (1974): 19–42. Volume 40, No. 1.

"Soviet Blessing Goes to Goodman." *The New York Times*, 3 June 1962, 13.

"Soviet Now Bans Phonograph Jazz Records; Calls Our Music 'Bourgeois Music.'" *The New York Times*, 9 January 1927, 6.

"Soviet Sweetens Tone on Some Types of Jazz." *The New York Times*, 19 March 1955, 17.

"Soviet Arts Trace Political Pattern." *The New York Times*, 10 February 1948, 12.

Spiro, Peter J. "The Paradox of American Power: Why the World's Only Superpower Can't Go It Alone by Joseph S. Nye, Jr." *The American Journal of International Law* 97, no. 3 (2003): 731–734.

Starr, S. Frederick. *Red & Hot: The Fate of Jazz in the Soviet Union*. New York: Limelight Editions, 2004.

Steinmetz, Leon. "The Four Soviet Cultures." *National Review* 39, no. 20 (1987): 32.

Sulzberger, C. L. "Restrictions on U.S. Press Growing in Soviet Sphere." *The New York Times*, 3 November 1947, 8.

"Swing is the Thing in Germany." *The New York Times*, 14 November 1937, 95.

"Swing Sessions with Bill Gottlieb." *The Washington Post*, 18 August 1940, A7.

"Talking About 'Tribe' Moving from Stereotypes to Analysis." 1997. http://www.africaaction.org/bp/ethzul.htm.

Tagore, Rabindranath. *The Religion of Man*. New Dehli: Rupa & Co., 2005.

Tantner, Anton ."Jazz Youth Subcultures in Nazi Europe." *ISHA Journal* (February 1994): 22–23.

Tatum, Stephen. *Inventing Billy the Kid*. Albuquerque: University of New Mexico Press, 1982.

Taylor, Frederick W. *The Principles of Scientific Management*. New York: W. W. Norton & Company, 1967.

Taylor, Jeffrey. "Louis Armstrong, Earl Hines, and 'Weather Bird.'" *The Music Quarterly* (1988): 1–40. Volume 82, No. 1.

"Tha Dogg Pound feat. Crooked I Gangsta Rap." 12 July 2005. http://www.lyricsstyle.com/t/thadoggpound/gangstarap.html.

"The Glue of Society." *The Economist*, 16 July 2005, 16.

Thelonious Monk Institute of Jazz, "Jazz in America." http://www.jazzinamerica.org/lp.asp?LPOrder=3&Grade=8&PageID=205.

Thomas, Jr., Robert McG. "Willis Conover Is Dead at 75; Aimed Jazz at the Soviet Bloc." *The New York Times*, 19 May 1996. http://query.nytimes.com/gst/fullpage.html?res=9E04E6DD1E39F93AA25756C0A960958260

"Thomas 'Tommy' Ladnier (1900–1939)." 2 May 2005. http://www.redhotjazz.com/Ladnier.html.

Tolstoy, Leo. *The Kingdom of God is Within You.* Lincoln: University of Nebraska Press, 1985.

Tomlinson, Gary. "Cultural Dialogues and Jazz: A White Historian Signifies." *Black Music Journal* 11, no. 2 (1991): 229–264.

"Total Quality Management." Wikipedia, 4 July 2005. http://en.wikipedia.org/wiki/Total_quality_management.

Trachtenberg, Alan. "The Rainbow and the Grid." *American Quarterly* 16, no. 1 (1964): 3–19.

"A Trumpeter Unmuted." Newsweek, October 2004. http://www.msnbc.msn.com/id/6212850/site/newsweek/.

"UNT Presents Honorary Degree to King of Thailand in March Ceremony." 4 July 2004. http://www.unt.edu/inhouse/april22004/thailandannounce.htm.

Verba, Cynthia. *Music and the French Enlightenment: Reconstruction of a Dialogue*, 1750–1764. New York: Oxford University Press, 1993.

"'Voice' Is Reported Upsetting Kremlin." *The New York Times.* 28 May 1950, 3.

Von Eschen, Penny M. *Satchmo Blows Up the World: Jazz Ambassadors Play the Cold War.* Cambridge, Mass.: Harvard University Press, 2004.

Von Kuehnelt-Leddihn, Erik. Introduction to *Democracy in America*. Volume 1. New Rochelle, New York, 1966.

Vonnegut, Kurt. *Man Without a Country.* Steven Stories Press, 2004.

Walser, Robert. "Out of Notes: Signification, Interpretation, and the Problem of Miles Davis." *The Music Quarterly* (1993). Volume 77, No. 2. pg. 343-365.

West, Cornell. *Democracy Matters: Winning the Fight Against Imperialism.* The Penguin Press HC, 2004.

"Wild Ones." *The Guardian*, 11 December 2004. http://www.guardian.co.uk/arts/features/story/0,11710,1370298,00.html.

Williams, John Carlos. *Paterson.* New Directions Publishing Corporation, 1995.

Wilmer, Valerie. *Jazz People.* Da Capo Press, 1991.

Wilson, Bruce. "Ukrainians Refuse to Accept Kremlin's Man after Rigged Election Flashback to the Cold War." *The Advertiser*, 27 November 2004.

Wines, Michael. "Republicans' Boomerang." *The New York Times.* 6 January 1996, 1.

Wittgenstein, Ludwig. *The Blue and Brown Books.* New York: Perennial, 1942.

Whiteman, Paul, and Mary Margaret McBride. *Jazz.* New York: Arno Press, 1974.

Whitman, Walt. *An American Primer.* Edited by Horace Traubel. Boston: Small, Maynard & Company, 1904.

Whitman, Walt. *Democratic Vistas.* Walter Scott Publishing, 1970. London.

"Wynton Marsalis' Insight on Jazz." *Blackenterprise.com*, 1 July 2005. http://www.blackenterprise.com/exclusivesekopen.asp?id=1212&p=1.

Yeats, W. B. *Autobiographies.* Edited by William H. O'Donnell and Douglas N. Archibald. New York: Scribner, 1999.

"You're the Top. 2 May 2005. http://www.assumption.edu/dept/history/HI14Net/Porterlyrics.html.

Zabor, Rafi. *The Bear Comes Home.* New York: W. W. Norton & Company, 1998.

Zingg, Paul J. "Diamond in the Rough: Baseball and the Study of American Sports History." *The History Teacher* 19, no. 3 (1986): 385–403.

Zinn, Howard. "The Power and the Glory: Myths of American Exceptionalism." *Boston Review.* http://bostonreview.net/BR30.3/zinn.html.

FOR TOMORROW

SAVING THE MUSIC OF TODAY, FOR THE WORLD OF TOMORROW

As part of the social royalty initiative developed between Kabir Sehgal and Better World Books, a portion of proceeds from the sale of this book will go towards bringing the music back to New Orleans. Music For Tomorrow is a non-profit organization that provides resources to enable communities in need of assistance after Hurricane Katrina to continue music traditions. These traditions are an important part of a shared cultural heritage, which Music For Tomorrow wishes to preserve. The organization achieves this by awarding grants to musicians and ensembles, presenting or subsidizing concert series, and supporting music institutions that protect our musical heritage. Music For Tomorrow is committed to providing aid to the city of New Orleans by helping displaced musicians return to the city through grants for housing and living, by helping musicians already back in the Crescent City through the subsidization of concerts and with need based grants, and through a partnership with the New Orleans Jazz Orchestra.